· BELARUS ·

Westview Series on the Post-Soviet Republics

Alexander J. Motyl, Series Editor

Published in cooperation with the
Nationality and Siberian Studies Program
of The Harriman Institute, Columbia University

▪ (BELARUS) ▪
At a Crossroads in History

JAN ZAPRUDNIK

WESTVIEW PRESS
Boulder · San Francisco · Oxford

Westview Series on the Post-Soviet Republics

Published in 1993 in the United States of America by Westview Press, Inc., 5500 Central Avenue, Boulder, Colorado 80301-2877, and in the United Kingdom by Westview Press, 36 Lonsdale Road, Summertown, Oxford OX2 7EW

Library of Congress Cataloging-in-Publication Data
Zaprudnik ĪA.
   Belarus: at a crossroads in history / Jan Zaprudnik.
      p.   cm. — (Westview series on the post-Soviet republics)
   Includes bibliographical references and index.
   ISBN 0-8133-1339-2. — ISBN 0-8133-1794-0 (pbk.)
   1. Belarus—History.   I. Title.   II. Series.
DK507.54.Z37   1993
947'.65—dc20   92-42923
                                                                              CIP

Printed and bound in the United States of America

∞   The paper used in this publication meets the requirements
      of the American National Standard for Permanence of Paper
      for Printed Library Materials Z39.48-1984.

10   9   8   7   6   5   4   3   2

· Contents ·

Belarusan-Ukrainian Relations, 218
Belarusan-Lithuanian Relations, 220
Belarusan-Latvian Relations, 222
Belarusan-Jewish Relations, 222
Belarus Within the Context of the World, 224
Notes, 226

· Tables and Illustrations ·

Photos

· Preface ·

Before the precipitous demise of the Soviet empire in 1990–1991, very few people in the West were aware of the existence of the Belarusan political state—in spite of the fact that the Belarusan (Byelorussian) SSR had been a member of the United Nations since 1945. Even fewer Westerners knew anything about the centuries-long history of the Belarusan people and their aspirations for self-government and independence. The sudden and profound changes in the political structure of Eastern Europe in the 1990s and the active role played by Belarus in these changes, coupled with the area's geostrategic importance, warrant a closer look at this republic, which became a stage in the dramatic expiration of the last big empire, the USSR.

It was the speaker of the Belarusan Supreme Council—Stanislaŭ Šuškievič (Shushkevich)—who invited Russian President Boris Yeltsin and Ukrainian President Leonid Kravchuk to the Bielavieža Forest in Belarus in early December 1991. Then and there the three leaders decided to administer a coup de grâce to the moribund Soviet Union of President Mikhail Gorbachev. Belarus's capital, Miensk, became the seat of the Commonwealth of Independent States (CIS).

Since the momentous date of July 27, 1990, when the Belarusan Parliament declared national sovereignty, the Republic of Belarus has been struggling to establish itself in the international arena as a nation-state with its own agenda. As with many other emerging East European democracies, the parliament in Belarus was still dominated by former Communists in 1993. But the republic's legislature has been stimulated by a resourceful democratic opposition that has steered the legislative process toward both cultural survival of the Belarusan people and development of a polity with human rights guarantees and political stability for Belarus's multiethnic society.

Traditionally, whenever Belarus was written about in Western source books (authored predominantly by exponents of the Russophile school of historiography), it was treated as an "appendix" to a larger political unit, whether to Kievan Ruś in ancient times, Poland in the late Middle Ages, or Russia and the Soviet Union in the ensuing periods. But in such descriptions of a country as part of a larger whole, that country's wholeness and uniqueness are often either distorted or negated. The wider "imperial" context in which Belarus was presented by Russian, Soviet, and Western authors has entailed emphases and criteria that led to derogation of the identity and national strivings of the Belarusans. Such authors have failed to present the Belarusan nation from within, as it were, in the light of its own dynamics and aspirations. Terminological problems—differences in the meanings of key geographic and national names between the past and the present—have further contributed to the distortion and misunderstanding of Belarus's historical heritage.

Written today, a history of the Belarusan nation as it emerges from a period of subjugation and submission must necessarily look into the country's past for facts to illuminate its current behavior and to facilitate an understanding of present-day claims, controversies, and impediments. As historical consciousness is a part of political awareness, in today's Belarus the past has become a potent argument in shaping programs for the future. In the realm of intraethnic relations these programs deserve a closer look, for they may contain some qualities worth emulating in the modern world, where diversity has become a source of violent eruptions and dismay for the rest of the international community. Having found themselves at the crossroads of history in the center of Europe, between East and West, remembering their tragic past experiences, the Belarusans have been groping for solutions that would protect individual and group rights as well as guarantee the peaceful cohabitation of various ethnic and religious entities. Because of its central geographical location, Belarus has a considerable potential for becoming an important member-state of the European Community connecting Western Europe and the Eurasian continent and for serving as an example of a peaceful multiethnic and multireligious society. Familiarity with the past and present of Belarus will indeed facilitate the task of Belarus's integration into the international family.

I have the pleasant duty of expressing my gratitude to the following individuals who, each in his or her own way, contributed to this volume by providing help with published material, language and computer advice, editorial and technical help, criticism, and encouragement: Anthony Adamovich, Adam Akulich, Joseph Arciuch, Vaclaŭ Bahdanovič, Hienadź Buraŭkin, Uladzimir Hierasimovič, Hieorhi Jahoraŭ, Jaŭhien Jaŭmienaŭ, Vitaŭt Kipel, Zora Kipel, Siarhiej Kryčeŭski, Jaŭhien Lecka, Adam Maldzis, Alexander Motyl, Uladzimir Novik, Zianon Paźniak, Archer Puddington, Jury Rahula, Vitali Rusak, Anatol Shavzin, Anton Shukieloyts,

Iosif Siaredzič, Halina Siarhiejeva, Alex Silwanowicz, Walter Stankievich, Aleh Trusaǔ, Vitaǔt Tumash, Victor Tur, and Vera Zaprudnik.

Special thanks go to my friend Professor Thomas E. Bird, of the City University of New York, for his continuous editorial guidance and insights.

Jan Zaprudnik

· A Note on Terminology ·

In this book the spelling of Belarus and many of its cities and citizens varies. This is due to the following:

1. Several languages were used on Belarusan territory—Belarusan, Polish, Russian—resulting in spelling variations (Skaryna–Skoryna–Skorina; Kalinoŭski–Kalinowski–Kalinovskiy).
2. Names were changed by various governing authorities (Navahradak–Nowogródek–Novogrudok; Byelorussia–Belarus; Miensk—Minsk).
3. When spelled in the Belarusan Latin alphabet, names are rendered differently than in their English version (Šuškievič–Shushkevich; Kiebič–Kebich).

Whenever a name is used by this author, it is the Belarusan variant spelled according to the Belarusan Latin alphabet rules.

▪ The Belarusan Alphabet ▪

Letter	Pronunciation	Letter	Pronunciation
a	a (in *ah*)	o	o (in *horse*)
b	b	p	p
c	ts (in *tsetse*)	r	r
ć	ts (palatalized)	s	s
č	ch	ś	s (palatalized)
d	d	š	sh
e	e (in *ten*)	t	t
f	f	u	u (in *rule*)
g	g (in *go*)	ŭ	w (in *how*)
h	h (in *have*)	v	v
i	i (in *machine*)	y	y (in *Mary*)
j	y (in *boy*)	z	z (in *zero*)
k	k	ź	z (palatalized)
l	l (in *million*)	ž	s (in *pleasure*)
ł	l (in *table*)	ch	ch (in *chutzpah*)
m	m	dz	dz (in *adze*)
n	n	dž	j (in *jet*)
ń	n (in *onion*)		

· Belarus at a Glance ·

Geography

Belarus occupies an area of 80,154 square miles (207,600 square kilometers), about three times as large as Belgium and the Netherlands combined. Its neighbors are as follows: Russia to the east, Poland to the west, Ukraine to the south, Lithuania to the northwest, and Latvia to the north. Situated 160 miles at its closest point from the Baltic Sea, Belarus has a temperate continental climate, with winter lasting between 105 and 145 days and summer up to 150 days. Its major rivers are the Dnieper, Nieman, Prypiat, and West Dvina. Approximately one-third of its territory is covered by forests and woods. The landscape is flat, 525 feet above sea level on average and 1,135 feet at the highest point.

The major cities of Belarus are the capital Miensk (also spelled Mensk or Minsk), with a population of 1,800,000 in 1992; Homiel (Gomel), population 506,000; Mahiloŭ (Mogilev), population 363,000; Viciebsk (Vitebsk), population 356,000; Brest, population 269,000; and Hrodna (Grodno), population 255,000.

People

According to the Soviet census of 1989, Belarus had 10,128,000 inhabitants: 7,900,000 Belarusans (77.8 percent), 1,300,000 Russians (13.2 percent), 417,000 Poles (4.1 percent), 290,000 Ukrainians (2.9 percent), 112,000 Jews (1.1 percent), and 71,000 others (0.9 percent). Of the total population in 1992, 67 percent were urban dwellers and 33 percent were rural. Life expectancy was 72 years.

The major religious groups in Belarus are Orthodox Christians (approximately 75 percent of the population), Catholics (approximately 10 percent), Protestants (especially Baptists), Uniates, Jews, and Muslims.

Government

The government of Belarus is of the parliamentary type, with a unicameral legislature (the Supreme Council) whose speaker acts as head of state.

The prime minister is appointed by the parliament, which also confirms all ministers. The Declaration on State Sovereignty of the Belarusan SSR was adopted on July 27, 1990 (now a national holiday). Independence was declared on August 25, 1991, in the wake of the Moscow putsch.

The major political parties of Belarus are as follows: the Joint Democratic Party of Belarus, the Belarusan Social-Democratic Union (Hramada), the Belarusan Peasant Party, the Belarusan Peasant Union, the Belarusan Christian-Democratic Association, the Belarusan Ecological Union, the National Democratic Party of Belarus, the Party of Communists of Belarus, and the Belarusan Association of Servicemen. In addition, the Belarusan Popular Front serves as a fulcrum of opposition for the various parties.

As this book goes to press, the speaker of parliament is Stanislaŭ Šuškievič (Stanislav Shushkevich), and the prime minister is Viačaslaŭ Kiebič (Vyacheslav Kebich).

Military

Of the 240,000 troops stationed in Belarus in 1992, about 90,000 constitute a national army consisting of land army, air force, and strategic units. Other troops, armed with nuclear weapons, remain subordinated to the commander of the Commonwealth of Independent States (CIS) forces.

Communications

Of the 28 daily newspapers in Belarus (total circulation in 1992: 2,738,000), the principal ones are *Narodnaja hazieta* (People's newspaper), *Sovetskaya Belorussiya* (Soviet Belarus), *Zviazda* (Star), *Litaratura i mastactva* (Literature and art), *Znamya yunosti* (The banner of youth), *Nastaŭnickaja hazieta* (Teachers' newspaper), *Belorusskaya niva* (Belarusan field), and *Svaboda* (Liberty). In addition, there are 303 radios, 315 television sets, and 108 telephones for every 1,000 Belarusan residents.

Economy

Belarus's workforce comprises 5.1 million people (every eighth one of whom has a higher education): 3.6 million are employed by the government, 100,000 have jobs in the private sector, and the rest work in collective farms and other activities.

The country's natural resources include potash salt, rocksalt, peat, oil, lignite, coal, iron ores, slates, bituminous shale, construction materials, mineral waters, arable land, and forests.

Industries account for 70 percent of the gross national product; the main ones are engineering, chemicals, woodworking, light manufacturing, and food processing. The agricultural sector produces grain, flax, potatoes, beets, meat, milk, and eggs.

The share of the Soviet Union's external debt assumed by Belarus in 1991 was 4.13 percent of the total, or $2.5 to 2.7 billion. When the USSR's gold reserves were reapportioned among the republics of the former union, Belarus was allotted 6.1 tons of gold.

In 1992 inflation stood at about 23 percent monthly.

Foreign Trade

Among the former Soviet republics, Russia and Ukraine are Belarus's major trading partners. In 1991 Belarus exported industrial goods and chemicals in the amount of about 500 million convertible rubles to all of these republics as well as to Poland, Bulgaria, Hungary, Germany, Austria, Yugoslavia, the Netherlands, Cuba, Afghanistan, China, and Egypt.

In the same year Belarus imported goods in the amount of about 250 million convertible rubles from Poland, Germany, Japan, Yugoslavia, the Netherlands, Austria, and Switzerland.

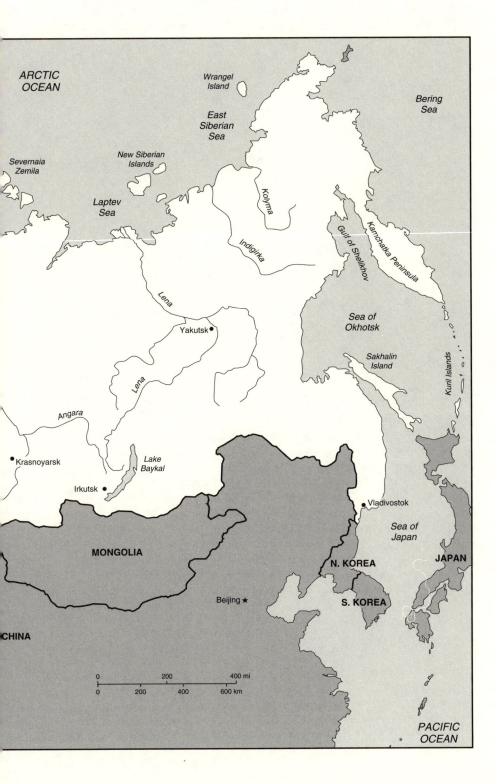

ONE

From Statehood to Decline and Oppression

THE NAME

Changed Content in a Familiar Form

One of the difficulties facing Belarus is recognition of its individuality and national character. Part of the problem lies in the country's name—or rather names, for there have been several throughout the history of the Belarusan people.

It is true that a rose by any other name would smell as sweet. But not a nation's name to its people. The national name is the epitome of the people's past. It contains the people's triumphs and tragedies, and their sense of belonging. It also reflects their collective journey through the expanse of time; it guards their historical continuum. But as the Bard implies, the name is not immutable; it changes, as does the content with which one invests it. The term *Prussians* originally referred to a Baltic tribe inhabiting an area between the estuaries of the Vistula and Nieman rivers. Conquered and assimilated by the Germans, this tribe left them its name— thus, ironically, "surviving" in their annihilators, the Prussians of the Fredericks and Bismarck. Similar semantic metamorphoses occurred elsewhere at different times. At the dawn of their history, a contemporary Slavic people—the Bulgarians—were not Slavs but Turks. One is also reminded here of the Holy *Roman* Empire, which in the sixteenth century was essentially the kingdom of *Germany*.

Ruś

Ruś—distortingly translated by many as "Russia"—was a patch of land in the triangle formed by three cities; Kiev, Chernigov, and Pereyaslavl in present-day Ukraine. But as a result of the expansion of the Kievan Ruś state, which spread during the tenth century over the vast territories of Novgorod, Pskov, Polacak, Muscovy, and other regions, Ruś ac-

1

quired a new meaning; its scope was substantially changed. And when the center of power in that empire moved by the mid-fourteenth century to Muscovy, the quintessential Ruś went with it. The Kievan state crumbled in the twelfth century; Kiev was destroyed by the Mongols in 1240; and Moscow, which by the end of the fifteenth century had proclaimed itself the "Third and Last Rome," took upon itself the imperial program of "gathering in all the Ruśias." Hence the primary meaning of the term *Ruś* was "Christian Orthodox," connoting the religious and cultural patrimony of the Byzantine and Kievan empires.

Belaya Ruś, Belaruś

The history of the name *Belaya Ruś* (variously translated as "White Russia," "White Ruthenia," "Byelorussia," "Byelorussiya," or "Belarus") is quite different from the history of the East Slavic Belarusan people. The name originated in the twelfth century and initially designated various parts of northwestern Russia or Ukraine. Since the fourteenth century it has also been applied to eastern territories of present-day Belarus.

The meaning of *White* in *White Russia*, as applied to present-day *Bela*rus, is something of a puzzle. Historians have proposed various imaginative, if conflicting, explanations for the term.[1] *White* could refer to the beauty of the land, for instance, or to the abundance of snow, to the white complexion of the people or to freedom and independence. Concerning the last of these meanings, we read in *Belorusskaya SSR na mezhdunarodnoy arene* (The Belarusan SSR in the international arena), edited by the republic's foreign affairs minister, Kuźma Kisialoŭ, that "the word 'white,' as opposed to 'black,' meant in those distant times free, independent. In the course of many centuries the Belarusans in stubborn struggle defended their independence, language, culture, and national way of life."[2] Another plausible explanation of *White* and *Black* in conjunction with Ruś has been given recently by historian Kastuś Tarasaŭ. Both adjectives, according to him, have a religious context. The term *beloruski* was used for the first time by Prince Andrei Bogolubski who, having sacked Kiev in 1169, assumed the title Prince *beloruski* to underscore true Orthodox faith. In the middle of the next century, when areas east and south of Ruś were conquered by the Mongols, *White* was applied to the Smolensk land, which remained free. But in 1267 the Tatars took Smolensk. Then, says Kastuś Tarasaŭ, "the Polacak, Viciebsk, and Mahiloŭ lands [lying farther to the west and south] began to be called White Ruś which the Tatars were unable to subordinate."[3] As for *Black Ruś*, by which the western Belarusan lands around the cities of Navahradak and Hrodna (Grodno) were known, Tarasaŭ notes that the term was not a self-appelation. Rather, it was used originally by the German Knights of the Cross to indicate their

Orthodox "schismatic" or heathen character, which served the Knights to justify their aggression.

The name *Belarus* (pronounced *byeh-lah-RooS*), which in its contemporary meaning signifies either the modern Belarusan state or the entire ethnographic area settled by the Belarusans, dates back only to the last decade of the nineteenth century, when the Belarusan political movement began to develop. Its earlier variant was *Belaya Ruś*. The geographic imprecision of its meaning in 1891 is best described in *Entsiklopedicheski Slovar'*, which states: "At various times, parts of the western half of what is now Russia were included under this name, while today it designates only the Mogilev [Mahiloŭ] and not the entire Vitebsk [Viciebsk] gubernias."[4] The imprecision deepens when one reads in the same text the description of *Belorussiya* (Belarus): "Formerly, Belorussiya mainly embraced the principalities of Polotsk, Vitebsk, and Smolensk. Presently, Belorussiya includes mainly the Minsk, Mogilev, Vitebsk, and the western part of the Smolensk gubernias."[5] It should be noted that neither the western gubernia of Vilna (Vilnius) nor that of Hrodna, where Belarusans constituted the largest population group, was incorporated in the earlier descriptions of *Belaya Ruś* or *Belorussiya*. Therefore, none of these terms, as they were used in the past, should be equated with the ethnic territory inhabited by the Belarusans today.

Historical Lićviny ("Lithuanians")

The ancestors of the Belarusans have been known throughout history under various names. Of these one is particularly important because it provides a key to understanding the Belarusan people's role in the history of the medieval empire known as the Grand Duchy of Litva (Lithuania), Ruś, and Samogitia. The lengthy name of this state is often abbreviated—whether for purely practical reasons or because of ulterior motives—to the Grand Duchy of Lithuania (GDL), or simply to Lithuania. The GDL was a polyethnic dynastic empire where local customs and the Christian Church were respected and where new Lithuanian rulers, still pagan, underwent acculturation by the ruled. The GDL began expanding in the mid-thirteenth century; at its territorial peak two centuries later, it stretched from the Baltic coast to the Black Sea, encompassing all of Belarus, a large part of Ukraine, and some Russian lands. In 1430 the ratio of these areas to Lithuania proper was approximately twelve to one.[6] At the time of the political union between the GDL and the kingdom of Poland in 1569, when Ukraine was transferred from the GDL to the Polish kingdom, Belarus remained in the duchy. During this period, some Lithuanian princes embraced eastern-rite Christianity, and Belarusan was the official language of the ducal chancellery and courts.

Having lived in the Grand Duchy of Lithuania for five hundred years before being incorporated into the Russian empire in the latter part of the eighteenth century, Eastern Slavs known today as Belarusans had been calling themselves and were called by others *lićviny* or *litoŭcy* ("Lithuanians"). The ethnographic encyclopedia *Etnahrafija Bielarusi*, recently published in Minsk, explains this nomenclatural problem as follows:

> *Litviny, lićviny* is the name of the inhabitants of the Grand Duchy of Lithuania, mainly western Belarusans and eastern Lithuanians, in the period of the fourteenth to eighteenth centuries. The name appears for the first time in Polish historical sources (chronicles and annals) in the fourteenth century. In the Belarusan-Lithuanian chronicles and other documents of the fourteenth to sixteenth centuries the name *litviny, lićviny* was associated in the ethnogenetic aspect with the legendary Roman settlers headed by the Prince Palemon and, in the territorial aspect, with the original location of the toponym *Litva*—to the west of Minsk between the rivers of Nieman and Vilia where a mixed Balto-Slavic population lived. ... In the sixteenth to eighteenth centuries the term acquired the character of a politonym designating the entire population of the Grand Duchy of Lithuania from the state-political viewpoint. ... The inhabitants of Bielaja Ruś called themselves *litviny-bielaruscy*.[7]

Toponymic names of *Litva* survived on Belarusan territory well into the twentieth century. For example, the city of Brest—through which one enters Belarus going by train from Warsaw to Moscow, and which is scores of miles away from ethnic Lithuanian territory—was still called Brest-Litovsk in 1918. And Polish authors writing of Belarus's capital, Minsk, in past centuries refer to it as *Minsk Litewski* ("Lithuanian") to distinguish it from Minsk Mazowiecki in Poland.

Over the centuries, various parts of present-day Belarus have had different names in Russian administrative nomenclature, including such nineteenth-century designations for the entire country as *Severo-Zapadnyi Kray* (North-western region), *Zapadnyi Kray* (Western region), *the Western gubernias, Western Russia,* or simply *Russia.* These terms resulted from the tsar's prohibition of the name *Belarus* in 1840.

We must therefore keep in mind that, "just as the term 'Lithuania' was applied to a territory larger than that occupied by the Lithuanian people, so the term 'Belarus' fell short of covering the territory inhabited by Belarusans."[8]

There are several English terms for Belarus. White Russia, an early variant, is still found on many maps and globes. And until September 19, 1991, the official spelling was *Byelorussia,* spelled by some scholars *Belorussia.* On that day, the Supreme Soviet (parliament) of the Byelorussian Soviet Socialist Republic (BSSR) decided to change the name of the state to

Typical rural landscape of Belarus. Photo by Michail Żylinski. Courtesy of *Narodnaja hazieta* (People's newspaper).

Respublika Bielaruś. The Western media and the republic's UN representation rendered the new name in English as the Republic of Belarus.

Of the two adjectival forms, *Belarusian* retains a trace of the old official version and *Belarusan* is closer to the original term, *bielaruski.*

THE LAND

The course of early Belarusan history was defined primarily by the country's waterways, as in so many other parts of the world. Belarus's 10,800 lakes attracted early settlers. And the Dnieper River enabled ancient merchants and adventurous Vikings to go south toward Kiev and Byzantium, whereas the Dvina secured access to the Baltic Sea and the Hanseatic cities. The upper regions of the Dnieper and the Dvina provided connections with the Volga basin, opening the way south to the Caspian Sea, Persia, and the Arab world. The Prypiat' River in the southern part of the country has served as a bridge between the Dnieper and the Vistula in Poland. A network of more than 20,000 tributaries—48 of them at least 100 kilometers long—cover Belarus's inland.

The Dnieper and the Dvina exerted the strongest impact on the course of earliest historical developments. Lying close to each other in their upper regions, they constituted a highway system of tributaries and portages "from the Varangians to the Greeks"—that is, from Scandinavia to

Byzantium. Along this trade route, cities and towns were founded; some, including Polacak (Polotsk), Smolensk, Viciebsk (Vitebsk), Turaŭ (Turov), and Pinsk, became the centers of powerful principalities.

Foreign travelers visiting Belarus in the fifteenth to seventeenth centuries were impressed by the abundance of thick forests, whose wealth was extolled in a magnificent Latin poem of 1523. "Our forests," wrote Nicolai Hussoviani (Husoŭski), a native of Belarus, "are an endless storehouse and blessing for the country. Caravans of foreign ships come to us with their glittering overseas goods."[9]

Belarus is a flat country. On average, it lies 530 feet above sea level. Diagonally through the land, from southwest to northeast, runs a swath of slightly elevated and hilly territory. This is the route—the shortest between Warsaw and Moscow—that the armies of Napoleon and Hitler took on their way to the center of the Russian empire. The Russian armies of Alexander I and Stalin followed the same path pushing west. Indeed, geopolitics has weighed heavily on the entire course of Belarusan history, including the most recent developments. For example, as a result of the republic's location within the Soviet Union and the fact that one-third of Belarus's territory is covered by forests, a disproportionately high number of Soviet nuclear arms have been placed within the republic, some of them on twenty-four missile bases.[10] It is not without justification that the Soviet press used to call Belarus "the Western Gate of the Soviet Union." Belarus's history and even the national character of its people bear the heavy imprint of this geopolitical fact.

The history of Belarus includes a north-south axis in the ninth to thirteenth centuries, when events were shaped by relations of the Polacakan (Belarusan) princes with Novgorod and Kiev; and a west-east axis beginning in the mid-thirteenth century, when Belarusan territories became the central part of the Grand Duchy of Litva, Ruś, and Samogitia, which in turn came into conflict with an expanding Muscovite state.

THE PEOPLE

In schoolbooks, the ethnic makeup of the Belarusan people is explained rather simply as the merger of three early East Slavic tribes of Kryvičans who settled in the north (in the city of Polacak), Drehavičans in the south (Turaŭ and Pinsk) and Radzimičans in the southeast (Homiel, or Gomel). But for scholars the matter is much more complex and controversial.

For more than a century, ethnographers and historians have been debating the ethnic origin of the Belarusans—whether they are of "pure" Slavic stock or a mixture of Slavs and Balts. Strong opinions have been expressed by proponents of each side because any answer to this question has ideological and political implications. In 1919 Mitrafan Doŭnar-

Belarusan national costumes. Courtesy of the Belarusan American Association in New York.

Zapolski argued the cause for an independent Belarusan state: "By their historical and ethnographic particularities the Belarusans are the purest of the Slavic tribes who have preserved both the external appearance of a Slav, many traits of his psyche, and even his way of life."[11] Similar views were propounded by such other Belarusan historians as Vaclaŭ Lastoŭski (1881–1938) and Usievalad Ihnatoŭski (1881–1931). Since the early 1890s, however, evidence had been accumulating to support the opposite opinion—that there was a strong Baltic substratum in the ethnogenetic makeup of the Belarusans. Linguists were the first scholars to call attention to such a possibility.

In 1894 Piotr Golubovsky observed that those descendants of the Kryvičans who spoke Belarusan, unlike their eastern Russian-speaking relatives who came from the same tribe, "fell in prehistoric times under a different ethnic influence."[12] During the next several decades, enough evidence accumulated in the fields of archeology, ethnography, linguistics, toponymy, anthropology, and so on, to enable a Moscow scholar, Valeri V. Sedov, to write a monograph on the ethnogenesis of the Belarusans. Sedov's thesis goes as follows: Originally, the Belarusan area was settled by Baltic tribes. They had been living there for almost two millennia when, around the sixth century A.D., Slavic newcomers began to move in. The process was slow and peaceful. The small separated communities of Balts in the Upper Dnieper region had no military or political organization. Therefore, the Slavs were able to move deep into the area, sometimes in scattered groups. As a result of such uncoordinated movement, islets of East-Baltic population found themselves among Slavs at the end of the first millennium A.D. The assimilation of the Balts, according to Sedov, was facilitated by their linguistic proximity to the Slavs. Sedov thus concludes:

> The ancestors of the Belarusans are to an equal extent both the newly-arrived bearers of the Slavic tongue, who settled in the Upper Dnieper and Upper Dvina rivers during the second half of the first millennium A.D., and the local population which had lived here for about two millennia and who spoke dialects of the Baltic linguistic group.[13]

Sedov's opinions on this matter, published in Moscow in 1970, were viewed as heresy in Minsk. There, the academician and Party guardian of Belarusan historians, Laŭren Abecedarski, on the eve of the appearance of the Sedov monograph, lashed out at unnamed scholars for maintaining that, in Abecedarski's words, "the Belarusans, having come from the West with their culture which had long been Baltic ... differed significantly from all other people of the Slavic tongue."[14] Abecedarski's invective was directed against the "servants of American imperialism." But soon it became obvious that the "enemy" was closer at home. In April 1974 Piotr

Mašeraŭ (Masherov), first secretary of the Communist Party of Belarus, delivered a "serious reprimand" to the Party Bureau of the Belarusan Academy's Department of Social Sciences for "walking on the leash of politically unstable individuals" and allowing the department "to approve undertakings without thinking of their possible negative results as was the case with a scheduled symposium on the ethnogenesis of the Belarusans."[15]

The controversy about the ethnogenesis of the Belarusans has been as much an issue of politics and ideology as one of scholarship. Such matters usually are. History, held the notable British historian Edward Hallett Carr, has a dual function: "to enable man to understand the society of the past and to increase his mastery over the society of the present."[16] Indeed, historical awareness has always been at the basis of political consciousness.

In the former Soviet Union a strictly obligatory view about the origin of the three East Slavic peoples—Russians, Ukrainians, and Belarusans—was maintained since Stalin's time. All three nationalities, according to the official dogma that Stalin inherited along with the tsarist empire, sprang from the same Old-Ruśian root. The trifurcation of the Old-Ruśian "nationality" (*narodnost'*), according to this school of thought, came about as a result of the feudal disintegration of Kievan Ruś and the conquest of Slavic territories by Lithuanian and Polish princes and landlords. Of course, this conquest left the Muscovites the task of liberating those "Russian" lands and reuniting them again in a single state, now with Moscow as the center. Obviously, the theory of the Baltic substratum in the ethnogenesis of the Belarusans—with its implication that the formation of the Grand Duchy of Lithuania, Ruś, and Samogitia may have been a result not so much of conquests as of peaceful processes—undermines Moscow's rationale for westward expansion, depriving it of moral ground and political justification.

The issue of the Baltic substratum in the ethnic make-up of the Belarusans continues to reverberate as does the problem of the purported existence of the unified Old-Ruśian nationality. The dynamics of current developments in the area dredge up arguments from every possible quarter, including historiography.

EARLY PRINCIPALITIES

The Past Feeds the Present

Perestroika has liberated Belarus's past from the prison of Russified Communist dogmas. History has once again become a field of free inquiry, scholarly discussions, speculations, and—inevitably—journalistic simplifications. The past and the present have merged once more into a natural relationship that impinges upon the future and confirms the perspicacity of the nineteenth-century historian Jacob Burckhardt, who said that history is "the record of what one age finds worthy of note in another." The "worthiness" of the past emerges from the needs of the present, as demonstrated by Belarus's foreign minister, Piotr Kraučanka (Kravchenka) when, in September 1991, he addressed the General Assembly of the United Nations. Kraučanka, underscoring his nation's historical experience, made reference to the distant past. "Today we note with pride," he said, "that the traditions of Belarusan statehood have a centuries-old history. It has been embodied in various forms of a state system and was at its peak in the Middle Ages."[17]

The Polacak Principality

The earliest embodiment of statehood on Belarusan territories were the principalities of Polacak, Turaŭ, and Navahradak (Novohorodak); named after their respective main cities. Ruled toward the end of the tenth century from Kiev, they asserted themselves early on as independent or semi-independent dominions. This was especially true of Polacak, the largest of the three.

The Polacak principality, occupying more than a half of present-day Belarus, was settled by a tribe of Kryvičans, one of the largest groups of East Slavs who moved into the area in the sixth century A.D. The territory occupied by the Kryvičans stretched beyond the confines of the Polacakan princes. Farther east another Kryvičan center of power arose, the Smolensk principality, sometimes Polacak's rival, occasionally its ally. The land of Polacak had other major cities: Viciebsk, Orša, Miensk (Minsk), and Druck. Begun as outposts of the expanding domain of the Polacak sovereign, they developed into commercial nuclei of their own and, around the end of the eleventh century, amid feudal contention, themselves aspired to self-rule.

Similar developments took place over the same period of time in the Turaŭ principality, where the cities of Pinsk, Brest, Sluck, and Kleck were founded sometime during the course of the eighth to ninth centuries.

The city of Polacak is mentioned for the first time in the twelfth-century Ruśian *Primary Chronicle*. It is named there under the year 862 A.D. as a colony given by the Norman prince Rurik, the ruler of the northern city of Novgorod, to one of his vassals. Rurik's descendants established themselves in the following century as the princely dynasty in Kiev and built the mighty Kievan state. After a brief period of subjugation to Kiev, Polacak managed to assert its independence in the last quarter of the tenth century under prince Rahvalod, who was either of Scandinavian origin (like Rurik) or of Slavic stock.[18]

Historical beginnings of Belarus: Location of tribes in and around future Belarus toward the ninth century.

The Story of Princess Rahnieda

Belarusan political history during the Kievan Ruś period opens with violence, rape, and marital drama, according to popular legend recorded by early chronicles. The perpetrator of the alleged crime was no less a figure than the future Christianizer of Ruś, Kievan prince St. Vladimir himself. In his younger pre-Christian days Vladimir ruled Novgorod, which was given to him in appanage by his father Svyatoslav (d. 972), the warrior-builder of the Kievan empire. To Vladimir's dismay his father gave the prestigious Kievan seat to another son, Vladimir's half-brother Yaropolk. Knowing he would have to fight for Kiev, Vladimir decided to secure himself an ally by marrying Rahnieda, the daughter of the Polacak prince, Rahvalod. She, however, preferred Yaropolk. Rahnieda not only pricked Vladimir's pride by her refusal but also injured his ego by calling him *rabynič* (born of a servant). Rumor had it that Vladimir's mother was a servant in the household of the grand prince Svyatoslav. This was sufficient pretext for Vladimir and his cunning uncle Dobrinya to descend on Polacak, kill Rahnieda's parents and two of her brothers, and force the princess to become his wife. Soon afterward, Vladimir gained the Kievan seat by killing his half-brother Yaropolk. Rahnieda gave birth to a boy, whom she named Iziaslaŭ. She continued to hate her husband, however, not only for having killed her family but also because of his ties to other women, including the wife of the slain Yaropolk. Hurt and neglected, Rahnieda decided to kill her husband in his sleep. But the scheme did not work: Vladimir awoke in time and thwarted his wife's revenge. He wanted to punish Rahnieda by death; but, as the chronicler tells us, their young son, Iziaslaŭ, made him change his mind. Iziaslaŭ stood up for his mother. With a sword in his hand he said: "Don't think that you are all by yourself here!" Impressed by the courage of his first-born, Vladimir decided to banish both of them to their native Polacak and even ordered a city built for the two of them, appropriately named Iziaslaŭ (today known as Zaslaŭje, located near Miensk). According to legend, Rahnieda became a nun, taking the name of Anastasia, and spent the rest of her life in a monastery near the newly built city of Iziaslaŭ, where she died around the year 1000.

The image of the tragic Rahnieda has sunk deep into the memory of the Belarusan people. There are numerous tales of the heartbroken princess who wanders across her native land consoling those in grief, healing the wounds of injured soldiers, and helping the unfortunate.

The story of Rahnieda and Vladimir epitomizes the early north-south axis of Belarus's history and Polacak's struggle for independence. Straddling the two major trade routes along the Dnieper and Dvina rivers, the Polacak Kryvičans had to contend with two centers of power, Novgorod to the north and Kiev to the south, linked by tradition and dynastic bonds. The history of the interrelationship of Kiev and Novgorod in the feudal period, says Ukrainian historian Piotr P. Tolochko, "testifies that between these two major centers of the land close and permanent ties existed—economic, cultural, and politico-administrative."[19]

The political origin of the principality of Polacak was similar to that of Kiev and Novgorod. All three shared the same written Church-Slavonic language and Christian values. The unifying impact of Christianity, however, should not be overrated. Christianization of the wider masses was a rather prolonged process, and elements of paganism among them survived well into the next several centuries. Approximately 95 percent of the population lived in rural areas, where cultural inertia was very strong. Medieval allegiance was primarily to the local tribe. In the twelfth century, the city of Polacak was known for its popular town assembly, the *veche*, which resembled its Italian contemporary, the Milanese *Parlamento*, where all citizens, even those of modest means, could participate. A student of ancient Ruś, Vadim Wilinbachow, rightly notes that "each Slav felt himself to be primarily a part of his own tribe and his own rural community. ... The Drevlan was first of all a Drevlan and the Kryvičan a Kryvičan. ... The Old-Ruśian state organization was incapable of abolishing tribal borders."[20] The strength of this tribal cohesiveness asserted itself when the Old-Ruśian state disintegrated, along tribal lines, toward the end of the twelfth century. Similar occurrences took place in the Russia of 1917 and in the Soviet Union of 1991.

The bias of prerevolutionary Russian and Soviet historiography claims the existence in Kievan Ruś of a unified "Old-Ruśian nationality" (*narodnost'*), allegedly out of which the (Great) Russian, Ukrainian, and Belarusan peoples emerged beginning in the fourteenth century. But such a nationality did not exist. It could not have—there was no concept for it. A common Christian religion, where this religion took root or was enforced, and the written Church Slavonic language (based on Old Bulgarian), used by few, were outweighed by tribal ties and local customs that were deeply imbedded in the minds of medieval people. Neither did the endless internecine wars contribute to a sense of "All-Ruśian nationality." Claims of the existence of such a nationality constitute a post-factum political stratagem, an attempt to justify the later expansion of Muscovy, which grew into the Great-Russian tsarist and later Communist empire.

Geography Dictates a Policy of Independence

The Polacak principality came into conflict with Novgorod and Kiev as a result of its strategic location between them on the route from Scandinavia to Byzantium. The land of the Kryvičans had its own dynasty that remembered the tragic death of their forebear, Rahvalod, at the hands of a Novgorod-Kiev ruler. "Since then," recorded the chronicler, "Rahvalod's grandchildren have been drawing the sword." Polacakan princes did not participate in the continuous infighting to occupy the Kievan seat; indeed, they rarely took part in common military undertakings on behalf of the entire Ruśian land.

After the early death of Rahnieda (Anastasia) around 1000 A.D. and the premature departure of her son Iziaslaŭ in 1001, Polacak underwent two successful reigns by Iziaslaŭ's son, Bračyslaŭ (d. 1044), and grandson,

Usiaslaŭ the Bewitcher (d. 1101). (This sobriquet probably came from an adversarial Kievan chronicler.) With changing fortunes, they fought against Kiev and Novgorod and succeeded in aggrandizing their domain into areas occupied by the related tribe of Drehavičans to the south, as well as into the Baltic territories to the west along the Dvina River, far away from Polacak where the Livs, Semigals, and other tribes became Polacak's tributaries. "In the first half of the eleventh century," notes Leonid V. Alekseyev, a specialist on the period, "the political boundaries of the Polacak Land were finally settled."[21] To crown the achievements of his father and assert himself as coequal to the other grand princes, Usiaslaŭ ordered the construction in Polacak of St. Sophia Cathedral to match the cathedrals in Kiev and Novgorod built in 1037 and 1050, respectively. The building, erected between 1044 and 1066, demonstrated originality in its architecture. A contemporary of William the Conqueror, the king of England from 1066 to 1087, Usiaslaŭ had a long, glorious, and turbulent reign. His name was immortalized by the anonymous twelfth-century author of the Ruśian poetic masterpiece, *The Lay of Igor's Host* (the Slavic equivalent of the Western classical epic, *Song of Roland*), in which Usiaslaŭ is depicted with warmth and sympathy.

Christianization Brings Culture

Christianity came to Belarus soon after Rahnieda's husband, Kievan grand prince Vladimir, baptized his subjects in 988. The Byzantine variant of Christianity became the state religion and was spread throughout the realm by force of decree. Some historians believe that Polacak's first bishopric emerged as early as 992 and that Turaŭ's came in 1005.[22]

The Christianization of Ruś brought to the Polacak Land not only literacy, education, and arts but also a softening of manners. Such progress is best illustrated by the life and deeds of St. Euphrosyne of Polacak (ca. 1120–1173), a granddaughter of the great Usiaslaŭ. Christened Pradslava, the young princess chose to become a nun. She transcribed books, initiated the building of churches and monasteries, and founded schools, libraries, and orphanages. St. Euphrosyne is remarkable not only for her works but also for her courage and devotion to Christian ideals. During the Second Crusade she visited the Holy Land on a pilgrimage to Jerusalem where she died in 1173 and soon afterward was canonized. Revered today by both Orthodox and Catholics as patron of Belarus, she symbolizes the civilizing power of Christianity. Her name was immortalized by (among other things) a splendid gem-studded cross created at Euphrosyne's behest by a local master, Lazar Bohša. Of exquisite beauty, the relic survived centuries of turbulence until World War II, when it mysteriously disappeared. In its attempts to trace the whereabouts of this treasure, the

(*Left*) An icon of St. Euphrosyne of Polacak (1120–1173), first Belarusan saint and educator. Courtesy of the F. Skaryna National Research and Educational Center in Miensk. (*Right*) The Cross of St. Euphrosyne made in 1161 by Lazar Bohša. Courtesy of the F. Skaryna National Research and Educational Center in Miensk.

government of the Republic of Belarus has looked virtually everywhere, examining even private collections in the United States.

Historian Leonid Alekseyev concludes his detailed description of the Polacak Land with the following summary:

> Maintaining independent ties with Byzantium and Western Europe and perhaps with the East, Polacak became a major cultural center with its own original school of architecture which infused the best traditions of the contemporary world culture, with monasteries as centers of education and literacy, where chronicles were composed as was done in Kiev, Novgorod, and other major centers of Ruś.[23]

The Turaŭ Principality

Another principality in the territory of the future Belarus was that of Turaŭ (Turov), to the south of Polacak. It stretched along the Prypiat' River, a tributary of the Dnieper, which connects the south-flowing Dnieper with the Vistula River in Poland. Situated closer to Kiev than to Polacak and smaller in size, the Turaŭ principality was for some time an appanage of the Kievan dynasty. Its princes kept rotating, some moving up to the center of power in Kiev. However, "the occupation of the Kievan seat did not automatically entail possession of the Turaŭ Land."[24] In the spirit of the age, Turaŭ princes, undoubtedly reflecting the wishes of the local nobility and merchants, strove to defend their own interests, which were in conflict with those of the central authority. After half a century of subordination to the rulers of Kiev, by 1162, Prince Jury Jaraslavič managed to "obtain recognition of the Turaŭ's Land independence, preserve relations with its powerful neighbors, and gain the support of the Kievan prince."[25]

The second half of the twelfth century was for Turaŭ "a time of political flourishing."[26] In this early period, the most illustrious representative of the Turaŭ principality was Bishop Kiryla of Turaŭ (ca. 1130 to ca. 1182), who was canonized for his devotion to the church and his eloquence as a preacher. Some of Kiryla's homilies and prayers have survived and are still studied for their literary merits.

As the twelfth century wore on and feudalization progressed, the Kievan conglomerate of principalities fragmented as a result of the proliferation of local "dynasties" that were warring with one another. The same process also affected the principalities of Polacak, Turaŭ, and Smolensk, among others. In the meantime, the authority of Polacak was challenged by other centers within the boundaries of the realm, such as Miensk, Viciebsk, and Druck. The importance of Turaŭ declined as well, because of the challenge brought by Pinsk, Sluck, and other centers. Gradually, during the last quarter of the twelfth century and the first half of the thirteenth, the thrust of events shifted from the north-south axis of Belarusan history to the east-west line of development.

The Center of Power Shifts from Polacak to Navahradak

The thirteenth century witnessed dramatic events and profound changes in northeastern Europe both along the shores of the Baltic Sea and farther inland to the east. These changes also affected the lands of Polacak, Turaŭ-Pinsk, and Navahradak (Novagorodok, Novohorodak), the latter lying to the west of the former two and encompassing the Baltic tribes of Yatvegians, Lithuanians, and Letts.

A seed of turbulence in this area was planted in 1186, when the Polacakan "King Waldemar" (Uladzimier) granted the German missionary Bishop Meynard the right to proselytize among Uladzimier's vassals, the Livs and Letts in the lower region of the Dvina River.[27] Fifteen years later, in 1201, German missionaries, following the merchants of the Hanseatic cities who traded with the East, founded the city of Riga (Latvia's present-day capital) at the estuary of the Dvina River. There, in 1202, one of Meynard's successors, Bishop Albert of Bremen, established the religious order of Knights of the Sword. The order's task was to spearhead Christianization of the pagans for the papacy and territorial expansion for the Germans. Soon Polacak began to feel the pressure of the sword bearers. It was a time of growing hatred between the Byzantines and the Latins, resulting from the outrages committed by the Crusaders and the sacking by the Latins of Constantinople in 1204. In 1210, after several clashes with the Germans, Prince Uladzimier was forced to sign a peace treaty with Bishop Albert and a commercial agreement with the city of Riga. This interlude did not last long, however. By 1214 Polacak had lost to the Knights of the Sword its western vassal cities on the banks of the Dvina, Kukenois, and Hercyke. Superior in their armaments, the knights kept advancing. By 1264 their possessions had reached the border of the Polacak Land proper. The Polacak prince Hieradzien had to settle for a compromise. His agreement with the order specified the rights of German merchants in the Polacak principality and similar rights of Polacakan traders in Riga.[28]

Added to the pressure along the Dvina River in the northwest of Belarus was a new force to the southwest, exerted by another order of German Christian warriors, the Knights of the Cross (also known as the Teutonic Order). After crusading in the Holy Land, they were invited in 1228 by a Polish prince, Conrad of Mazovia, to fight the pagan Baltic tribes of Prussians. Soon the Teutons extended their forays into the neighboring pagan lands of Yatvegians, Lithuanians, and the East Slavic inhabitants of Belarus. Although the latter had already been Christianized in the Byzantine rite by missionaries from Constantinople, they remained schismatics in the eyes of the Crusaders because of the split in 1054 between Rome and Constantinople. In the remaining years of the century, following the destruction of Kiev by the Mongols in 1240, the Belarusan lands were beset by incursions from the Tatars in the south and the Teutons in the west. Local warring did not stop either; among the new participants, the Lithuanian princes, was Mindoŭh (Mindaugas) (ca. 1200–1263), who became a major figure.

Mindoŭh's Consolidation of Lithuania and Ruś

Emerging around 1238 as a dominant ruler over eastern Lithuania, Mindoŭh found himself in the west Belarusan town of Navahradak—apparently as a result of continuing strife with his Lithuanian adversaries. According to one chronicle, Mindoŭh and many of his boyars "received the Christian faith from ... the East" in 1246.[29] From Navahradak he launched his conquests and consolidation of a new confederated state consisting of east Lithuanian and west Belarusan territories—namely, the Grand Duchy of Lithuania and Ruś (Samogitia, the area now known as western Lithuania, was added in the mid-fifteenth century to the name of the state.)

Mindoŭh left a record as an able but ruthless politician. Facing difficulties in his struggle with the princes of Halich, Volhynia, and other Ruśian lands to the south, he engaged the Teutonic Knights as allies by promising them to convert to Catholicism. The knights even secured for him a crown from the pope, and the ceremony of his coronation as a Christian king was duly held in Navahradak in 1251. In the face of subsequent wars and further political shuffles, however, Mindoŭh was pressed by the Samogitian Prince Treniota to renounce Christianity as a condition of uniting the country under Mindoŭh's rule and found it expedient to apostasize. He was murdered by his rivals in 1263.

Mindoŭh's son Vojšalk (d. 1268) expanded his father's domain eastward by adding the lands of Polacak and Viciebsk. Like his father, Vojšalk combined religion and politics. He not only converted to eastern-rite Christianity but also took monastic vows and perpetuated his name by building a monastery at Laŭryšava near the capital of Navahradak. Because the Ruśian lands, including Belarus, had obtained literacy along with Christianity by the end of the tenth century (in contrast to the majority of Lithuanians, who remained pagan until 1386), the Ruśian language became the vehicle of the ducal chancellery, courts, chronicles, and various official transactions. It continued in this role until the end of the seventeenth century, when it was replaced by Polish. The common written language of the East Slavs—Belarusans, Ukrainians, and Russians—began differentiating in the thirteenth century and gradually developed into the three national languages by the end of the fifteenth century. Inasmuch as the Old Belarusan language was used by the ducal chancellery since its establishment in the fourteenth century, Belarusan is one of the earliest official vernaculars in Europe. (It was also in Europe that, for example, the use of Castilian was ordered for use in Spanish government records during the thirteenth century, English achieved official recognition in 1362, and the Parisian dialect of French achieved such recognition in 1400.)

The fourteenth century witnessed further territorial and political growth of the Grand Duchy during the 1315–1341 reign of Grand Duke Hedymin (Gediminas), who transferred the capital from Navahradak to Vilnia (Vilnius) in 1323, and the 1341–1377 reign of Grand Duke Alhierd (Algirdas). Both rulers had close marital and cultural ties with the Slavic world. Hedymin was married three times. There is little evidence to suggest that his wives were Orthodox, although five of his seven sons were known to be. More evidence was left by Hedymin's son Alhierd, whose twenty relatives' names, notes historian Marceli Kosman, indicate a "progressive Ruthenization of the dynasty."[30] This conclusion is understandable in view of the far-reaching eastward and southward expansion of the duchy and Vilnia's political ambition to rival the aspiring aggrandizers of Muscovy—Grand Duke Ivan Kalita (1325–1340), known as the Money Bag, and his descendants.

Contrary to the claims of some authors (including those of the old Soviet school of history) about the conquest of Belarusans and their domination by Lithuanians in the Grand Duchy, history has recorded neither any major battles between the two neighboring peoples nor any facts of ethnic oppression. On the contrary, the formation of the Grand Duchy was accomplished largely through voluntary arrangements, including marriages, and occurred as a consequence of centuries-long interspersed cohabitation of Slavic and Baltic tribes before the rise of the common state. The Christianity and literacy that had been practiced in Belarusan lands for almost four centuries before the Christianization of Lithuania ensured the prominent role of the Belarusan territories within the Duchy, where local customs were well preserved and the language of which had gained official status and was used even in Lithuanian ethnic areas. To speak of the Grand Duchy of Lithuania, Ruś, and Samogitia as purely or even predominantly a Lithuanian state, then, is to distort the past by investing it with terms and concepts from an entirely different era.

To strengthen his claims to Christian lands in the East, Grand Duke Hedymin established an Orthodox metropolitanate for his duchy in about 1317, foreseeing that Moscow would use the powerful religious pretext of reuniting Christians under the banner of Orthodoxy that it had inherited from Byzantium via Kievan Ruś. Indeed, by 1325 metropolitans of the destroyed city of Kiev had settled permanently in Moscow and succeeded in turning it into the ecclesiastical capital of Russia.

Grand Duke Alhierd, twice married to Ruśian princesses (although he remained pagan himself), continued his father's eastern policy of adding new lands; with his victorious armies he even reached the gates of Moscow. His territorial ambitions, according to Oscar Halecki, were summarized in the statement that *"omnis Russia* ought to belong to the Lithuanians."[31] During the next several decades, the program of "gathering All Ruś" was conducted from both Vilnia and Moscow, with seemingly equal chances for success. This idea of uniting all of Eastern Europe under one monarch was still alive as late as the beginning of the seventeenth century, during Muscovy's "time of troubles" (1603–1613), when a Polish king of Swedish lineage, Sigismund III, tried to gain acceptance as Russia's tsar.

In 1380 Dmitry Donskoy (1350–1389), duke of Moscow and grand duke of Vladimir, defeated the Tatar armies in the Battle of Kulikovo, thereby securing for his descendants the right of succession without approval by the Tatar khan and launching Muscovy on its imperial course. A collision between the Grand Duchy of Lithuania and Donskoy's heirs was inevitable because of their mutually exclusive claims to territories settled by adherents of the same Orthodox Church.

THE DYNASTIC UNION WITH POLAND

Meanwhile, a development took place that drastically changed the further course of East European history. In 1385 one of Alhierd's twelve sons, Grand Duke Jahaila (Jogailo in Lithuanian, Jagiello in Polish), and members of his dynasty decided to unite the Grand Duchy of Lithuania and Ruś with the kingdom of Poland through Jahaila's marriage to the Polish queen. This step was mutually beneficial for both sides: Jahaila, emerging from a disastrous civil war, was pressed for allies in his struggle with the Teutonic Knights as well as with rising Muscovy. And the Poles, with their twelve-year old Queen Jadwiga (a daughter of the widow of Louis of Hungary) needed a king to stave off complications of succession as well as to engage an ally in resisting the German threat. This was not the first case of Lithuano-Polish dynastic rapprochement. Half a century earlier, in 1325, Grand Duke Hedymin's daughter Aldona was married to the Polish King Casimir. Now, however, the matrimony was coupled more deeply with geopolitics. Jahaila consented to unite his duchy with the Crown of Poland; to convert Lithuania, the last heathen country of Europe, to Latin Christianity; and to fight for the return of Polish lands conquered by the Germans. In 1386 Jahaila, whose Orthodox christened name was Jakaŭ

(Jacob), was rechristened Wladyslaw and crowned king of Poland while retaining the title of supreme duke of Lithuania and Ruś. The title of grand duke was passed to his Orthodox brother Skirhaila (Ivan). This momentous step closely and dramatically interconnected the destinies of Poles, Lithuanians, Belarusans, and Ukrainians for the next 500 years.

In 1387, to advance conversion to Catholicism in the duchy, a ducal privilege granted the Catholic Church vast estates exempting that property, as well as the lands of nobility who accepted the new religion, from state obligations and levies. The first Catholic churches in Belarus were founded in Miensk and Brest around 1390.

Jahaila's acceptance of the Polish crown affected Belarus in two far-reaching ways. First, the Belarusan lands were launched on a path of developing political institutions and culture based on or influenced by Western models while preserving some Old-Ruśian cultural elements. Especially fruitful progress was made during the sixteenth century. Second, the Belarusan people, Christianized originally in the Byzantine rite, became multiconfessional as a result of the advantages Catholicism enjoyed in the Grand Duchy, followed by the Reformation, Counter-Reformation, and Polish as well as Russian counterpressures. Over the centuries, however, the peoples of the Grand Duchy of Lithuania, Ruś, and Samogitia, were able to work out a peaceful modus vivendi marked by religious tolerance and interethnic cooperation among Belarusans and Lithuanians, Orthodox and Catholics, Jews and Tatars. Kings and grand dukes (sometimes in the same person), limited in their power by the growing assertiveness of the nobility and mindful of the common needs of the realm, did manage to regulate relationships among their subjects and avoid large-scale internal bloodshed caused by religious differences. These two aspects of past experience, ingrained in the national memory, have manifested themselves quite clearly in present-day Belarus, thus sparing the republic violent clashes.

Grand Duke Vitaŭt's Thrust to the East

The reign of Jahaila, King Wladyslaw II of Poland and grand duke of Lithuania and Ruś (1386–1434), though quite successful on the whole, was accompanied by political turbulence between the two states and within the Grand Duchy itself. The problem was that the act of the union, personal in nature, was interpreted differently by the Polish and Lithuanian sides: The Poles stressed incorporation whereas the Lithuanians insisted on the duchy's autonomy. Moreover, the privileges given by the grand duke to the Lithuanian nobility who accepted Catholicism evoked resentment among their Slavic counterparts. In addition, there was friction within the ruling stratum itself; its members, some of them Orthodox, were scattered as the Grand Duke's deputies throughout the vast duchy.

The greatest challenge King Jahaila faced came from his resourceful cousin Vitaŭt (Vytautas), whose venerable father Grand Duke Keistut (Kestutis) was treacherously murdered in 1382 when Jahaila fought him for consolidation of power. Ceding Samogitia to his ally, the German Knights, Vitaŭt concentrated on conquests in the east and south so as to secure a power base for himself as a counterweight to Jahaila's Poland. At the beginning of Vitaŭt's campaign, Muscovy and the Golden Horde favored his separatism. The marriage in 1391 of Vitaŭt's daughter Sophia to Vasili, Grand Duke of Muscovy, was arranged as an event of great political importance.[32] By 1392 Vitaŭt was strong enough to gain recognition from King Jahaila as de facto ruler of the Grand Duchy while returning, by way of compromise, an acknowledgment of the formal existence of the union. Around 1395 Vitaŭt assumed the title of grand duke of Lithuania and Ruś. And in 1398 he was proclaimed by the Duchy's feudal lords to be the official head of the independent state. Moreover, the Teutonic Order, with the consent of the Holy Roman Emperor, sanctioned him as "the King of Lithuania and Ruś."[33]

But Vitaŭt was not destined to enjoy the title. His eastern policy and the ambitions he attached to it suffered a crushing blow when the Lithuanian armies were defeated by the Tatars on the Vorskla River in 1399. This event marked a turning point in Grand Duke Vitaŭt's relations with King Jahaila and changed his attitude toward the union with Poland. The Vorskla disaster made Vitaŭt more willing to cooperate with Cracow. In 1401 the union between the two states was reconfirmed on the condition that Vitaŭt remain the ruler of the duchy for life but in close cooperation with the Crown against common enemies, of whom the German Knights constituted the most immediate threat. The confrontation with the Teutons came to a head in 1410, when the combined forces of Poland and the Grand Duchy, commanded by King Jahaila, dealt a crushing blow to the Order in the famous Battle of Grunwald.

One of the results of the shared victory over the Germans was the reinforcement of the Lithuano-Polish union in 1413. In a Diet at Horodlo castle, forty-seven noble Lithuanian families received from the same number of Polish families their coats-of-arms. Some new administrative units were introduced into Lithuania on the Polish model, and high ecclesiastical and civil positions in the duchy were made accessible to Catholics only in order to assure Rome that the Grunwald defeat of the German Crusaders did not spell a retreat of Catholicism in the region. At the same time, Poland and the Grand Duchy reconfirmed their union by agreeing not to elect a king or grand duke without having each other's consent.

Grand Duke Vitaŭt's remaining years in power, until his death in 1430, were devoted mainly to enlarging eastern and southern territories of Ruś—especially after 1422, when Poland and the Grand Duchy signed the Melno peace treaty with the Teutonic Knights, thereby somewhat improving the Polish frontier and returning Samogitia to Lithuania. In a stabilized situation on the western front, Vitaŭt reverted to his uncle Alhierd's dream of "gathering all the Ruśias" under his helm.

At the end of Vitaŭt's rule, the Grand Duchy of Lithuania, Ruś, and Samogitia reached its territorial peak, having expanded to include the Smolensk and Vyazma areas in the northeast as well as the Black Sea coast in the south. Vitaŭt seemed to have achieved everything but a royal crown. Indeed, he was on the point of receiving even that through the efforts of Poland's adversary, king of the Romans, and future emperor of the Holy Roman Empire, Sigismund of Luxemburg. Even the day of the coronation was set; but the crown was intercepted by the vigilant Poles shortly before the great warrior and statesman died in 1430. The Lithuano-Polish union, threatened by Grand Duke Vitaŭt's separatist aspirations, received a boost in King Jahaila's fourth marriage to Belarusan Princess Sophie Halšanskaja of Druck,[34] who gave the aging monarch much-hoped-for sons.

Further Rapprochement with Poland

Immediately after Vitaŭt's death a dynastic war broke out, triggered by discrimination against the Orthodox in the duchy. Their champion was none other than King Jahaila's brother, Grand Duke Svidryhaila, supported by the nobility of the Ruśian lands. He fought his uncle, Žyhimont (Sigismund), whom the Lithuanian Catholic lords proclaimed grand duke. To appease the revolt, King Jahaila issued two charters in 1432 and 1434 by which the feudal lords of closer-lying Ruśian lands were given equal rights with those of the Catholics except for the right to membership in the grand ducal council. The equality spelled out in these charters was reiterated and reinforced in 1447 when Grand Duke Kazimir was about to add king of Poland to his titles. To ensure the loyalty of the nobility and church hierarchs of his expansive Ruśian lands, especially in view of Moscow's claim to the lands of "Kievan heritage," Grand Duke Kazimir chose to forgo a number of levies and duties that the nobility traditionally performed for the state. Moreover, any new obligations to be imposed on the landlords had to receive an approval by their council. The feudalization of the lands had its social concomitant—namely, the enserfment of peasants who had been placed by the charters into the jurisdiction of manorial courts while the lords agreed not to accept any fugitives.

As a result of territorial expansion and wars, the prerogatives and estates of the landed nobility grew significantly during the reign of Grand

Duke Jahaila and his successors. Whereas at the end of the fourteenth century at least 80 percent of the duchy's inhabitants lived on the ducal lands and enjoyed personal freedom, at the end of the first quarter of the sixteenth century that percentage had dropped to about 30. In the same period, the landlords' estates grew to include 65 percent of the total land, with 5 percent of the remainder belonging to the church.[35] Although the central authority remained very powerful until the mid-sixteenth century, the charters of 1387, 1413, 1432, 1434, and 1447 marked an important evolution—the emergence of a new social and political force, the boyars, later referred to by the Polish term *szlachta*, meaning gentry. Over the next hundred years, this new stratum gradually asserted itself vis-à-vis the ducal and royal authority, on the one hand, and that of the great magnates, descendants of Rahvalod and Hedymin, on the other. In the second half of the fifteenth century, a new representative body, the General Diet (*valny sojm*), began to meet periodically to settle vital issues. Initially limited to include representatives of the nobility and gentry of the so-called Lithuanian Land (i.e., eastern Lithuania and western and central Belarus), the institution had widened by the beginning of the sixteenth century to include two delegates from every county in the land. In addition, the right was given to every member of the gentry class to attend the Diet. This process of legal and judicial emancipation of the nobility was modeled essentially on the Polish example, thus making the union between the two states increasingly more attractive to the key section of society.

CITIES, TOWNS, AND TRADE

During the fifteenth and sixteenth centuries cities and small towns in Belarus underwent considerable growth. The charter of 1447 named fifteen urban centers in the territory of the Grand Duchy of Lithuania, of which seven were in Belarus. The most important of these were Polacak, Viciebsk, Biareście (Brest), and Miensk (Minsk). In the sixteenth century, Mahiloŭ (Mogilev) joined their ranks. This process of growth continued into the seventeenth century, by which time 40 cities and more than 400 small towns had been added to the territory of Belarus. Of course, cities in those times were much smaller than those of today; none exceeded 10,000 inhabitants. In the mid-seventeenth century, of the 2.9 million people in Belarus, 150,000 resided in the cities and 250,000 in the small towns—a combined total of approximately 12 percent of all inhabitants of the country.[36] The urban population was replenished mainly from the surrounding rural areas. In the sixteenth century, therefore, (in contrast to the nineteenth), the cities in Belarus were at least 80 percent ethnically Belarusan. Jews made up between 2 and 8 percent of the town dwellers. The names of streets in some cities indicate other nationalities as well: German, Russian,

Lithuanian, Tatar.[37] The capital of Vilnia, where Catholicism had been actively promoted since Grand Duke Jahaila's conversion in 1386, retained its Orthodox outlook: The Orthodox churches—nearly twenty of them—still outnumbered the Catholic ones around the mid-sixteenth century.[38]

A majority of the dwellers in larger towns were artisans, craftsmen, and merchants engaged in metal-, wood-, and leatherworking as well as in trade. By the first half of the seventeenth century nearly 200 different trades and specialized crafts had emerged. Many of the goods manufactured by the craftsmen were sold in internal markets. High on the list of items exported were wax, furs, tar, bacon, hops, flax seeds, hemp, and grain. Most were destined for the ports and towns of Poland, Ukraine, Romania, Hungary, Turkey, Russia, and the Baltic. Imports consisted of English and German woolen textiles, Dutch and Westphalian linen, herring, wine, iron, copper, lead, various metals, and luxuries. Belarus was also an important transit route for Russian goods going west as well as for Russia's imports.

The central authority of Belarus, interested in increasing revenues from the towns by shielding them from feudal lords, supported their development through charters implemented by the so-called Magdeburg Statutes for a measure of municipal self-rule. Modeled after German examples, these charters, with modifications taking local customs and conditions into account, were granted to Vilnia (1387), Brest (1390), Hrodna (1391 and 1496), Sluck (1441), Polacak (1498), Miensk (1499), Mahiloŭ (1577), Pinsk (1581), Viciebsk (1597), and other towns.[39] However, the Magdeburg Statutes affected only those inhabitants who, at the time the charters were granted, were free from feudal obligations. Because the central authority could not liberate municipalities from feudal mortmain, a seigniorial regime survived in towns late into the eighteenth century, thus preventing the emergence of a viable third estate. Towns in the Grand Duchy, as well as those in Poland, did not have the resiliency of cities in Northern Italy, Flanders, or Germany. Nevertheless, the Magdeburg Statutes gave rise to a class of entrepreneurs and craftsmen who, when the time came, became receivers and propagators of the ideas of humanism and the Reformation.

Artisans and craftsmen of the larger Belarusan towns were organized into guilds. In the city of Mahiloŭ, for example, seventeen different guilds were active during the first half of the seventeenth century. Compared to their West European counterparts, however, the Belarusan guilds were less regulated; they were also less influential politically because of the feudal character of the cities. An explanation is found in the fact that some towns in the Grand Duchy of Lithuania developed on private lands and were administered by the landowners—lords, churches, and monasteries. In Western Europe this development had occurred at an earlier stage, in the period from the eleventh to fourteenth centuries, accompanied by the municipalities' struggle for and establishment of their autonomy. But in both the Grand Duchy of Lithuania and Poland, the seignorial regime was much more resistant to change. Around the mid-seventeenth century, 15 of the 40 Belarusan cities and more than half of the 400 small towns belonged to great magnates, were situated on their land, and were administered by them. The authority of the magnate, notes historian Anatol Hryckievič (Gritskevich), was almost absolute. Supreme arbiter over his subjects, he appointed his deputies and commissars to run the city. He was even considered the patron of churches of all denominations, including synagogues, on his territory—an interesting expression of the ecumenical and interreligious spirit and credal toleration for which the Grand Duchy of Lithuania, Ruś, and Samogitia was known, especially in its early period. The owner of the town(s) also kept under his command garrisons of soldiers, who were not submitted to any higher state authority. In short, great magnates in the Grand Duchy appropriated for themselves certain prerogatives of the national government.[40] These freedoms of the great feudal lords later became a considerable hindrance to the efficient management of the state, especially in view of the military pressures of Muscovy.

PRESSURE FROM EAST AND WEST

After Grand Duke Jahaila was crowned king of Poland in 1386, the Grand Duchy of Lithuania, Ruś, and Samogitia became part of a limited monarchy in which the grand duke and the king (sometimes two different persons, father and son) were circumscribed in their power by tradition and the personal character of the union. The great magnates of the duchy jealously defended the separateness of their state in order to preserve their own privileged position vis-à-vis lesser lords and the gentry. But the political clout of the magnates and their resistance to a closer association with Poland was gradually undermined by the duchy's gentry, whose voice in political matters continued to grow. Especially significant was the charter of 1413, the so-called Union of Horodlo. Along with an emphasis on the duchy's independence, the document widened the political rights of the Catholic nobility, including the rights of the gentry vis-à-vis the great magnates, as was the case in Poland. Although the Orthodox lords and gentry were left out of these provisions, their inequality was mitigated by the charters of 1432, 1434, and 1447, which laid a foundation for the legal rights of the entire upper class.[41] "From now on," according to historian Vladimir I. Picheta, "the gentry decisively puts itself on the side of the union [with Poland], being interested in full equality with the Poles and in weakening the influence of the Lithuanian magnates."[42] The charters of 1447 and 1492, given respectively by Grand Dukes Kazimir and Alexander as newly enthroned kings of Poland, established and confirmed a Lords' Council (*pany-rada*) whose consent was mandatory for any important decision of the grand duke. The promulgation in 1529 of the Code of Laws of the Grand Duchy of Lithuania confirmed and reinforced the ascendancy of the magnates.

In 1567, two years before the conclusion of the real union with Poland, there were twenty-nine great feudal landlords in the Grand Duchy (thirteen of Lithuanian origin, nine of Belarusan, five of Ukrainian, and two of Russian). Although they made up only 1 percent of the total number of feudal lords, they possessed more than 42 percent of the peasant households.[43]

The Muscovite Threat

The gentry's attraction to the Polish model was soon reinforced by the growing menace of Muscovy. Since its victory over the Tatars in 1380, the principality of Moscow, with its law of primogeniture, had been accumulating both territories and ideological accoutrements of power. In 1448 it began to install its own metropolitans without Constantinople's approval. And in 1472 its grand duke, Ivan III (1462–1505), married a Byzantine princess and assumed the role of the Defender of Orthodoxy. The threat he saw came not so much from the twice-fallen Constantinople (with reference to its acceptance of the 1439 Florentine religious union with Rome and its subjugation since 1453 to the Turks) as from the Grand Duchy of Lithuania, Ruś, and Samogitia. Not only was the latter in union with Catholic Poland, but, inasmuch as it consisted mostly of Ruśian lands, it also still cherished the old ambition "to control all the Russias and thus the whole of Eastern Europe."[44]

By 1480, having incorporated the principalities of Yaroslavl, Rostov, and mighty Novgorod, Muscovy finally got rid of the Tatar overlordship, thus assuming the stature of all-Russian hub. The Crimean khanate, an enemy of the Golden Horde, became Ivan's important ally in attacking the southern rim of the Grand Duchy of Lithuania, Ruś, and Samogitia. In 1482 the Crimean Tatars sacked Kiev. Three years later, Moscow subdued the northwestern principality of Tver and raised claims to all the territories of Kievan Ruś. Whereas the Crimean Tatars continued their incursions into the Ukrainian and Belarusan regions (45 raids between 1500 and 1569), Ivan III, in two wars against the Grand Duchy of Lithuania (1487–1494 and 1500–1503), annexed a swath of territories reaching as far west as the cities of Chernigov, Bransk, and Homiel, which were occupied. Alexander, grand duke of Lithuania (1492–1506) and king of Poland (1501–1506), in the hopes of appeasing his aggressive neighbor, married Ivan's daughter Helen in 1494; but this did not stop the conflict. As in many European countries of the period, religious and national considerations took precedence over dynastic ones.

Attempts to Separate the Orthodox Metropolia from Moscow

The Grand Duchy's dukes and Poland's kings, aware of the power of appealing for reunification of their Orthodox lands with Muscovy, counteracted by building up the autonomy of the duchy's Orthodox Church. Back in the 1370s, Grand Duke Alhierd had obtained from Constantinople a separate metropolitan for his lands. Grand Duke Vitaŭt did the same in 1415. Vitaŭt ordered the convocation of an Orthodox Church council in Navahradak, where a nephew of the previous Metropolitan Kipryjan (1374–1406), a Bulgarian by the name of Ryhor Tsamblak, was elected head. He was consecrated in Navahradak, and this ancient city of the Duchy replaced Kiev as the metropolitan see in order to shorten the distance to Vilnia and escape incursions by the Crimean Tatars. Although the patriarch, objecting to a bifurcation of the Ruśian Metropolia, refused to confirm the new hierarch for the Grand Duchy, Constantinople eventually reconciled itself with the practice of the Grand Duchy of Lithuania electing its own head of the Orthodox Church. The final split between the metropolias of the Grand Duchy of Lithuania and Muscovy occurred in 1458, when Rome, in union with Constantinople since 1439, confirmed the appointment by Patriarch Mammas of Ryhor Baŭharyn as uniate metropolitan of "Kiev, Lithuania, and All Ruś."[45] Invariably, metropolitans of both centers of power, those in Navahradak-Vilnia and those in Moscow, carried in their respective titles the name of "Kiev and All Ruś" as a reflection of the ambitious strivings of those two centers for hegemony in Eastern Europe.

Another attempt at uniting the Catholics and Orthodox was made in 1458 when Pope Pius II confirmed Ryhor Baŭharyn as metropolitan of "Kiev, Lithuania, and All Ruś" after Baŭharyn was blessed for that post by the pro-uniate patriarch of Constantinople. Ten years later, however, Metropolitan Ryhor renounced the union with Rome, as did the Patriarch of Constantinople in 1472. In the same year, Grand Duke of Moscow Ivan III married the Byzantine Princess Sophia Paleologue and became, as it were, the Supreme Defender of Orthodoxy. It was at this historic juncture, around the turn of the fifteenth century, that a Russian monk Philothei evolved the theory of Moscow as the "Third Rome"—that is, the ultimate bastion of true Christian faith, after the first two centers, Rome and Constantinople, had fallen. Thus religious motivations became a vital ideological and emotional component in Muscovy's *Drang nach Westen* less than a century after the German Crusaders were defeated by a common effort of Poland and the Grand Duchy on the battlefield of Grunwald in 1410.

THE UNION WITH POLAND

Throughout the sixteenth century, inducements for a union between the Grand Duchy and Poland continued along both political and religious lines. In 1500 Grand Duke Alexander, Ivan III's son-in-law, granted the metropolitan see of his duchy to Bishop Iosif Baŭharynovič of Smolensk, who started promoting union with Catholics. The following year, a papal decree had allowed those people living in the regions of Vilnia, Kiev, Lutsk, and Samogitia, among others to be converted to Catholicism without rebaptism.[46] In the same year, Grand Duke Alexander, after being elected king of Poland, signed a document, the Mielnik Union, consenting to a full merger of his duchy and the Kingdom of Poland. Although the Diet of the duchy refused to ratify the Mielnik Union, the tendency to unite was clearly present.

Meanwhile, the situation on the eastern border grew more menacing, to the great disadvantage of the Grand Duchy. After several wars the city of Smolensk, an important outpost, was lost to the enemy in 1514. A brief armistice was interrupted in 1533 when Grand Duke Vasili III of Muscovy died, leaving behind his infant son, the future Ivan IV (Ivan the Terrible). The war lasted until 1537, without resulting in any important territorial gains. But a major change in the situation occurred in 1558 when Ivan IV (who "upgraded" his title from grand duke to tsar in 1547) opened a military campaign for conquest of Belarus and Livonia, both of which lay between his realm and the Baltic Sea. The Muscovites achieved a major victory in 1563 by taking the rich and strategically important city of Polacak from which they took an immense loot in treasures and up to 50,000 military and civilian prisoners. The Catholic and Jewish inhabitants of the city who refused to convert to Orthodoxy were drowned in the Dvina River.[47] Polacak remained in Russian hands until 1579.

In 1562, during the war with Muscovy, the gentry of the Grand Duchy, exploiting the thrust of the moment, formed a so-called confederation (i.e., a temporary military-political agreement) and demanded closer ties with Poland. These actions brought about an abrogation of the discriminatory features of the non-Catholic provisions of the Horodlo Union (1415) and reinforced a large part of the lesser nobility in its drive for further rapprochement with the Crown. What had started as a personal union between the Grand Duchy and Poland in 1386 turned into a real federation in 1569, concluded in the Polish city of Lublin after six months of wrangling about the new relationship between the two states.

The Lublin Union, which left a fair amount of autonomy to the Grand Duchy, was a result of the confluence of three developmental currents: (1) The Grand Duchy's gentry, which by the mid-sixteenth century had gained considerable political leverage and economic rights, modeled

largely on the Polish pattern, saw in the Union a furtherance of its influence. (2) A certain institutional similarity had developed between the two
states in the sphere of administration (territorial division, courts, property
laws, etc.), thus facilitating coalescence. (3) Wars with Muscovy had over-
taxed the limited human and financial resources of the Grand Duchy, thus
prompting a search for an ally.

The great magnates of the duchy, anxious to preserve their privileged
position and weary of cultural amalgamation, tenaciously resisted attempts by the Polish side at Lublin to incorporate the duchy into the
Crown of Poland. Nor was the lesser nobility willing to renounce the
duchy's independence. The end result was a compromise, with some territorial losses for the duchy. Its Ukrainian territories—Podlachia, Volhynia,
and the Kiev region—were incorporated into the Polish Crown. Both contracting parties were from now on to constitute "one indivisible body,"
with a common Diet convoked in Warsaw and a commonly elected monarch. A single currency was introduced, but to be coined separately by
each state under its own stamp. And the new oath by the Lithuanian and
Ruśian dignitaries was now to be given only to the king and Crown of Poland. At the same time, the Grand Duchy preserved its separate name, institutions, army, treasury, judicial system, and ancient privileges, as well
as a separate official language—Belarusan.[48]

Controversy over the Significance of the Union

Historians have never ceased arguing about what kind of confederated
state the Commonwealth of Poland became after the Lublin Union of 1569
and how much unification had been achieved between the Grand Duchy
and the Crown. Whereas Polish authors tend to emphasize the voluntary
character of the merger and its beneficial effects, historians of other nationalities participating in the Commonwealth take a more critical view,
stressing ruse and coercion on the part of the Poles. Polish legal historian
Juliusz Bardach, in his balanced study on the Lublin Union, looking for
"pluses and minuses," admits that "Poland's centuries-long effort at expansion into the eastern territories, generally speaking, ended in a fiasco."
But he also sees a plus for the Polish side—an enrichment of Polish culture
through the talents of Polonized Ukrainians, Belarusans, and Lithuanians.
Of course, one's gain is another's sacrifice, and Bardach concedes as
much: "The loss resulting from the assimilation of the upper social strata
certainly had negative results for the peoples of Lithuania and Western
Ruś by depriving them of leaders, natural for those times."[49]

In "those times" the magnates and the gentry of the Grand Duchy of
Lithuania, Ruś, and Samogitia did not think in post–French Revolution
nationalistic terms; rather, they had their own patriotic values and a sense

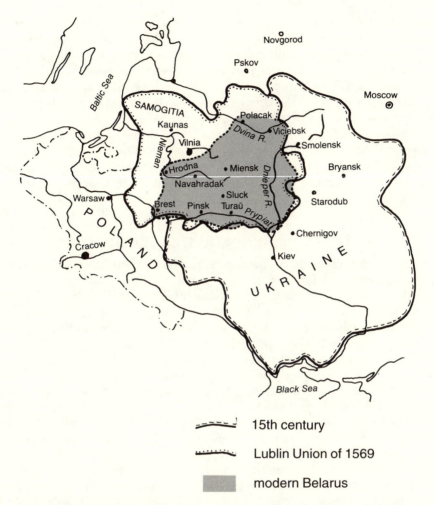

Grand Duchy of Lithuania, Ruś, and Samogitia in the fifteenth century and after the Lublin Union of 1569 with Poland.

of separateness that they did not want to dilute in the newly formed federation. Unable to resist the prevailing trend in Lublin, the nobility of the duchy later reclaimed some of its lost positions. For example, the Lublin Union established the right of Poles to acquire landed estates in the Grand Duchy, and the duchy's subjects to acquire same in Poland. This right, however, was flatly denied by the third edition of the Statute of the Grand Duchy of Lithuania promulgated in 1588. The new king of Poland and grand duke of Lithuania Sigismund III Vasa "promised and swore under

oath" not to give any church or civic property or official positions to anyone—including "neighbors of this realm"—except those born in Lithuania, Ruś, Samogitia, and other lands belonging to the duchy.[50] This example is indicative of the strain between the two subjects of the federation
that lasted until the latter quarter of the eighteenth century, when the
Commonwealth was dismembered by Russia, Prussia, and Austria in
three consecutive onslaughts (1772, 1793, and 1795).

The legal barriers designed to prevent Polish penetration into Lithuania and Belarus (Ukraine after 1569 remained part of the Kingdom of Poland) were ineffective. If anything, such penetration was greatly facilitated and accelerated by the Reformation and the Catholic Counter-
Reformation.

REFORMATION AND COUNTER-REFORMATION

Ideas relating to the Renaissance, humanism, and the Reformation
were widely accessible in Belarus as a result of trade contacts with Germany, solidarity with the Czech Hussite movement in the first half of the
fifteenth century, and the attendance at Western universities by young
men from the duchy. According to some scholars,[51] Francišak Skaryna (ca.
1490–1552?), the translator-publisher of the Belarusan-language Bible, met
in 1523 in Wittenberg with Philipp Melanchton and Martin Luther for a
discussion of religious matters but parted in disagreement. Skaryna—
who, in addition to his baccalaureate from the University of Cracow, held
a doctorate in medicine from Padua University—may have participated in
the preparation of the first Statute of the Grand Duchy of Lithuania. His
leonardian interests and pursuits contributed significantly to the popularity of Reformation ideas in Belarus. Lutheranism, however, did not spread
in Belarus beyond some urban merchant groups, mainly those of German
origin. Rather, it was Calvinism that the great magnates readily espoused,
led by the most powerful of them, Prince Mikalaj Radzivil, who had huge
estates throughout the duchy. Benefiting from the tolerant attitude of
Grand Duke (1544–1548) and later King Sigismund Augustus (1548–1572),
Calvinism also gained adherence among businessmen, tradespeople, and
artisans in many towns. Protestant communities with their prayer houses,
schools, and hospitals were founded in larger and smaller towns: Vilnia,
Navahradak, Viciebsk, Miensk, Sluck, and others.

A factor that contributed to the spread of Reformation ideas was the
rather poor intellectual and ethical condition of both the Catholic and the
Orthodox clergy. Moreover, little attempt seems to have been made to
remedy that situation. In Belarusan medieval literature there were no
counterparts of the French anticlerical *fabliaux*, of Boccaccio's *Decameron*,
or of Ruechlin's blistering *The Letters of Obscure Men* that would expose

Francišak Skaryna (1490?–1552?), doctor of medicine and translator and publisher of the Bible in Old Belarusan (1517–1519). Courtesy of the Belarusan Institute of Arts and Sciences in New York.

and cure the most egregious obscurantism and misbehavior. Calvinist preacher and polemicist Symon Budny was not far from the truth when he wrote in his *Katekhisis* (1562) of the clergy: "They themselves know little truth and prohibit those who would like to teach."[52] And a desire for learning kept growing under the impact of Belarus's ties with the West.

As elsewhere in Europe, great magnates who resented the privileges of the clergy, especially their exemptions from taxation and military levies, found in the Reformation an opportunity to appropriate landed property of the Catholic and Orthodox churches. Similar economic and juridical reasons were at work in the cities self-governed under the Magdeburg Statutes. "The striving of city dwellers to rid themselves of the Church's jurisdiction," notes V. I. Picheta, "was one of the reasons for the spread of the Reformation movement among the urban population."[53] However, the rule of "Cuius regio, eius religio," prevalent in Germany, did not apply in Belarus, where both the denizens of the countryside and the vast majority of the townsfolk remained Orthodox. The reason for this resistance was that most of the magnates had been Polonized, and attachment to the faith of their forebears was seen by a majority of Belarusans as a matter of national survival. The use of the Belarusan language in Protestant publications, schools, and worship services, prompted undoubtedly by patriotic motivations on the part of many, was widely viewed as an instrument used by the upper class to advance its own economic and political goals.

In western parts of Belarus, ideas of antitrinitarianism (Arianism) found wide acceptance. The main proponents of these ideas were Symon Budny (ca. 1530–1593), the aforementioned Calvinist preacher, who wrote in Belarusan, Polish, and Latin; and Vasil Ciapinski (1530?–1603?), best known for his translation into Belarusan of some books of the New Testament.

Lively debates evoked by the Reformation and a flood of polemical publications turned out by numerous printing houses contributed significantly to the development of the Belarusan literary language, which would eventually become the basis for the modern Belarusan revival after the "twilight zone" of the eighteenth and first half of the nineteenth centuries.

The Catholic counteraction to Protestantism gained momentum following the arrival of Jesuits in Vilnia in the year of the Lublin Union (1569), and their opening of a series of colleges in Vilnia (1570), Polacak (1581), and Niasviž (1584), a town in western Belarus that belonged to Prince Radzivil. The new King Stefan Batory (1576–1586) generously granted the Jesuit Order lands and privileges. Indeed, the Order was soon in possession of lands with 16,000 serfs; in the city of Polacak approximately a quarter of the landed property belonged to them.[54] The king used the Catholic Church not only to combat the Reformation but also to stem the dissatisfaction of the duchy's magnates with the Lublin Union, an action that reduced the magnates to a minority within the federal structure of government. The cause of the Counter-Reformation gained even a stronger proponent in the person of the new King Sigismund III Vasa (1587–1632), a devout Catholic who was very much interested in a religious union within his Commonwealth between the Catholics and Orthodox. Such a union was much desired as a unifying factor in a state where vast eastern territories shared the same East Christian rite with the covetous Muscovy.

THE GOLDEN AGE OF BELARUSAN CULTURE

The past is connected to the present in the sense that the latter selects what is important of yore and uses it as building blocks of the future. In the modern Belarusan revival, historical culture has been such a building block. The rebellious spirit of nationalism takes its endurance from culture because culture embodies and symbolizes historical continuity, thus generating an impulse for action and furnishing the necessary moral strength for political struggle.

As stated in the draft of the new Constitution of the Republic of Belarus, modern Belarusans pride themselves on having a "centuries-long history of the development of Belarusan statehood," as reflected, inter alia, in "the Statutes of the Grand Duchy of Lithuania."[55]

The Statutes of the Grand Duchy of Lithuania—which, as codes of law, were promulgated in 1529, 1566, and 1588—stand as a monument to the role played by Belarusan culture in the early period of the Grand Duchy. Written in Belarusan, the official language of the ducal chancellery, these statutes contain local-custom laws as well as decisions of the administration and courts. The fifteenth and sixteenth centuries left behind a wealth of documents—including historical chronicles, original literary works and translations of the classics, religious treatises, and biblical studies—that attest to the fruitful development of Belarusan culture in the Grand Duchy of Lithuania. Some of these riches have been published in recent decades (see Bibliography at the conclusion of this volume), but many remain virtually inaccessible. For example, the *Litoŭskaja Metryka* (Lithuanian archive), a collection of about 600 volumes of documents from the grand ducal chancellery, is still kept, unpublished, in the Central Archive in Moscow, essentially beyond the reach of most researchers. Moreover, although an international commission has been at work in recent years with a mandate to publish the material, little is known of its achievements. The *Metryka* contains manuscripts from the period of the fourteenth to the eighteenth centuries. The documents from the fifteenth century and the

Sixteenth-century castle at Mir in the Hrodna region. Courtesy of the F. Skaryna National Research and Educational Center in Miensk.

greater part of the sixteenth were written in Belarusan, whereas those from the later periods are largely in Polish and partly in Latin. Historian V. I. Picheta, Pičeta who specialized in the sixteenth century, has written:

> The documents of the Lithuanian Archive are a living indicator of the dominance of "Ruśian" (Belarusan) culture in the Grand Duchy of Lithuania, as a result of which this state in the fifteenth to sixteenth centuries was more 'Ruśian' (Belarusan) than Lithuanian. The Lithuanian Archive is a phenomenon of extraordinary significance in the history of the Belarusan people's culture.[56]

Cultural development in Belarus, as part of the Grand Duchy in union with Poland, was influenced by ties with Western Europe, to which Belarusan merchants shifted their trade as a result of wars with Muscovy during most of the sixteenth century. The demand by European markets for agricultural products and goods from forests in the East fueled the economic growth and prosperity of the cities of Vilnia, Bierascie (Brest), Polacak, Miensk, Hrodna (Grodno), and others. The nobility and burghers could afford to send their sons to study at the universities of Koenigsberg, Heidelberg, Leipzig, Louvain, Basel, and Padua. These contacts brought Renaissance culture and humanism into Belarus, enriching the development of native talents. Translation and publication of the Bible into Belarusan, with commentaries by Francišak Skaryna (1517–1519); Skaryna's other publishing and educational activities in Vilnia; a widening of the gentry's role in the affairs of the state; and the growth of city self-government under the Magdeburg Statutes—all of these factors ensured a fertile reception in Belarus of Renaissance and humanist ideas and values. Henrik Birnbaum, in his thorough study "Some Aspects of the Slavonic Renaissance," noted that "it was only in western Russia or, to be exact, in the Ukraine and in Belorussia, that any truly humanist literature ever flourished."[57] This historical exposure to diverse intellectual currents brought about by the Renaissance, coupled with traditional religious tolerance, is a major source of cultural difference between Belarus and its eastern neighbor, Russia, whose society was bonded by the tsars to a single Orthodox Russian Truth.

The sixteenth century is generally viewed as a time of maturation of the Belarusan national consciousness, of which the major component was the language. Although Belarusan had not come of age, as it were, terminologically (all three tongues—Ukrainian, Belarusan, and Russian—were still called "Ruśian," thus strongly connoting Kievan Eastern Christianity), in terms of phonetics, vocabulary, and grammar they were sufficiently differentiated to be considered independent. The Belarusan language had been developing under the strong impact of its role as the official medium of the ducal chancellery, courts, chronicles, and diplomacy. "Even Catholic clergy used this [Ruśian] language in many instances," says Polish historian Marceli Kosman in his discussion of Belarusan culture in the fifteenth and first half of the sixteenth centuries.[58] Indeed, Belarusans of the period were fully conscious of the place occupied by their language in national life. Leu Sapieha, a "Lithuanian" magnate and editor of the third (1588) statute of the Grand Duchy, wrote in the preface in his native Belarusan: "If a people should be ashamed for not knowing its rights, the more so should we be who have their rights written down not in some foreign tongue but in our own language."[59]

In 1621, at a time when many Belarusan and Lithuanian noble families embraced the Polish language, poet Jan Kazimir Paškievič wrote: "Poland flourishes with Latin, Lithuania flourishes with Ruśian; there you cannot get along without the former, here you would look foolish without the latter."[60]

RELIGIOUS UNION AND ITS POLITICAL AFTERMATH

The political Union of Lublin three decades later produced a religious concomitant. Following turbulent discussions and maneuverings, the council of clergy and laymen convoked in the border city of Brest in 1596 recognized the supreme authority of the pope and accepted some fundamental dogmas of the Catholic Church while preserving the Eastern-rite liturgy.

With the Polish element dominating the political life of the Commonwealth, the religious union unavoidably became an instrument of the Polonization of Belarusans and Ukrainians and as such was widely resisted, especially in eastern Belarus and Ukraine, the latter having been incorporated into the Polish Crown since the Lublin Union. Historically, both the rulers and the people of the Grand Duchy of Lithuania were remarkably tolerant of other religions; but when masses of Belarusans and Ukrainians did not follow their hierarchs into the union with Rome, a flood of oppressive acts was unleashed against the Orthodox by the royal authorities as well as by Catholic and Uniate activists. In 1622 King Sigismund III prohibited any public polemics against the Catholics. A wave of takeovers of Orthodox Church buildings and monasteries swept Belarus. Just as Protestants a century earlier had taken over Catholic churches, now the Uniates, instigated and supported by state authorities and the Vatican, did the same to Orthodox shrines. Catholicism, having lost much ground to the Reformation in Western Europe, found a small counterweight in the East.

The great magnates, having secularized church lands and reacting to more radical groups of Protestants, such as Antitrinitarians and Socinians, returned to the fold of the old confession, helped by a concerted effort of the Jesuits. The Catholic Church came out of this struggle even stronger because many of those who left the Orthodox Church for Calvinism also embraced Catholicism. Orthodox Confraternities—which were hubs of educational and publishing activity, especially in Vilnia, during the years of the Reformation upsurge—ceased to be active by the mid-seventeenth century. Meanwhile, Eastern Ukraine under Polish rule was turning into a hotbed of resistance. Many Belarusans, dissatisfied with social conditions and opposing the growing pressure to join the Uniate Church, fled south into the Ukrainian steppes to join the Cossack hosts. Under the impact of wars with Muscovy and Ukraine (1604–1618, 1632–1634, 1648–1654, 1654–1667), and following Polonization of the upper strata, conditions for the development of Belarusan culture deteriorated severely. In 1696, by decision of the General Confederation in Warsaw, the Belarusan language in the Grand Duchy lost its official status and was replaced by Polish. More-

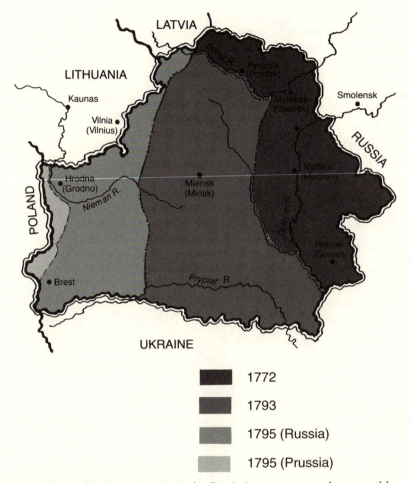

Annexations of Belarusan territories by Russia in 1772, 1793, and 1795, and by Prussia in 1795.

over, Catholicism became increasingly identified as the "Polish creed," thus deepening and complicating the Russo-Polish antagonism.

In their geopolitical striving toward Western Europe, the tsars used the convenient pretext of "liberating" their co-religionists of the "Russian faith." The Commonwealth of Poland, burdened with constitutional crises and internal dissent among its multiethnic and multireligious components, was in no position to resist both Prussian and Russian pressure. In his wars with Sweden at the beginning of the eighteenth century, Tsar Peter I (1682–1725) used Belarusan territories at will and his diplomats freely interfered with legislative matters of the Commonwealth Diet. As historian Oscar Halecki describes it, "Peter the Great was gradually turning Poland into a Russian protectorate."[61] Empress Catherine II (1762–1796) continued Peter I's policy even more aggressively, exploiting the paralysis of the Polish Diet, whose ability to act was hampered by the unanimity rule (*liberum veto*). Claiming to defend the rights of "dissidents" within the Commonwealth, she also demanded the return of more than 300,000 Russian peasants and their families, who, attracted by "Polish freedoms," fled to the Commonwealth.[62] The German-born Russian empress had little difficulty persuading the ambitious Prussian King Frederick II and Austrian monarch Maria Theresa to join in a conspiracy to dismember the weakened gentry republic that was the Commonwealth of Poland. The three partitions of 1772, 1793, and 1795, had a major historic impact on the Belarusan people: After more than 400 years of common life with Lithuania and Poland, Belarus was entirely incorporated into the empire of the Romanovs. And the Romanovs in turn, having appropriated the religious heritage of Kievan Ruś, reiterated their claim to Belarus as their ancient patrimony.

In 1839 the Uniate Church in Belarus, to which about three-quarters of the population adhered,[63] was forcibly converted to Russian Orthodoxy. The name *Belarus* was officially banned, replaced either by the names of individual gubernias or by the term, *West Russia* (with such variants as *North-West Russia* and *North-Western Province*).

NOTES

1. For a detailed discussion of this term, see Nicholas Vakar, "The Name 'White Russia,'" *The American Slavic and East European Review*, Vol. 8, No. 3 (1949); I. U. Čakvin, and I. A. Jucho, "Bielaja Ruś," *Etnahrafija Bielarusi. Encyklapiedyja* (Minsk: Bielaruskaja Savieckaja Encyklapiedyja, 1989), p. 77.

2. K. V. Kiselev, ed., *Belorusskaya SSR na mezhdunarodnoy arene* (The Belarusan SSR in the international arena) (Moscow: Mezhdunarodnyie otnosheniya, 1964), pp. 12–13.

3. Kastuś Tarasaŭ, *Pamiać pra lehiendy. Postaci bielaruskaj minuŭščyny* (Remembrance of legends: Personalities of the Belarusan past) (Minsk: Polymia, 1980), pp. 45–46.

4. *Entsiklopedicheski Slovar'* (Encyclopedic dictionary), Vol. 5 (St. Petersburg: Brockhaus-Yefron, 1891), p. 173.

5. *Ibid.*, p. 231.

6. See N. N. Ulashchik, *Vvedeniye v izucheniye belorussko-litovskogo letopisaniya* (Introduction to the study of the Belarusan-Lithuanian chronicles) (Moscow: Nauka, 1985), p. 20, fn. 54. According to another scholar, Lithuanian territory proper in the GDL constituted "barely one-fifteenth" of the whole. See Marceli Kosman, *Historia Bialorusi* (Wroclaw-Warszawa: Ossolinskich, 1979), p. 74.

7. I. U. Čakvin, "Litviny, lićviny," *Etnahrafija Bielarusi. Encyklapiedyja*, p. 291.

8. N. N. Ulashchik, *Predposylki krestyanskoy reformy 1861 g. v Litve i Zapadnoy Belorussii* (Bases of the land reform of 1861 in Lithuania and West Belarus) (Moscow: Nauka, 1965), p. 6, fn. 2.

9. Nicolai Hussoviani, quoted in Mikola Husoŭski, *Piesnia pra zubra* (The song of the bison) (Minsk: Mastackaja litaratura, 1973), p. 23.

10. A member of the republic's parliament, Hienadź Hrušavy, told Radio Liberty that "about 40 percent of all nuclear missile installations in the European part of the USSR are located on Belorussian territory." See *Report on the USSR*, Munich, August 31, 1990, p. 13. Regarding the twenty-four military bases on the republic's territory, see *7 dney* (Seven days), Minsk, August, 20–26, 1990.

11. M. Dovnar-Zapolsky, "Osnovy gosudarstvennosti Belorussii" (The grounds for Belarus's statehood), *Nioman*, No. 2 (Minsk, 1990), p. 133.

12. Piotr Golubovsky, quoted in Yu. Šerech, *Problems in the Formation of Belorussian*. Supplement to *Word* (Journal of the Linguistic Circle of New York), Vol. 9 (December 1953), p. 82.

13. V. V. Sedov, *Slavyane Verkhnego Podneprov'ya i Podvin'ya* (The Slavs of the Upper Regions of the Dnieper and Dvina rivers) (Moscow: Nauka, 1970), pp. 6, 192.

14. L. Abecedarski, *U sviatle nieabvieržnych faktaŭ* (In the light of undeniable facts) (Minsk: Holas Radzimy, 1969), p. 9.

15. *Zviazda* (Star), Minsk, April 30, 1974.

16. Edward Hallett Carr, *What Is History?* (New York: Vintage, 1961), p. 69.

17. Republic of Belarus, Mission to the United Nations, *Statement by Pyotr Kravchanka, Minister for Foreign Affairs of the Republic of Belarus in the General Debate of the Forty-Sixth Session of the United Nations General Assembly*. Press Release, New York, September 28, 1991, p. 1.

18. For an etymological analysis of the names of Rahvalod and his daughter Rahnieda, see Chviedar Kryvanos, "Rahvalod i Rahnieda: zahadkavyja imiony" (Rahvalod's and Rahnieda's mysterious names), *Čyrvonaja zmiena*, Minsk, September 15, 1991.

19. P. P. Tolochko, *Drevnyaya Ruś. Ocherki sotsialno-politicheskoy istorii* (Ancient Ruś: An outline of sociopolitical history) (Kiev: Naukova dumka, 1987), p. 136.

20. V. Wilinbachow, "Struktura kultury staroruskiej w wiekach X–XII" (The structure of Old-Ruśian culture in the tenth to twelfth centuries), *Kwartalnik Historyczny*, Rocznik 79 (Warsaw, 1972), p. 837.

21. L. V. Alekseyev, *Polotskaya zemlya (Ocherki istorii severnoy Belorussii) v IX–XIII vv.* (The Polacak Land: An outline of the history of Northern Belarus [in the ninth to thirteenth centuries]) (Moscow: Nauka, 1966), p. 220.

22. Archbishop Afanasiy, *Belarus v istoricheskoy gosudarstvennoy i tserkovnoy zhizni* (Belarus in historical, state, and church life) (Buenos Aires, 1966), p. 69.

23. Alekseyev, *Polotskaya zemlya*, p. 291.

24. P. F. Lysenko, *Goroda Turovskoy zemli* (Cities of the Turaŭ land) (Minsk: Nauka i tekhnika, 1974), p. 28.

25. *Ibid.*, p. 30.

26. I. U. Budovnits, *Obshchestvenno-politicheskaya mysl' drevney Rusi* (The socio-political thought of Ancient Ruś) (Moscow: Academy of Sciences of the USSR, 1960), p. 261.

27. Alekseyev, *Polotskaya zemlya*, p. 282.

28. Mikola Jermalovič, *Staražytnaja Bielaruś. Polacki i novaharodski pieryjady* (Ancient Belarus: The Polacak and Novaharodak periods) (Minsk: Mastackaja litaratura, 1990), pp. 327–328.

29. *Ibid.*, p. 318.

30. Marceli Kosman, *Historia Bialorusi* (Wroclaw: Ossolineum, 1979), p. 63.

31. Oscar Halecki, *Borderlands of Western Civilization: A History of East Central Europe* (New York: Ronald Press, 1952), p. 112.

32. I. B. Grekov, *Vostochnaya Yevropa i upadok Zolotoy Ordy (na rubezhe XIV–XV vv.)* (Eastern Europe and the fall of the Golden Horde [at the Turn of the Fourteenth and Fifteenth Centuries]) (Moscow: Nauka, 1975), pp. 195, 199.

33. *Ibid.*, pp. 206–207.

34. Oscar Halecki in *Borderlands of Western Civilization*, p. 125, speaks of the king's "fourth marriage with a Lithuanian princess" without using the name of Sophie Halšanskaja. Since the princess came from Druck near Orša in northeastern Belarus, we again see how differently the term *Lithuanian* was used in the past. In addition, a vivid description of Grand duke Vitaŭt's matchmaking on behalf of the king is quoted from a chronicle by Iosif Jucho in his book *Krynicy bielaruska-litoŭskaha prava* (Sources of the Belarusan-Lithuanian laws) (Minsk: Belarus, 1991), p. 145. It is worth noting that Jahaila's wedding took place not in Cracow or Vilnia but in Navahradak, the first capital of the Grand Duchy, thus indicating the king's sense of history and respect for tradition.

35. Academy of Sciences of the BSSR, *Istoriya Belorusskoy SSR* (Minsk: Nauka i tekhnika, 1977), p. 42; Jerzy Ochmánski, *Historia Litwy* (Wroclaw: Ossolineum, 1982), p. 136.

36. Academy of Sciences of the BSSR, *Istoriya Belorusskoy SSR*, pp. 41, 47.

37. Z. Yu. Kopysski, *Ekonomicheskoye razvitiye gorodov Belorussii (XVI–XVII vv.)* (Economic development of Belarusan cities [Sixteenth to Seventeenth Centuries] (Minsk: Nauka i tekhnika, 1966), pp. 50–51.

38. Juryj Labyncaŭ, *Pačataje Skarynam. Bielaruskaja drukavanaja litaratura epochi Reniesansu* (What Was Begun by Skaryna: Printed works of Belarusan literature in the period of the Renaissance) (Minsk: Mastackaja litaratura, 1990), p. 60. In Navahradak, the first capital of the Grand Duchy of Lithuania, where King Jahaila married his last wife, there were ten Orthodox churches and only one Catholic Church one hundred years later. See *Francysk Skaryna i jaho čas. Encyklapiedyčny daviednik* (Francis Skaryna and his times: Encyclopedic reference book) (Minsk: Belarusan Soviet Encyclopedia, 1988), p. 458.

39. I. A. Yukho, *Pravovoye polozheniye naseleniya Belorussii v XVI v.* (The legal status of the population of Belarus in the sixteenth century) (Minsk: Belarusan State University, 1978), pp. 55–56.

40. A. P. Gritskevich, *Chastnovladelcheskiye goroda Belorussii v XVI–XVII vv. (Sotsialno-ekonomicheskoye issledovaniye istorii gorodov)* (Privately owned cities of

Belarus in the sixteenth to eighteenth centuries [A socioeconomic study of the history of cities]) (Minsk: Nauka i tekhnika, 1975), pp. 148–149.

41. J. Jucho, *Krynicy bielaruska-litoŭskaha prava* p. 40.

42. V. I. Picheta, *Belorussiya i Litva XV–XVI vv. (issledovaniya po istorii sotsialno-ekonomicheskogo, politicheskogo i kulturnogo razvitiya)* (Belarus and Lithuania of the fifteenth to sixteenth centuries [Studies in the history of socioeconomic, political and cultural development]) (Moscow: Academy of Sciences of the USSR, 1961), p. 535.

43. *Statut Vialikaha Kniastva Litoŭskaha 1588. Teksty. Daviednik. Kamientaryi* (The Statute of the Grand Duchy of Lithuania: Texts, References, Commentaries) (Minsk: Belarusan Soviet Encyclopedia), p. 500.

44. Halecki, *Borderlands of Western Civilization*, p. 136.

45. Archbishop Afansiy, *Belarus v istoricheskoy gosudarstvennoy i tserkovnoy zhizni*, p. 113.

46. Juryj Labyncaŭ, *Pačataje Skarynam*, p. 60.

47. Mikhail Bez-Karnilovich, *Istoricheskiye svedeniya o primechatelneyshikh mestakh v Belorussii* (Historical information on the most remarkable locations in Belarus) (St. Petersburg, 1855), pp. 80–81.

48. V. I. Picheta, *Belorussiya i Litva XV–XVI vv.*, pp. 559–561; Juliusz Bardach, *Studia z ustroju i prawa Wielkiego Ksiestwa Litewskiego XIV–XVII w.* (Studies on administration and laws of the Grand Duchy of Lithuania from the fourteenth to seventeenth centuries) (Warsaw: Panstwowe Wydawnictwo Naukowe, 1970), pp. 56–57.

49. Bardach, *op. cit.*, pp. 62, 63.

50. *Statut Vialikaha Kniastva Litoŭskaha 1588*, pp. 118, 366.

51. *Francysk Skaryna i jaho čas. Encyklapiedčny daviednik* (Francis Skaryna and his time: Encyclopedic reference book) (Minsk: Bielaruskaja Savieckaja Encyklapiedyja, 1988), p. 399.

52. Symon Budny, quoted in Picheta *op. cit.*, p. 689.

53. Picheta, *op. cit.*, p. 677.

54. *Historyja Bielaruskaj SSR*, Vol. 1 (Minsk: Navuka i technika, 1972), p. 232.

55. *Narodnaja hazieta*, Minsk, December 3, 1991.

56. V. I. Picheta, *Belorussiya i Litva XV–XVI vv.*, p. 650.

57. Henrik Birnbaum, "Some Aspects of the Slavonic Renaissance," *Slavonic and East European Review*, Vol. 47, No. 108 (London, January 1969), p. 48.

58. Kosman, *Historia Bialorusi*, p. 93.

59. Leu Sapieha, quoted in *Statut Vialikaha Kniastva Litoŭskaha 1588. Teksty. Daviednik. Kamientaryi*, pp. 48, 506.

60. Jan Kazimir Paškievič, quoted in U. V. Aničenka, K. S. Usovič, *Kalasy rodnaj movy* (Ears of corn of the native language) (Minsk: Univiersiteckaje, 1990), p. 8.

61. Halecki, *op. cit.*, p. 233.

62. V. P. Gritskevich, "Razmeri i prichiny massovogo begstva russkikh zhiteley v Litvu i Belorussiyu vo vtoroy polovine XVIII veka (po opublikovannym russkim istochnikam)" (Dimensions of and reasons for the mass flight of Russian inhabitants to Lithuania and Belarus in the second half of the eighteenth century [according

to Russian published sources]), unpublished article given to me by the author in 1991, p. 6.

63. A. P. Hryckievič, "Relihijnaje pytannie i zniešniaja palityka caryzmu pierad padzielam Rečy Paspalitaj," (The religious question and the foreign policy of tsarism before the partition of the Commonwealth), *Viesci Akademii Navuk BSSR. Sieryja hramadskich navuk* (Proceedings of the Academy of Sciences of the BSSR, Social Sciences Series), No. 6 (Minsk, 1973), pp. 62, 63.

TWO

The Emergence and Embodiment of the Belarusan National Idea

INTEGRATION INTO THE EMPIRE

The partition of the Commonwealth of Poland fulfilled Moscow's age-old goal with regard to Belarus. That goal was encapsulated in the two highest titles of Russian rulers—one sacerdotal (Patriarch of *All Ruś'*), the other temporal ("Tsar of Great, Little, *and White* Ruś"). The latter component in the tsar's title was added by Peter I's father, Aleksei Mikhailovich, in the 1650s. Catherine II, aware of having achieved the goal of "gathering All Ruś," ordered the minting of a commemorative medal with the inscription (containing a flagrant distortion of history): "What had been torn away, I returned." "Returning" Belarus, with a population at the time of more than 3 million inhabitants, into the fold of the empire required, however, much more than simple military occupation. There was a linguistic and religious gap to be bridged and a historical memory to be altered.

During the period between 1596, the year of the religious Union of Brest, and 1796, when the empress died, most of the Belarusan nobility, gentry, and many burghers had been thoroughly Polonized, whereas more than 80 percent of the peasantry (four-fifths of the population), with their native language preserved, had been brought over to the Uniate Church.[1] The Uniate clergy, graduates of the Jesuit collegiums and Piarist schools that had been active in a dozen Belarusan cities since the seventeenth century, spoke better Polish and Latin than the language of their flock. Concepts of religion and nationality were inseparably welded: Orthodoxy was Russian, Catholicism was Polish, and Uniatism was plebeian, associated with Eastern rites but Western ecclesiastical allegiance.

The nineteenth century saw a succession of cultural and armed conflicts between the Russian and Polish elements fighting for the soul of Belarus. In the course of these clashes, the idea of Belarusan nationhood and a political state based on this concept had emerged slowly and painfully, and was precariously incarnated by the end of World War I—first in the form of the Belarusan Democratic Republic and then in that of the Byelorussian Soviet Socialist Republic.

At the beginning of the nineteenth century, however, the road to nationhood for Belarusans was barely perceptible, inasmuch as the Commonwealth of Poland had transformed itself from a federated state into a unitary one, with the Polish language accepted by nearly the entire upper class and almost all of the burghers. The extent of the political and cultural merger, obliterating all traces of the Grand Duchy of Lithuania, Ruś, and Samogitia, is best reflected in the Commonwealth's Constitution of May 3, 1791: The document refers to the common state exclusively as Poland and mentions no other peoples but the Poles. During the first fifty years of the Russian regime in Belarus, both the position of the Polonized gentry and the role of the Polish language remained basically intact. The nobles who took an oath to the new sovereign, Catherine II, received the same rights and privileges as those enjoyed by the Russian nobility. Those who refused to take the oath of allegiance lost their lands but not their freedom. The gentry, somewhat limited by the arbitrariness of its status, preserved the right of self-government and local assemblies. The towns were less fortunate. Most of them, except for several major cities, were deprived of the self-rule earlier provided for by the Magdeburg Statutes.

In 1802 St. Petersburg introduced its administrative system into the acquired Belarusan territories by establishing five gubernias with centers in the cities of Viciebsk, Mahiloŭ, Miensk, Grodno, and Vilnia.

Anxious to fortify the social base in the annexed region, Catherine II and her successor, Paul I (1796–1801), distributed freely to their bureaucrats and military commanders landed estates with more than 200,000 male serfs. This policy of land distribution, and the grafting of a Russian ethnic element into the "North-Western Province" (Belarus's official name since 1840), was continued throughout the century, especially as a response to the uprisings of 1830 and 1863.

In the area of religious and cultural policies, the Russian regime in Belarus was initially mild and tolerant toward Polish interests. Paradoxically, Empress Catherine II turned herself into a protectress of the Jesuits when the Order was banned by Pope Clement XIV in 1773. In 1774 she allowed the establishment of a Belarusan Catholic Diocese with full rights of property and religious ceremony. And in 1812, the Jesuit Collegium (high school) in Polacak was upgraded to an academy. Jesuit schools and printing presses continued to work until 1820, when they were banned.

At the beginning of the nineteenth century Russia established a Ministry of Education, the first in its history. Another part of this reform was the creation in 1803 of the Vilnia Educational District encompassing all of Lithuania, Belarus, and right-bank Ukraine. The purpose underlying the establishment of this district was "to weaken the political role of the Polish nobility and the Catholic Church while bolstering the role of the Russian nobility."[2] But the young and idealistic Tsar Alexander I was less of a Russophile than were his ministers. At the head of the Vilnia Educational District he placed his close friend Prince Adam Czartoryski, an ardent Polish patriot. As a result, the basic language of instruction in the district's schools remained Polish. Russian was taught only if pupils were interested in it. And there were not too many of these. "The Polonization of Belarusan youth through the school acquired its widest extent in the period of 1803–1823 when the Curator of the Vilnia Educational District was the Polish magnate A. Czartoryski," states the Belarusan Soviet Encyclopedia. "Teaching in Belarusan in the schools of the district was prohibited."[3]

In 1803 the Vilnia Imperial University was founded as a replacement for the higher educational institution that had been in existence since 1579. The university became not only a center of enlightenment for the region but also a nucleus for patriotic youth—whether Polish, Belarusan, or Lithuanian—in search of ways to liberate the *Patria* from alien domination. Though theoretically accessible to anyone, secondary and higher education was virtually limited to children of the nobility, who in turn were almost exclusively of Polish disposition; hence the prevailing spirit at the university was Polish. Nevertheless, this institution played an exceedingly important role in the Belarusan reawakening. Many of its teachers and students came from Belarus and, quite naturally, became involved in activities on its behalf.

Local intelligentsia and patriots attached great expectations to Napoleon, who was redrawing the map of Europe and on whose side a considerable number of Polish legionnaires had fought. Memories of the 1794 uprising, led by Tadeusz Kosciuszko (of Belarusan lineage) in defense of Poland's 1791 Constitution, were still fresh. Thus the establishment of the Duchy of Warsaw, under French control as dictated by the Tilsit Treaty in 1807, was viewed by many as a first step toward the dismantling of the infamous partitions of the Commonwealth of Poland. However, Napoleon wove his own plans and in 1810, taking into consideration Tsar Alexander I's views, gave the Russian monarch a promise not to restore Poland's independence.

1812: THE TURNING POINT
TOWARD RUSSIFICATION

In 1812 the situation changed dramatically. Napoleon (whose army of 600,000 included almost 100,000 Polish troops) undertook a march on Moscow that ended in the well-known disaster of that year. There were conjectural plans, on both the Russian and French sides, to restore the Grand Duchy of Lithuania and the Kingdom of Poland, but neither materialized. As far as Belarus was concerned, the most notable project was the one submitted to Tsar Alexander I in 1811 by Count Michal Kleafas Ahinski (Oginski). On behalf of a group of political friends who did not want to accept the full merger of the Grand Duchy with Poland, Ahinski drafted a manifesto and a constitution that intended to restore the Grand Duchy of Lithuania, with the tsar's lieutenant at its head. The duchy was to consist of the gubernias of Vilnia, Hrodna (including the region of Bielastok), Miensk, Viciebsk, Mahiloŭ, Volhynia, Podolia, (including the region of Tarnopol), and Kiev.[4] But the events of 1812 and of the ensuing years overtook this and other projects entertained by the Poles with French support. The cause of Poland's freedom and restoration of the Commonwealth, whatever its chances might have been, was lost in 1812 for another 100 years.

During the six-month occupation of Belarus by the French, Belarusan peasants not only fought marauding foreign soldiers but also used the occasion to pillage the estates of their landlords. These events did not go unnoticed by the tsarist government, which had to choose between the dissatisfied peasantry, deemed to be "Russian," and the unfaithful Polonized nobility. The government chose the latter; class solidarity prevailed. The tsar's manifesto of December 12, 1812, ordered a halt to confiscation of the lands of those who had collaborated with Napoleon, and the property already taken away was restored. A victorious Alexander I magnanimously agreed in this document to "commit the entire past to eternal oblivion and deep silence."[5]

Vilnia University

The forbearance of St. Petersburg toward the Polish character of the "returned" lands lasted several more years, thanks partially to the friendship between the liberal Alexander I, who was crowned king of a territorially reduced Poland, and Prince Adam Czartoryski. But post-Napoleonic Eastern Europe, touched by the fiery motto of *Liberté, Egalité, Fraternité* and the religion of the revolution, was not in any condition to forget "the entire past" and remain in "deep silence." On the contrary, the vogue of romanticism and the explosive power of nationalism became potent propellants for action. Especially restless were the students. Groups of patriotic activists sprang up at Vilnia University. Their views were formed under the influence of Joachim Lelewel, a noted Polish historian and professor at the same university. The best known of these groups was the society of Philomaths, whose basic concerns were social and political reforms as well as restitution of the Commonwealth's independence.

Among the Philomaths was Adam Mickiewicz, the foremost Polish poet, born in Navahradak, and his friend from the same area, Adam Čačot (Czeczot), also a poet and a noted Belarusan folklorist. Another group at Vilnia University was made up of history enthusiasts, mainly Uniates from the Bielastok region, who were fascinated with the role being played by the Belarusan language in the Grand Duchy of Lithuania and saw it as a basis for national revival.[6]

The activity of these clandestine student societies did not last long, however. In 1823 the groups were disbanded and their leaders, among them the two aforementioned poets, were exiled. By that time, Tsar Alexander had shed his tolerance of the Polish cause in what was now officially considered to be Western Russia. The school curriculum now stressed religion and social subjects at the expense of the natural sciences. Control over the schools became stricter. Youth from Belarus and Lithuania were forbidden to study at higher schools in Poland or farther in the West. And to weaken the influence of Vilnia University, the tsar subordinated the educational institutions of the Mahiloǔ and Viciebsk gubernias to the St. Petersburg Educational District.

The monarchical regime took a sharper reactionary course in the wake of the Russian officers' revolt that was staged in December 1825 following Tsar Alexander's death. The so-called Decembrists, some of them located in Belarus, conspired against autocracy and serfdom but, lacking support among the soldiers, were crushed swiftly and severely. Alexander's autocratic brother, Nicholas I (d. 1855), drastically changed the nature of the regime, especially in relation to the gubernias that had been "returned." As a consequence, some schools of the Vilnia Educational District were placed under surveillance by the military. In 1827 conversion of Uniates to Catholicism was forbidden by a decree. St. Petersburg was indeed intent on wrestling "Western Russia" from Polish cultural domination.

THE 1830 INSURRECTION AND ITS AFTERMATH

In November 1830 the Polish insurrection broke out in Warsaw, with the goal of reconstituting the Commonwealth of 1772. The uprising was supported in Lithuania and in western parts of Belarus. At the beginning of 1831 a committee was formed in Vilnia to coordinate operations. However, because the committee was dominated by landlords, it failed to gain wide popular support. In May 1831 the Polish national government decided to send a regular military unit to Belarus and Lithuania to generate wider backing. It met with moderate success. Among the 10,000 insurgents in the northwestern part of Belarus there were peasants and burghers along with intelligentsia, students, and Catholic clergy.[7]

The tsarist government reacted to the uprising with severity. Martial law was introduced immediately in western parts of Belarus as well as in Lithuania and right-bank Ukraine. By a decree of December 21, 1830, the estates of landlords who had fled to the Kingdom of Poland were confiscated. Many officials of Polish background were fired from their jobs. By August 1831 the uprising had been crushed militarily; what followed was a string of administrative measures designed to secure Belarus's "everlasting Russian" character. In the same year, the 1588 Statute of the Grand Duchy of Lithuania was abrogated and replaced with the Russian code in the eastern Viciebsk and Mahiloŭ gubernias.

Upon the recommendation of Mikhail Muravyov, a Decembrist-turned-reactionary who served in various capacities in Belarus, a school reform was introduced. Its first "victim" was Vilnia University, closed in 1832. The educational establishments at Catholic monasteries were transformed into secular Russian high schools. A teachers' seminary was established in Viciebsk with the task of preparing the "right" kind of pedagogues. And in 1836 the Polish language was banned from the schools in the gubernias of Viciebsk and Mahiloŭ, followed five years later by the remaining gubernias of Belarus.

In 1839 a council of Uniate hierarchs held in the ancient city of Polacak renounced the 1596 Union of Brest and, claiming to act on behalf of 3,303 clergymen and monks, declared themselves reunited with the Orthodox Church of "Mother Russia." The Uniate Church had a following among more than 80 percent of Belarusan peasants, who in turn made up 90 percent of the entire population of Belarus.

The motto on the commemorative medal struck to celebrate the occasion, "Separated by Violence, Reunited by Love," was immediately belied by the coercion and brutal force used by the tsarist authorities to implement the conversion.[8] History repeated itself in a paradox: Violence at the beginning of the seventeenth century, when Orthodox individuals were being forced into the religious union of 1596, returned two centuries later to avenge itself on the innocent.

The liquidation of the Uniate Church was followed in 1840 by the abrogation of the 1588 Statute in the remaining gubernias of the former Grand Duchy. Finally, in the same year, the names *Belarus* and *Litva* were banned from official use. From now on the area would be known as the North-Western Province, Western Russia, or simply Russia.

In 1841 the Catholic Theological Academy was transferred from Vilnia to St. Petersburg, closer to the center of surveillance. This action was taken in order to shore up the three pillars of tsarism—Orthodoxy, Autocracy, and (Russian) Nationality—in the North-Western Province. But the tide of development went the other way.

The title page of the Belarusan-language Statute of the Grand Duchy of Lithuania, 1588 edition. Courtesy of the Belarusan Institute of Arts and Sciences in New York.

LITERARY AWAKENING

The first half of the nineteenth century witnessed the awakening of nationalities and the rise of nationalism as a repercussion of the French Revolution and Napoleonic upheaval. The Quadruple Alliance (Britain, Prussia, Austria, and Russia), which in 1815 decided at Vienna to keep Europe tranquil in disregard of nationalist aspirations, brought out revolutionaries who called for an alliance of the people. The writings of the German cultural historian Johann Herder (1744–1803), who argued that each national organism has its own distinct personality, or "folk spirit", and the first successful national uprising of the Greeks in 1821, fired people's imaginations and directed attention to the past as a source of that unique "folk spirit." The publication of the medieval sources of the Germans, *Monumenta Germaniae historica,* accomplished under the motto *Sanctus amor patriae dat animum* (The sacred love of the fatherland inspires us), directed the attention of the Belarusan intelligentsia to their own "folk" and artistic oral tradition. The revolutions of 1830 in France and Belgium, inspired by nationalist ideas, instilled optimism among the patriotic youths in the former Commonwealth of Poland. And although efforts at national liberation in Poland and the former Grand Duchy of Lithuania failed, determination and hope persisted among the romantic enthusiasts of the Fatherland. Throughout regenerating Europe, the greatest hopes were pinned on culture, particularly literature, which, according to Johann Herder, was "the surest measure of a nation's growth."[9]

Herder also wrote of the Slavic peoples:

> Since many fine and useful contributions have been made to the history of this people for several of its regions, it is desirable to fill the gaps in our knowledge of others as well. The dwindling remnants of their customs, songs, and legends should be collected, and finally there should be painted a history of the family as a whole, a history appropriate to the canvas of mankind.[10]

After a two-century dormancy, Belarusan literature had to start its growth from the bottom up, inasmuch as it lacked readership in the upper strata of the society. The language used by the gentry was Polish, and Russian was increasingly becoming the medium of the officialdom; Belarusan was spoken only by the peasantry and sections of urban dwellers. True, the Golden Age of Belarusan culture had left behind some memories, which eventually became an impulse for the nascent literary movement. In 1843 a certain Cytovič wrote with nostalgia in a Russian magazine, by way of introducing to its readership an anonymous Belarusan poem: "Now, the Lithuanian Statute has been forgotten, but there was time when its language was official and even had its own grammar."[11] In the same year, a political refugee in Paris, Adam Mickiewicz, lecturing on Slavic literatures, expressed this appreciation of the Belarusan language with which he was intimately familiar: "Belarusan which is also called Russinian or Lithuanian … is spoken by about ten million people. This is the richest and purest speech of ancient origin and marvelously developed. In the period of Lithuania's independence great princes used it in their diplomatic correspondence."[12] And Mickiewicz's countryman and friend Adam Čačot, who, unlike his more talented colleague, committed himself to the cause of collecting Belarusan folklore and imitated its forms in his own poems, indicated in 1846 that there were still old landlords who loved to use Belarusan among themselves and in contacts with their peasants.[13]

It was among such "old-timers" that the first attempt was made to use the everyday Belarusan language for literary expression. In the early 1820s a travesty of Virgil's *Aeneid* gained great popularity, filled as it was with descriptions of contemporary Belarusan peasant life. Patterned after similar parodies in Russian and Ukrainian, the Belarusan "Aeneid Turned Inside Out" was "extremely popular amongst the minor gentry" and "drew attention to the literary possibilities of the Byelorussian language."[14] Later, at the end of the 1830s, another anonymous poem, "Taras on Parnassus," smoother in style and purer in language, gained wide popularity.

Such literature, however, could circulate only in manuscript form because Polish and Russian journals were forbidden to publish works in Belarusan.[15] The tsarist government, in claiming Belarus as a "Russian" province, adamantly refused to allow usage and development of the Belarusan language. It preferred to see the use of Polish in the North-Western Province because, from the government's point of view, it was easier to counteract Catholic Poles than Belarusans who were either Catholic or Orthodox or, secretly after 1839, Uniate. This attitude of the tsarist regime toward Belarusans, along with the fact that Belarus had been for more than 300 years part of the Commonwealth of Poland, explains why the beginnings of Belarusan literature are closely connected with Polish culture and language. Most of the Belarusan writers of the nineteenth century wrote in both languages, Polish and Belarusan. Ideologically, they were supportive of the cause of Polish independence, but not at the cost of Belarus's individuality. A case in point is Aleksandar Rypinski (1811–1900?), a participant in the 1830 uprising who initially saw Belarus as a Polish province but, by the 1880s, had changed his views. Hurt by the disregard in some Polish histories of the literary achievements in Belarus, he asked another writer, Adam Pluh: "Maybe we are aspiring in vain to be

Vincuk Dunin-Marcinkievič (1807–1884), the first major Belarusan writer of the "Renewal" period. Courtesy of the Belarusan Institute of Arts and Sciences in New York.

with this hapless Poland, we who have been born in Ruś which also earlier used to be called Polish Siberia."[16]

The first major professional poet and playwright of the nineteenth century was Vincent Dunin-Marcinkievič (1807–1884). Like most of his contemporaries, he wrote in both Polish and Belarusan, but his Belarusan-language works are more impressive. Dunin-Marcinkievič undertook the ambitious task of translating into Belarusan the chef d'oeuvre of Mickiewicz, *Pan Tadeusz*. In translating this epic poem, which gives panoramic descriptions of the gentry life in Mickiewicz's native Navahradak region, Dunin-Marcinkievič demonstrated not only his own literary skills but also the capacity of Belarusan as a literary medium. It was of crucial importance that the fledgling Belarusan movement prove itself in the arena of language, the foundation of all national causes in Central and Eastern Europe. However, publication of Dunin-Marcinkievič's translation was stopped by a Russian censor in the midst of printing in 1859. The decision of the Main Office of Censorship was "not to allow use of the Polish alphabet in printing works in Belarusan dialect."[17] But Dunin-Marcinkievič did not want to use the Cyrillic (Russian) alphabet because, as he explained in his letter to the censor, "In our provinces, out of a hundred peasants perhaps ten could be found who can read Polish well, whilst, on the contrary, out of one thousand hardly one can be found who knows Russian."[18]

THE 1863 UPRISING

The defeat of Russia in the Crimean War (1853–1856) and the humiliating Treaty of Paris revealed the rot of the tsarist regime and intensified demands for reforms—above all, for the abolition of serfdom. During the first half of the nineteenth century, because of market demands for agricultural products, landlords took away from the peasants a sizable quantity of cultivated fields. In Belarus, the land tilled by peasants diminished from 66 percent of the total land at the beginning of the nineteenth century to about 50 percent in the 1850s. As a result, increasing numbers of peasants became landless. The management of the landlords' estates was, with few exceptions, inefficient, to the degree that landed estates employing 60 percent of serfs were mortgaged in 1859.[19]

Tsar Alexander II, who took over the reins of government in 1855 after the sudden death of his father, Nicholas I, decided to improve the internal situation by imposing a "revolution from above" and abolishing serfdom. This he did in 1861. The land reform, however, turned out to be a robbery of the peasants, who were given too little land for too high a price. The answer to the land reform was a wave of disturbances throughout the empire—including Poland, which became "practically a Russian province" after the 1830 uprising.[20]

Protests in Poland against the land deprivation were coupled with a national liberation movement and an attempt to restore the Commonwealth to its pre-1772 borders. A revolutionary mood was also in evidence in Belarus and Lithuania. A series of patriotic celebrations were held in Viciebsk, Vilnia, Hrodna, and other cities commemorating historic events from the Commonwealth's past. In addition, during 1861 in Belarus alone, 379 peasant protests were recorded; of these, 125 were quelled by police and military force.

Kastuś Kalinoŭski (1838–1864), publisher of the clandestine
newspaper *Mužyckaja Praŭda* (Peasants' truth) and leader of
the 1863–1864 uprising in Belarus. Courtesy of the Belarusan
Institute of Arts and Sciences in New York.

The atmosphere was ripe for an uprising. In Belarus, preparations for
this outcome commenced in July 1862, when the first issue of the clandestine newspaper *Mužyckaja Praŭda* (Peasants' truth) appeared. Behind the
publication stood a group of young radicals, of whom Kastuś Kalinoŭski
(1838–1864) was the most prominent. Principal contributor to the publication (seven issues of which were printed), Kalinoŭski became the leader of
the uprising in Belarus when it broke out two months after the Polish insurrection began in January 1863.

With his newspaper, as well as with his letters "from beneath the gallows," written in prison, Kalinoŭski aimed at three categories of audience:
first and foremost, the peasants; second, the faithful adherents of the Uniate Church, which had been officially abolished since 1839; and third,

those who cherished the Belarusan language (and were being discriminated against by tsarist authorities). The common denominator in all of these appeals was the assertion that life in the historic Commonwealth of Poland was immeasurably better than life under the tsars.

Reading Kalinoŭski's harangues today, one cannot help seeing a parallel between the situation of the 1860s and that of the 1990s in terms of political designs and results. "Six years have passed since the peasants' freedom began to be talked about," wrote Kalinoŭski in the first issue of his newspaper. "They have talked, discussed, and written a great deal, but they have done nothing. And this manifesto which the tsar, together with the Senate and the landlords, has written for us, is so stupid that the devil only knows what it resembles—there is no truth in it, there is no benefit whatsoever in it for us."[21]

Besides oppressive taxes and corvée, a basic source of grievance underlying the uprising was the recruitment of peasants for a twenty-five-year term of military service. This injustice contrasted sharply with past practices in the Commonwealth, where, as Kalinoŭski reminded, "whenever peasants wanted to go to war, they were immediately declassified from their peasant status and excused from performing corvée."[22]

It was during the second half of the nineteenth century that the Belarusan vernacular emerged as a mobilizing medium, and Kalinoŭski seized on this trend when he complained that "In our country, Fellows, they teach you in the schools only to read the Muscovite language for the purpose of turning you completely into Muscovites. ... You'll never hear a word in Polish, Lithuanian, or Byelorussian as the people want."[23]

The 1863 uprising had social, religious, and cultural dimensions. Quite naturally, there were divisions between the right wing (the landed nobility) and the left wing (the radical bourgeoisie and peasants). Tsarist propaganda aiming at the peasantry, of which the government was wary, stressed the fact that the uprising was dominated by the gentry. Indeed, about 70 percent of the insurgents belonged to that class. However, many of them were in fact landless, and lived in towns. About 75 percent of the insurgents came from urban areas, and only 18 percent were peasants.[24]

The uprising lasted until the late summer of 1863. Severe battles were fought throughout Belarus—especially in its western region, which was in closer cooperation with Poland. But the insurgents were no match for the 120,000-strong Russian elite troops, with whom nearly 260 encounters were fought, according to historian A. F. Smirnov. The Russians won in the majority of cases.[25]

The uprising of 1863 provoked harsh punishment of its participants and sympathizers in the North-Western Province, which now constituted the General-Governorship of Vilnia. Governor-General Muravyov well deserved the nicknames of "hangman" and Russifier. According to tsarist official sources for Belarus and Lithuania, 128 people were executed and more than 12,000 exiled to Siberia. The Polish language was banned from official places. Belarus was inundated with teachers, priests, and landlords from Russia. Poles were prohibited from acquiring landed estates. And the bulk of money collected as penalties and contributions financed the construction of Orthodox churches and the support of priests.[26]

An ideological by-product of these developments was the birth of Belarusan nationalism, of which Kastuś Kalinoŭski is considered the founding father. In his prison cell in Vilnia, before being hanged on March 22, 1864, Kalinoŭski wrote an impassioned plea to his people:

> Accept, my People, in sincerity my last words for it is as if they were written from the world beyond for your own welfare.
>
> There is no greater happiness on this earth, brothers, than if a man has intellect and learning. Only then will he manage to live in counsel and in plenty and only when he has prayed properly to God, will he deserve Heaven, for once he has enriched his intellect with learning, he will develop his affection and sincerely love all his kinsfolk.
>
> But just as day and night do not reign together, so also true learning does not go together with Muscovite slavery. As long as this lies over us, we shall have nothing. There will be no truth, no riches, no learning whatsoever. They will only drive us like cattle not to our well-being, but to our perdition.
>
> This is why, my People, as soon as you learn that your brothers from near Warsaw are fighting for truth and freedom, don't you stay behind either, but, grabbing whatever you can—a scythe or an ax—go as an entire community to fight for your human and national rights, for your faith, for your native country. For I say to you from beneath the gallows, my People, that only then will you live happily, when no Muscovite remains over you.[27]

Kalinoŭski's last letter "from beneath the gallows" has become a political credo of Belarusan nationalism.

POPULISTS AND THEIR PROGRAM
FOR "FEDERATED INDEPENDENCE"

One consequence of the 1863 uprising was a flood of ethnographic, linguistic, and historical publications in the ensuing decades that attempted to substantiate the "Russian" character of the North-Western Province. This activity coincided with the great debate in Russian society between the Westernizers and the Slavophiles as to whether Russia should tread the road of the West or go its own unique way of development. The second half of the nineteenth century was also an age of populism and pan-Slavism. The latter called for solidarity among the Slavs and the right of development for each Slavic people. Influenced by these trends and witnessing the ongoing contentions between the Russian and Polish sides, each claiming Belarus for itself, some young Belarusans began looking more closely at their own people and its past. And the answer they came up with was in favor of neither the Russians nor the Poles. The Belarusan Populists of the 1880s, wrote S. M. Sambuk, were "among the first in Russia [who] most fully defined the essential traits of the nation and on their basis proved the existence of an independent Belarusan nation."[28]

The Populist movement in Belarus was part of a wider phenomenon of the 1870s and 1880s known by the same name in Russian history. At the beginning of the 1870s a string of Populist organizations sprouted in Miensk, Mahiloŭ, Viciebsk, Hrodna, Sluck, and other towns. Under the guise of self-education, young people studied illegal Populist literature and discussed the future of their country. They also established contacts with countrymen enrolled in universities in Moscow, St. Petersburg, and other cities. From these circles came such well-known revolutionaries as Mikalaj Sudziloŭski, Ryhor Isajeŭ, and the later assassin of Tsar Alexander II (in 1881), Ihnat Hryniavicki.

In the early 1880s the Social-Revolutionary Group of Belarusans was founded. Struggling with growing persecution in the aftermath of Alexander II's violent death, the group managed to publish two issues of their clandestine magazine, *Homon* (Clamor), in St. Petersburg (where some of them were students). In the leading article of the first issue (in 1884), the publishers declared their firm intention to "put the first stone in the foundation of the federated independence of Belarus."[29] As was typical among the Populists throughout Russia, the Homonites pinned their hopes on the native intelligentsia. They wrote:

> The Belarusan people as a plebeian nation is still waiting for the emergence of their intelligentsia. Until now, they have been relinquishing from among themselves talents who served either Polish or Great Russian culture. Mutely but persistently they protested against treacherous attempts to Polonize or Russify them, and both cultures, forcibly foisted on them, failed to take root. Piously they preserved the foundations of their life while waiting for the emergence of their own intelligentsia who would not uproot those foundations but would develop and build on them. ... Then once more the Belarusan nationality will prove what has been proven many times by other plebeian nationalities (the Slavic peoples in Austria, the Finns in Finland, and others), that a low level of culture does not lead to its subjection, but on the contrary, subjection causes stagnation.[30]

Inspired by their belief in the salutary power of freedom, the Homonites called upon their followers to unite in the Social-Revolutionary Party of Belarusans. However, police surveillance following the assassination of Alexander II in 1881 was too intense to permit any sort of orga-

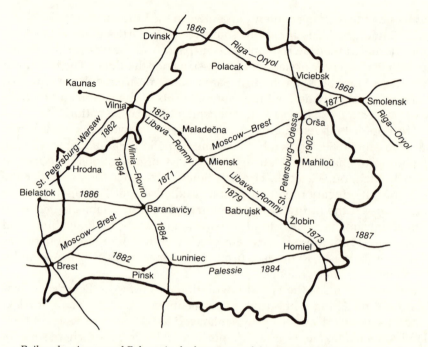

Railroads crisscrossed Belarus in the latter part of the nineteenth century in a testament to the country's central location.

nized revolutionary activity. By 1886 the echo of *Homon's* exhortations was muffled and its organizational activities had died out.

The Growth of Cities, Railroads, and Education

In the system of Russian capitalism of the last quarter of the nineteenth century, Belarus was less developed industrially than central Russia, Ukraine, the Baltic area, or Poland. The reason for this was the lack of natural resources and the persistence of the remnants of serfdom. However, because of the central location of Belarus, the government built a fairly developed network of railroads. By the end of the century more than 1,875 miles (3,000 kilometers) of railroads had been established in Belarus, along with a relatively dense network of waterways. Both facilitated the importation to Belarusan markets of goods from other areas. The local industry therefore specialized in processing agricultural and forest products as well as satisfying the needs of the population for everyday goods.

Between 1863 and 1897 (the latter being the year of the first systematic census in the empire), the population in Belarus grew by 94.5 percent from 3.3 million to 6.5 million. The number of city dwellers rose by nearly the same proportion (96.4 percent), from 330,000 to 648,000. However, the ratio of the urban population in Belarus remained the same (9.8 percent), whereas in the whole of European Russia the ratio grew (from 9.9 percent to 12.8 percent).[31]

At the end of the century, unemployment and poverty were rampant. According to some authorities, there were 3.6 million proletarians and half-proletarians in Belarus in 1897, mostly in rural areas.[32] This is one reason for the massive emigration from Belarus to the United States that occurred in the early 1900s.

The progress of education in Belarus during the second half of the century was considerably hampered by the persecutions that followed the 1863 uprising. In 1864 Belarus lost its only higher-education institution, the Agricultural Institute of Hory-Horki, in the Mahiloŭ region. Almost 2,000 students were dismissed from their schools for their role in the uprising. Discriminatory decrees against Catholic teachers and students affected not only Poles but also Belarusan Catholics, of whom there were about 750,000. The Ministry of Education knew quite well that the next line of defense against Polish interests and influence in Belarus was the classroom. With this in mind, the tsar in 1864 approved the transfer of all primary schools to the control of the Orthodox clergy. The Polish and Belarusan languages were totally banned from school buildings. Only the use of Russian was allowed in education.

Education expanded nevertheless, along with the growth of industry and cities. Consider the following statistics. In 1860 there were 576 educational institutions of all types (with 17,000 students); by 1868 the number of schools had risen to 1,391 (54,417 students); and by 1881 the number had increased again to 2,185 (63,584 students). Between 1864 and 1876 four teachers' seminaries were opened in Polacak, Niaśviž, Maladečna, and Śvislač.

Some authors have repeated the assertion that the literacy rate for Belarus "was the lowest among the peoples of European Russia."[33] But statistical evidence indicates that the proportion of literates in Belarus as of 1897 (among people nine to forty-nine years old) was 32 percent, compared to 29.6 and 27.9 percent in the Russian Federation and Ukraine, respectively.[34]

MEMORIES OF PAST GREATNESS PROVIDE HOPE

The tsarist policy of Russification in the North-Western Province faced a dilemma: What to allow and what to forbid? Having prohibited the name *Bielaruś*, and having banned the language from schools and creative writing, the government at the same time sponsored much publishing activity designed to prove the "Russianness" of the "Western gubernias."

Although most such projects referred to Belarus as "Western Russia," some of them, for scholarly or other reasons, had to use the term *Belaruś,* which Tsar Nicholas I had banned. Thus, lexicographer Ivan Nasovič published *The Dictionary of the Belarusan Language* in 1870, followed by *Belarusan Songs* in 1873. Ethnographers Paval Šejn, Mikalaj Nikifaroŭski, Piotr Biassonaŭ, and others published collections of "Belarusan" folksongs. And in 1884 linguist Jaŭchim Karski commenced publication of his studies devoted to "Belarusan speech," which culminated in *The Belarusans,* his monumental description of Belarusan language and literature (three volumes in seven parts, 1903–1922).

Along with censorship, Russian historical scholarship was involved in proving the Russian character of the North-Western Province. The Vilnia Archeological Commission alone published forty-nine volumes of historical documents (29,000 pages in folio) in 1864–1915.[35] The published documents were designed to prove what the tsarist government had in mind; but as N. N. Ulashchik observed, "Once documents are published, they take on a life of their own, and not infrequently prove quite another thing than the one their compilers and editors wanted while preparing for publication."[36]

It was Francišak Bahuševič (1840-1900), the "father" of modern Belarusan literature, who saw in those ancient documents a mirror of his nation's past and made an attempt to attract attention to them. In the foreword to his collection of poems, *Dudka bielaruskaja* (The Belarusan fife), published in Cracow in 1891 and smuggled into Belarus, he wrote: "I have read many old papers written two and three hundred years ago in our land by great lords, but in our purest language as if they were being written right now." Thus, he added, "our language is no less civilized and noble than French, German, or any other tongue." Comparing man's speech to the "vestment of the soul," the poet then exhorted his countrymen: "Do not abandon our Belarusan language lest you die!"[37] Indeed, Bahuševič's "Belarusan fife" "gave impetus to the Belarusan movement"[38] in spite of vigilant tsarist censors, on the one hand, and the animosity of enthusiasts of Polish and Russian culture, on the other.

THE 1897 CENSUS

In 1897 the first systematic census of the population of the Russian Empire was carried out. Its results, published in 1905, revealed that the five gubernias of the North-Western Province in which Belarusans constituted a majority (Mahiloŭ, Viciebsk, Miensk, Vilnia, and Hrodna) were inhabited by 8,518,247 people,[39] of whom 5,408,420 were Belarusans.[40] In the entire Belarusan ethnographic area, there were 5,886,000 Belarusans.[41] And in the five Belarusan gubernias there lived 1,202,129 Jews, 492,921 Russians, 424,236 Poles, 377,487 Ukrainians, 288,921 Lithuanians, 272,775 Latvians, 27,311 Germans, 8,448 Tatars, and 19,658 others.

The social categories of these nationalities break down as follows (with the percentage of each group living in towns noted in parentheses): nobility, 238,522 (28.7 percent); clergy, 21,849 (26.4 percent); merchants, 18,282 (81.0 percent); petty bourgeoisie, 1,781,908 (40.0 percent); peasants, 6,416,745 (3.4 percent); foreigners, 13,469 (29.6 percent); and others, 27,473 (49.0 percent).[42]

According to the same 1897 census, of the 5.4 million Belarusan speakers 81 percent belonged to the Orthodox religion, 18.5 percent were Catholic, .47 percent were Old-Believers, and .03 percent were Lutherans.[43] Belarusans, constituting 63.5 percent of the total population of the five gubernias, were essentially rural dwellers; only 2.6 percent lived in cities. In most Belarusan cities and towns, Jews constituted an overwhelming majority, up to 90 percent of the population. This was a result of the Empress Catherine's decree of 1794, which barred Jews (who were numerous in Belarus) from settling in Russian provinces; and of Tsar Alexander III's prohibition of 1883 against Jews settling outside cities and towns.[44]

The national consciousness of the Belarusans was just evolving. Toward the end of the nineteenth century, professionals who identified themselves as Belarusans were 40 percent of officials (čynoŭniki), 10 percent of jurists, 20 percent of doctors, 29 percent of post and telegraph employees, and 60 percent of teachers.[45] Thus we have an explanation for the difficulties faced by the Belarusan cultural revival and political movement, which at the beginning of the twentieth century had to rely for support on the lowest, most passive, and least educated social stratum, the peasantry.

"NAŠA NIVA" AND THE LITERARY REVIVAL

The literary potential of the Belarusan movement found its outlet and stimulus when, as a result of the 1905 revolution, the Russian government was forced to relax its policy toward national minorities. The State Duma (parliament) was instituted, and the ban on non-Russian languages was lifted. Vilnia, the ancient capital of the Grand Duchy, again became a bustling center of multicultural life. Of the more than sixty newspapers and magazines that appeared in the five Belarusan gubernias, most of them in Russian, two-thirds were published in Vilnia, including nine in Polish, nine in Yiddish, six in Lithuanian, and two in Belarusan.[46]

In 1906 activists of the Belarusan Socialist Union (Hramada) in Vilnia launched a weekly called Naša Dola (Our destiny). The newspaper immediately ran into trouble with the authorities because of its radical program. Foreseeing closure of the publication, which soon came about, the publishers initiated another weekly, *Naša Niva* (Our cornfield), a more successful periodical that lasted until 1915 and imprinted its name on an entire period of Belarusan history—*našaniŭstva*. Headed by the brothers Ivan and Anton Luckievič, the publishers assumed a more moderate course. In their first editorial they declared: "Do not think that we wish to serve only the gentry, or only the peasants. No, never! We want to be the servants of the whole long-suffering Belarusan nation." The newspaper, without being the official organ of the Belarusan Socialist Union, became a fulcrum of Belarusan cultural life. "*Naša Niva*," notes A. B. McMillin, "both reflected and guided the amazingly rapid development of literature at this time."[47] The newspaper successfully survived both financial difficulties and tsarist censorship until August 1915, when the German occupation of Vilnia interrupted its publication. The early twentieth century was a propitious time not only for Russian culture but for Belarusan literature as well. *Naša Niva* grouped around itself a constellation of young authors who wrote the classics of modern Belarusan literature. Among the most notable were Janka Kupala (1882–1942), Jakub Kolas (1882–1956), Ciotka (1876–1916), Maksim Harecki (1893-1939), Maksim Bahdanovič (1891–1917), Žmitrok Biadula (1886–1941), Aleś Harun (1887–1920), and Vaclaŭ Lastoŭski (1883–1938).

The leitmotif of their poems and prose—some marked by stern realism, others by nationalist romanticism—was the harsh, dehumanizing nature of peasant life. The bleak present was contrasted with the glorious distant past when the Belarusan was a free master of his destiny, enjoying the fruits of his labor and fame. The thirty-year-old Janka Kupala, "the Prophet of the Belarusan Rebirth," called on his country: "O young Bielaruś, come thou forth, take thy place of honour and fame among nations."[48] The idealization of the past had a concrete and practical application: It substituted for a program of national rebirth and liberation, which could not be expressed in the form of political platforms because of the oppressive regime. Literature, to paraphrase Alexander Solzhenitsyn's words from his Nobel Lecture, "kept preserving and protecting the nation's soul."

In 1910 Vaclaŭ Lastoŭski, a writer and self-educated historian, published in Vilnia his *Short History of Belarus*, the first Belarusan-language account of the country's past. Devoted to the "sons of Young Belarus," it demonstrated that in ancient times the Belarusan people had not only princes and nobility but literary achievements and high political standing as well.

The *Naša Niva* period (1906–1915) was also marked by a revival of Belarusan dramatic clubs and theater; by the establishment of publishing societies, student associations, reading rooms, and schools; and by the activities of Belarusan Catholics who in 1913 began publishing their newspaper *Bielarus* (1913–1915). Between 1908 and 1914, 77 titles of Belarusan books were published, totaling 226,660 copies.[49] All these activities, however, were conducted under highly unfavorable political and psychological conditions, given the generally accepted assumption that everything Belarusan was peasant, crude, and primitive. The impact of *Naša Niva*, whose circulation did not exceed 4,500 copies, was thus limited. There were also administrative barriers. As one scholar notes, "A ministerial order forbade the use of White Russian [Belarusan] in private assemblies, and soldiers were not allowed to receive letters from home written in their native language. In the schools the penalty for the use of the mother tongue amongst the pupils was expulsion."[50]

BELARUS BECOMES A MILITARY CAMP

The outbreak of World War I on August 1, 1914, turned Belarus into a theater of military operations. Strict martial law was introduced as of the first day of the war. All public meetings were banned, and the sale of newspapers and books could not be conducted without permission of the military authorities. Belarus absorbed a Russian army of 1.5 million men. Miensk alone had to accommodate 150,000 soldiers and military personnel. By the summer of 1915, when the Germans started their eastward advance, more than a million civilians had either fled or were expelled deep into Russia.

In the fall of 1915 one-third of Belarus found itself under German occupation, with Vilnia in the hands of the occupiers. By October 1917 two-thirds of Belarus had been occupied. After the Bolshevik coup in November 1917 and a brief interlude of peace negotiation at Brest-Litovsk, military operations were resumed and by March 1918 four-fifths of Belarus found itself under the German occupation. The Germans remained in the country until the end of 1918.

Belarusan life under the Germans was initially concentrated in Vilnia, where a number of *Naša Niva* adherents remained, including the most active of them, the brothers Ivan and Anton Luckievič. With a group of like-minded Lithuanians, Poles, and Jews, the Luckievičs tried to resuscitate the old concept of the Grand Duchy, which was favored by the Germans. Thus, on December 19, 1915, a declaration was published in four languages announcing the establishment of a "Confederation of the Grand Duchy of Lithuania" in which "all ethnic groups shall be guaranteed their rights." The authors of the declaration called upon all partners "to forget slander, strife, and mistrust in view of the great importance of this historic moment" and join the Confederation.[51] However, circumstances were very different from those of four to five centuries ago, and the initiators' romantic idea failed to germinate.

The March 1917 democratic revolution in Russia brought to every nationality in the area hopes for realizing the brand-new ideal of national independence. On the territories of the former Grand Duchy of Lithuania, Ruś, and Samogitia, which by the end of the eighteenth century had merged into the unified Commonwealth of Poland, each nationality worked zealously to attain its separate political status.

Within several weeks branches of the Belarusan Socialist Union and other political parties and cultural societies had sprung up in Miensk, Vilnia, and other towns of Belarus and Russia, including Moscow and Petrograd, where Belarusan workers and war refugees found themselves after the revolution of March 1917.

On the German side of the front, in Vilnia, the publishers of the discontinued *Naša Niva* launched a fresh semiweekly newspaper in February 1916. Called *Homan* (Clamor), it echoed the 1884 publication with its slogan of the "federated independence" of Belarus. The new *Homan* became a forum for Belarusan life and hopes of autonomy. Although the Germans did not particularly favor the Belarusan movement, they also did not object to it where it did not interfere with their war effort. In fact, the Belarusan language was recognized in 1916 as one of the official languages of the region.[52] Moreover, about 100 Belarusan primary schools were opened in the Vilnia district, with a teachers' college functioning in the town of Śvislač.

The Belarusan political cause surfaced for the first time in the international arena in 1916. In that year Ivan Luckievič and Vaclaŭ Lastoŭski attended the conferences of the Peoples of Russia at Stockholm, Sweden, and Lausanne, Switzerland, and made a plea to the international community to help the Belarusans in securing "the fullness of [their] cultural and political rights."[53]

As revolutionary Russia sank more deeply into the chaos of civil war, the protagonists of the Belarusan national idea had to struggle against many odds. First of all, there were about 1.5 million Russian soldiers in Belarus, ignorant of or opposed to Belarusan national aspirations. And the Belarusans themselves were divided on the subject of their political future. Political allegiances had strong cultural and religious underpinnings. Strivings for Belarusan separateness were seriously hampered by the general identification of Catholicism with Polishness and Orthodoxy with Russianness—a psychological heritage of the age-old Russo-Polish competition in the Belarusan lands.

The pronouncement of the Russian Provisional Government of peoples' rights to self-determination (April 10, 1917) as well as Lenin's Declaration of the Rights of the Peoples of Russia (November 15, 1917), both of which theoretically also recognized the right of the Belarusans to a separate status, were difficult to manifest in practical terms. The main obstacle was the fact that the political landscape in Belarus, where 97.4 percent of the urban population consisted of non-Belarusans, was dominated by Russian, Polish, and Jewish parties with their own goals not necessarily coinciding with—and in some cases antagonistic to—the Belarusan revival. The Bolshevik organizations, for example, operated in Belarus as branches of the Russian Social-Democratic Labor Party, which until the end of 1918, was opposed to the autonomy of Belarus. Thus the road to Belarusan nationhood, in both theoretical and practical terms, was all uphill and quite steep at that.

THE ALL-BELARUSAN CONGRESS DISPERSED

Belarusan political activities on a broader scale started in March 1917, when a conference of Belarusan organizations and parties took place in Miensk, with the statehood of Belarus as the main item on the agenda. The conference "expressed itself in favor of a republican democratic regime which would join the Russian Federal Democratic Republic as an autonomous state."[54]

The conference elected a sixteen-member Belarusan National Committee to spearhead the movement. In the ensuing months, a series of conventions of civic and military groups was held, periodicals advocating some degree of autonomy or independence were launched, and political alliances were concluded. Most parties in Belarus were of a Socialist orientation, acting either as independent entities or as chapters of All-Russian parties. The most vocal advocate of Belarus's autonomy was the aforementioned Belarusan Socialist Union; founded in 1902, it emerged again in 1917 with renewed vigor.

After the Bolsheviks seized power in Miensk on November 7, 1917, and failed to include the autonomy of Belarus in their program, the Great Belarusan Council issued an "Appeal to the Belarusan People," two days later calling on "Belarusan revolutionary democracy … never [to] permit the storm of disorder to engulf our sacred national cause of defending the freedom and rights of the Belarusan people."[55]

In mid-December of 1917 a coalition of Belarusan parties convened the All-Belarusan Congress in Miensk, at which 1,915 delegates represented local governments; social, political, and military organizations, including the Bolsheviks; and committees of Belarusan refugees. The congress proclaimed Belarus a democratic republic while refusing to recognize any other authority on its territory, meaning the Bolsheviks. As a result, the latter disbanded the congress on December 30, 1917. On the following day, the delegates handed over their power to the Council of the congress, whose executive committee continued to lead the national movement from underground.

Government of the Belarusan Democratic Republic (1918). Seated from left: Alaksandar Burbis, Ivan Sierada, Jazep Varonka, and Vasil Zacharka. Standing from left: Arkadź Smolič, Piotra Krečeŭski, Kanstantyn Jezavitaŭ, A. Aŭsianik, and Lavon Zajac. Courtesy of the F. Skaryna National Research and Educational Center in Miensk.

UNDER GERMAN OCCUPATION

On February 21, 1918, the Germans occupied Miensk. Their negotiations with the Bolsheviks produced a peace treaty (dated March 3, 1918) that divided Belarus among the neighboring states. Reacting to this diplomatic violence, the Executive Committee of the Council of the First All-Belarusan Congress published (on March 9, 1918), its Second Constituent Charter by which Belarus, "within the borders of the numerical majority of the Belarusan people," was proclaimed Belarusan Democratic Republic (BDR). Human rights and freedoms were specified in the charter.[56] support for the political aspirations of the Belarusans. Their response to the declaration of the BDR was forcefully negative, inasmuch as the Treaty of Brest-Litovsk (as Berlin explained in a later answer) specified that "Germany undertook an obligation not to support any new state creations on

Coat-of-arms of the Belarusan Democratic Republic (1918). Courtesy of the F. Skaryna National Research and Educational Center in Miensk.

the territory of former Russia."[57] The Council of the BDR, therefore, decided to act on its own and, on March 25, 1918, declared in its Third Constituent Charter: "From this time on, the Belarusan Democratic Republic is proclaimed an independent and free state. The peoples of Belarus themselves, under the aegis of the Constituent Assembly, shall determine the future national relations of Belarus."

BELARUS DIVIDED BETWEEN RUSSIA AND POLAND

The Bolsheviks, who for a long time had ignored the Belarusan national question and denied its importance, acknowledged their mistaken policy by the end of 1918. One of their leaders, Vilhelm Knoryn, wrote in 1924:

> The period of German occupation was at the same time a period of absorption by the masses of the idea of Belorussian independence, to which the Party should have given its attention. Under these circumstances the Party organizations of Moscow and Smolensk became convinced almost simultaneously that the establishment of the Belorussian Republic was necessary immediately.[58]

This was the "necessary" step for which the Belarusan sections within Lenin's Bolshevik Party fought during most of 1918. On December 20, 1918, the sixth regional conference of the Russian Communist Party (of Bolsheviks) in Smolensk converted into the First Congress of the Communist Party of Belarus and, on January 1, 1919, proclaimed the erection of the Belarusan Soviet Socialist Republic. Hardly a month had elapsed when the newly created republic was merged with Lithuania into the Lithuanian-Belarusan SSR. This maneuver was carried out in view of the war with Poland over the Belarusan and Lithuanian territories. In August 1919 Polish troops occupied the western half of Belarus, including the city of Miensk. Kaleidoscopic changes continued to evolve, however. In the summer of 1920 the Red Army swung westward as far as central Poland, where the "Miracle on the Vistula" took place and the Bolsheviks were again driven back to the East. Finally, in the fall of 1920, peace negotiations were begun in Riga. As they progressed and resulted in the westward withdrawal of Polish troops, the leadership of the Belarusan Democratic Republic organized an uprising against the oncoming Bolsheviks in the Sluck region. The Sluck Brigade of 10,000 men, however, could not save the situation. After five weeks of heavy battles and skirmishes, the survivors, poorly equipped and outnumbered, crossed over to the Polish side of the demarcation line where they had to lay down their arms.[59]

The Treaty of Riga, signed on March 18, 1921, divided Belarus between the Russian Soviet Federated Socialist Republic and Poland. The idea of a

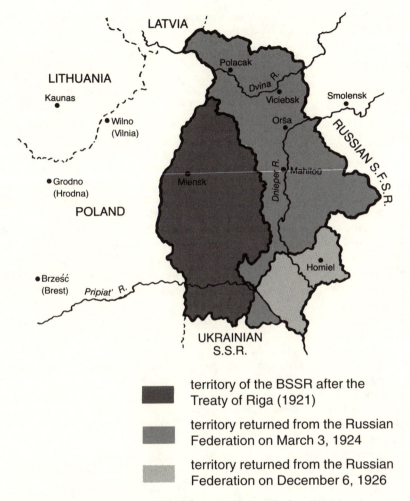

territory of the BSSR after the
Treaty of Riga (1921)

territory returned from the Russian
Federation on March 3, 1924

territory returned from the Russian
Federation on December 6, 1926

Territorial aggrandizement of the Belarusan SSR, 1924 and 1926.

Belarusan state failed to materialize in full. On the eastern side of the border the Belarusan SSR was established only on a small patch of territory (20,000 square miles) of the former Miensk gubernia, with a population of 1.5 million. Western Belarus was incorporated into the Polish state without any autonomous status.

NOTES

1. A. P. Hryckievič, "Relihijnaje pytannie i zniešniaja palityka caryzmu pierad padzielam Rečy Paspalitaj" (The religious question and foreign policy of tsarism on

the eve of the partition of the Commonwealth), *Viesci Akademii Navuk BSSR. Sieryja hramadskich navuk* (Proceedings of the Academy of Sciences of the BSSR: Social sciences series), No. 6 (Minsk, 1973), p. 63.

2. Academy of Sciences of the BSSR, Institute of History, *Historyja Bielaruskaj SSR*, Vol. 1 (Minsk: Navuka i technika, 1972), p. 508.

3. Academy of Sciences of the BSSR, *Bielaruskaja Savieckaja Encyklapiedyja*, Vol.3 (Minsk, 1971), p. 84.

4. Bronius Dundulis, *Napoléon et la Lituanie en 1812* (Paris: Alcan, 1940), p. 55.

5. Academy of Sciences of the Belarusan SSR, *Historyja Bielaruskaj SSR*, Vol. 1, p. 470.

6. Aleh Latyšonak, "Bielastoččyna i narodziny bielaruskaje dumki" (The Bielastok region and the birth of Belarusan thought), *Bielaruskija naviny. Biuleteń Bielaruskaha Demakratyčnaha Abjadnańnia* (Belarusan news: Bulletin of the Belarusan Democratic Union), No. 2 (Bielastok, July 1991), pp. 21–23.

7. Academy of Sciences of the BSSR, *Historyja Bielaruskaj SSR*, Vol. 1, pp. 574–577.

8. Archbishop Afanasiy, *Belarus v istoricheskoy gosudarstvennoy i tserkovnoy zhizni* (Belarus in historical state and church life) (Buenos Aires, 1966), pp. 224–226.

9. Johann Herder, quoted in Crane Brinton, John B. Christopher, and Robert Lee Wolff, *A History of Civilization*, Vol. 2, 3rd ed. (Englewood Cliffs, N.J.: Prentice-Hall, 1967), p. 139.

10. Herder, quoted in Hans Kohn, *Nationalism: Its Meaning and History* (New York: Van Nostrand, 1955), p. 108.

11. Cytovič, quoted in H. V. Kisialoŭ, comp., *Pačynalniki. Z historyka-litaraturnych materyjalaŭ XIX st.* (Initiators: From the nineteenth-century literary material pertaining to history) (Minsk: Navuka i technika, 1977), p. 8.

12. Adam Mickiewicz, quoted in A. A. Lojka and V. P. Rahojša, comps., *Bielaruskaja litaratura XIX stahoddzia. Chrestamatyja* (Belarusan literature of the nineteenth century: A reader), 2nd ed. (Minsk: Vyšejšaja škola, 1988), p. 32.

13. Kisialoŭ, *op. cit.*, p. 86.

14. Arnold B. McMillin, *The Vocabulary of the Byelorussian Literary Language in the Nineteenth Century* (London: Anglo-Byelorussian Society, 1973), p. 35.

15. Arnold B. McMillin, *A History of Byelorussian Literature: From Its Origins to the Present Day* (Giessen, Germany: Wilhelm Schmitz, 1977), p. 77.

16. Alaksandar Rypinski, quoted in Kisialoŭ, *op. cit.*, p. 176.

17. Kisialoŭ, *op. cit*, p. 136.

18. Vincent Dunin-Marcinkievič, quoted in Kisialoŭ, *op. cit.*, p. 134.

19. Academy of Sciences of the Belarusan SSR, *Istoriya Belorusskoy SSR* (Minsk: Nauka i tekhnika, 1977), p. 118.

20. Oscar Halecki, *Borderlands of Western Civilization* (New York: Ronald Press, 1952), p. 303.

21. Jan Zaprudnik and Thomas E. Bird, *The 1863 Uprising in Byelorussia: "Peasants' Truth" and "Letters from Beneath the Gallows" (Texts and commentaries)* (New York: Krečeŭski Foundation, 1980), p. 49.

22. *Ibid.*, p. 56.

23. *Ibid.*, pp. 54, 65.

24. Academy of Sciences of the Belarusan SSR, *Istoriya Belorusskoy SSR*, pp. 122, 123.

25. A. F. Smirnov, *Vosstaniye 1863 goda v Litve i Belorussii* (The Uprising of 1863 in Lithuania and Belarus) (Moscow: Academy of Sciences of the USSR, 1963), p. 346.

26. Academy of Sciences of the Belarusan SSR, *Historyja Bielaruskaj SSR, Vol. 2*, pp. 71–72. Somewhat higher figures are given in a Polish source: The total number exiled was 38,000, of whom 57 percent came from Lithuania and Belarus, 38 percent from the Kingdom of Poland, and 5 percent from Ukraine. See M. Kosman, *Historia Bialorusi* (Warsaw: Ossolineum, 1979), p. 235.

27. Zaprudnik and Bird, *op. cit.*, p. 68.

28. Susanna M. Sambuk, *Revolutsionnyie narodniki Belorussii (70-ye—nachalo 80-kh godov XIX v.)* (Revolutionary Populists of Belarus: The 1870s—Beginnings of the 1880s) (Minsk: Academy of Sciences, 1972), p.176.

29. A. Stankievič, "'Mužyckaja Praŭda' i 'Homon'" ("'Peasants' Truth" and "Clamor"), *Kalośsie* (Ears of grain), No. 1 (Wilno, 1935), p. 37.

30. S. Ch. Aleksandrovič, A. A. Lojka, and V. P. Rahojša, comps., *Bielaruskaja litaratura XIX stahoddzia. Chrestamatyja* (Belarusan literature of the nineteenth century: A reader) (Minsk: Vyšejšaja škola, 1971), pp. 193–194.

31. Academy of Sciences of the Belarusan SSR, *Historyja Bielaruskaj SSR*, Vol. 2, p. 126.

32. *Ibid.*, p. 128.

33. See, for example, Nicholas P. Vakar, *Belorussia: The Making of a Nation* (Cambridge, Mass.: Harvard University Press, 1956), p. 36.

34. Central Statistical Board at the Council of Ministers of the USSR, *Narodnoye obrazovaniye, nauka i kultura v SSSR. Statisticheskiy sbornik* (National education, science, and culture in the USSR: Book of statistics) (Moscow: Statistika, 1971), p. 21.

35. N. N. Ulashchik, *Ocherki po arkheografii i istochnikovedeniyu istorii Belorussii feodalnogo perioda* (An outline on archeography and sources of the history of Belarus of the feudal period) (Moscow: Nauka, 1973), pp. 64-65.

36. *Ibid.*, p. 15.

37. Francišak Bahuševič, *Tvory* (Works) (Minsk: Mastackaja litaratura, 1991), p. 16, 17.

38. Ye. F. Karski, *Belorusy. Khudozhestvennaya literatura na narodnom yazyke* (Belarusans: Literature in the vernacular), Vol. 3, part 3 (Petrograd, 1922), p. 153.

39. V. N. Pertsev, et al., eds., *Dokumenty i materialy po istorii Belorussii, 1900-1917* (Documents and material for the history of Belarus), Vol. 3 (Minsk: Academy of Sciences, 1953), p. 22.

40. Ye. F. Karski, *Etnograficheskaya karta belorusskago plemeni* (Ethnographic map of the Belarusan people), (Petrograd: Belarusan Regional Committee of the All-Russian Soviet of Peasant Deputies, 1917), p. 26.

41. Professor Karski recalled (in *ibid.*, p. 25) that back in 1903 he had found the number of Belarusans living in ethnographic Belarus to be substantially higher—8,317,961.

42. Calculated from Pertsev et al., *op. cit.*, p.27.

43. Karski, *Etnograficheskaya karta belorusskago plemeni*, p. 27.

44. Vakar, *op. cit.*, p. 34; U. M. Ihnatoŭski, *Karotki narys historyi Bielarusi* (A short outline of the history of Belarus), 5th ed.(Minsk: Bielaruś, 1991), p.171.

45. P. U. Cieraškovič, "Asnoŭnyja tendencyi razviccia bielaruskaha etnasu ŭ epochu kapitalizmu" (The main trends of development of the Belarusan ethnos in the epoch of capitalism), *Viesci AN BSSR. Sieryja hramadkich navuk* (Proceedings of the Academy of Sciences of the BSSR: Social sciences series), No. 5 (Minsk, 1986), p. 94.

46. Academy of Sciences of the Belarusan SSR, *Historyja Bielaruskaj SSR*, Vol. 2, p. 560.

47. McMillin, *A History of Byelorussian Literature*, p. 124.

48. Vera Rich, transl. *Like Water, Like Fire: An Anthology of Byelorussian Poetry from 1828 to the Present Day* (London: George Allen & Unwin, 1971), p. 60.

49. Academy of Sciences of the Belarusan SSR, *Historyja Bielaruskaj SSR*, Vol. 2, p. 566.

50. Inorodetz, pseud., *La Russie et les peuples allogènes* (Russia and the peoples of the outlying areas) (Berne, 1917), p. 128.

51. Vakar, *op. cit.*, p. 94.

52. *Homan*, Vilnia, July 18, 1916.

53. Ant. Adamovič, *"Jak duch zmahańnia Bielarusi" (Da 100-ch uhodkaŭ naradžeńnia Ivana Luckieviča)* ("Like the spirit of Belarus's struggle" [On the centenary of Ivan Luckievič's Birth] (New York: Bielarus, 1983), p. 21.

54. J. Mienski, "The Establishment of the Belorussian SSR," *Belorussian Review*, No. 1 (Munich: Institute for the Study of the USSR, 1955), p. 8.

55. *Ibid.*, p. 12.

56. Full texts of all three Constituent Charters of the Council of the Belarusan Democratic Republic in English translation can be found in *Zapisy* (Annals) of the Byelorussian Institute of Arts and Sciences, Vol. 13 (New York, 1975), pp. 95–98.

57. Mienski, *op. cit.*, p. 17.

58. Vilhelm Knoryn, quoted in Mienski (*op. cit.*, p. 18), from Knoryn, "Kamunistyčnaja partyja na Bielarusi" (The Communist Party in Belarus), *Bielaruś*(Minsk, 1924), p. 219.

59. Vitaŭt Kipel, "Armed Resistance," in Vitaŭt Kipel and Zora Kipel, eds, *Byelorussian Statehood: Reader and Bibliography* (New York: Belorussian Institute of Arts and Sciences, 1988), pp. 211–212.

THREE

Soviet and Polish Experiences in a Divided Belarus (1921–1941)

TWO CONTRASTING HALVES

In the year of the Treaty of Riga, which split Belarus into eastern and western parts, Soviet and Polish, a young philosopher-historian, Ihnat Abdziralovič, succinctly characterized the current historical juncture at which the Belarusans found themselves. He wrote:

> Everything brought to our people by uninvited patrons has turned to trash. The main prerequisite of social life, the possibility of creating, we lack. The experience we have gone through and the conditions we see around ourselves tell us that *we can guarantee the potential of social creativity only in the case of the absence, first of all, of foreign coercion.* From this there follows a conclusion about the necessity of political independence as the primary condition for a people to be itself. Belarusan political thought has begun working in this direction.[1]

Conditions for the realization of Belarusan political independence were quite different on the Soviet and Polish sides of the border. On the Soviet side there was a formal, albeit territorially reduced, Belarusan state with an international imprimatur. Article Two of the Russo-Polish Treaty of Riga (a Russian delegation there spoke on behalf of Soviet Belarus) stated: "Both contracting parties recognize the independence of Ukraine and Belarus in accordance with the principle of self-determination of peoples."[2] Not so on the Polish side. Warsaw, having wrested from the Bolsheviks extensive territories of Ukraine and Belarus that had been part of the historical Commonwealth, made every effort to amalgamate them both politically and culturally.

Under the Soviets, Lenin's nationality policy was turned initially into an instrument of combating the Whites and propagating a world revolution to other oppressed peoples. The institutionalization of the Belarusan national idea in the form of the Belarusan Soviet Socialist Republic (BSSR) had an immediate political application as well. Historian and political activist at the time of the proclamation of the BSSR, U. M. Ihnatoŭski, explained the sudden change of heart among the front-Bolsheviks in favor of Belarusan statehood in terms of their desire to "Bolshevize the Belarusan masses." Indeed, in little over a year the BSSR had become a contrastive example for 3.3 million Belarusans living under Polish rule.[3]

PROFITING FROM THE NEW ECONOMIC POLICY

The BSSR started as a tiny state of one-and-a-half million people on a fraction of Belarusan ethnographic territory. The size of the republic was a result of Moscow's politico-military maneuvering, in the context of the war with Poland and the latter's claims of Belarus as its historical patrimony.

After six years of devastating war (1914–1920) and constantly changing occupants, the recovery had to start from scratch. The non-Belarusan leaders of front-Bolshevism, captivated by the specter of world revolution, were initially adverse toward the idea of a Belarusan national state; nevertheless, their animosity allowed room for a policy of Belarusization. The composition of the republic's government itself, dominated initially by All-Russian Bolsheviks, changed in favor of Belarusan Communists, who advocated building a Belarusan National Home. Lenin's New Economic Policy (NEP) and a relative liberalism in the field of culture rendered the Soviet regime acceptable to some Western governments. In the early 1920s Soviet Russia concluded trade treaties with Britain, Poland, Germany, Italy, and other states. One cannot help but notice the striking situational parallel between 1922, when the Russians were invited to an international economic conference at Genoa, and 1992. In that earlier year, Soviet republics (which had not yet formed the USSR) had no diplomatic ties with the outside world. Accordingly, in January 1992 First Secretary of the Central Bureau of the Belarusan Communist Party, Vilhelm Knoryn, wrote as follows in an article entitled "We Want Recognition":

> The formal juridical recognition of the Soviet Republics by the Western countries would be a very important fact because it would give an opportunity for the Soviet Republics to use Western European markets and credits and to conduct more normal trade relations with Western Europe. This is essential for the development of our industry and the establishment of agriculture. ... The Soviet Republics have always agreed to make very significant concessions in order to be recognized by Western Europe.[4]

Who would contend that history does not repeat itself? It does; but not always. At any rate, there are many Belarusan patriots in the 1990s, especially from among the intelligentsia, who would like to see the repetition of Belarusization, a cultural phenomenon of the 1920s. Belarusization was a policy of favoring and fostering the Belarusan language in all spheres, including the higher echelons of the government and the Communist Party. It was historian Usievalad Ihnatoŭski, a Socialist-Revolutionary-turned-Communist and an influential commissar of education, who laid down the theoretical basis for the policy of Belarusization. This policy highlighted almost the entire decade of the 1920s. In December 1921 Ihnatoŭski published his "Theses" on the preparation of Party cadre work, entitled "The Belarusan National Question and the Communist Party."[5]

The departing premise for Ihnatoŭski's policy recommendations was the assertion that the Belarusan nation lacked class differentiation in the twentieth century. This was, he explained, a result of Polonization in the sixteenth to eighteenth centuries and Russification in the following 100 years. Thus, when the 1917 Bolshevik revolution abolished all *social* distinctions, for the Belarusans this outcome amounted to *national* liberation because "class and the national composition of the Belarusans almost coincided with each other." The Belarusan nation, according to Ihnatoŭski, consisted of the following social groups: 75 percent small landholders "ruined by the war," 14 percent landless peasants, and "an insignificant number of factory workers in villages and towns." "The only one standing aside," said Ihnatoŭski, "is the Belarusan homesteader whose political sympathies have been and are now tending toward the class of the large-landed bourgeoisie." With this social uniformity in view, Ihnatoŭski defined the policies of the Communist Party cadre:

It is necessary to penetrate into this thicket of Belarusan working people with Communist educational activities ... without fear of losing the purity of the Russian literary language. One must educate and involve in Communism the Belarusan rural semi-proletarian and proletarian in his familiar, native, routine, every-day Belarusan tongue.

Ihnatoŭski went further: He prescribed the linguistic Belarusization of all of national life. "Belarusan culture," he said, "is the culture of the working masses of Belarusans. It is a culture of the significant majority of these masses. ... We have to develop and strengthen the courts, administration, and organs of the economy and government, where use of Belarusan and familiarity with Belarusan culture and every-day life would agree with the needs of the majority of Belarus's working masses." This rationale became a guiding principle for the Communist Party of

Belarus for the remainder of the 1920s, until it collided with Stalin's design for collectivization and industrialization of the Soviet Union.

TERRITORIAL EXTENSION OF THE REPUBLIC

At the initiative of the Communist Party and the government of Belarus, and with Moscow's concurrence, the territory of the BSSR was extended in 1924 and 1926 to include Belarusan ethnographic areas that, as a result of the civil war and foreign intervention, had remained within the Russian republic. Thus the area of the BSSR increased from 20,000 square miles to 48,500 and the population from 1.5 million to almost 5 million.[6]

In 1926 the national composition of the population of the republic was as follows: Belarusans, 4,017,000 (80.6 percent); Jews, 407,000 (8.2 percent); Russians, 384,000 (7.7 percent); Poles, 98,000 (2.0 percent); Ukrainians, 35,000 (0.6 percent); and others, 42,000 (0.9 percent).[7]

Of the republic's total population of about 5 million, 82 percent lived in rural areas. Moreover, 91 percent of Belarusans were peasants. But with economic recovery and Belarusization of the governmental structures, villagers gradually began moving into towns. In the mid-1920s about forty percent of the urban inhabitants were former villagers. Belarusans, Jews, and Russians made up the urban population in a ratio of 40:40:15.[8]

In the central institutions of the republic, positions were filled by Belarusans, Jews, Russians, and others; see Table 3.1 for a breakdown of their numbers.

ECONOMIC RECOVERY AND SOCIAL DIFFERENTIATION

The economic effect of the NEP policy was very much in evidence in the Soviet Union by the mid-1920s. Financial reforms secured hard currency toward the end of 1924. And by 1925 the agricultural production in the BSSR had reached the 1913 level. The recovery was not as successful in industry, however. Although the overall restoration of industry was essentially completed in the Soviet Union by the end of 1925, the emphasis in the BSSR was placed on the heavy sector of production at the expense of consumer goods. In 1927 the republic had 410 industrial enterprises employing 32,000 workers. Production in light industry constituted only 62 percent of the 1913 level at the end of 1925. The large enterprises, of course, remained nationalized according to Lenin's dictum regarding the "commanding heights" of industry.

The private sector also grew, especially in the area of trade. In 1924–1925, 14,000 out of 16,000 trade enterprises were in private hands. Small

TABLE 3.1   Government Positions in the Belarusan SSR Occupied by Members of Various Nationalities (in percentages)

Positions	Belarusans	Jews	Russians	Others
Administration	51.3	24.8	18.0	5.9
Economy	30.8	49.3	13.0	6.9
Courts	26.3	42.1	21.1	11.5
Agriculture	59.5	10.1	24.1	5.3

Source: Ivan S. Lubachko, Belorussia Under Soviet Rule, 1917–1957 (Lexington: University of Kentucky Press, 1972), p. 69.

private shops and cooperatives produced about 70 percent of all goods in 1926–1927.

As a result of the 1923 Land Law Code, peasants increased their land-holdings by 25 percent relative to the pre-1917 period. Middle-class land-holders, constituting 60 percent of farms and holding around 70 percent of arable land, were becoming the main social force in rural areas. To increase efficiency many of these landholders resettled from large villages to their homesteads, thereby shortening the distance to their fields. By 1925 the level of agricultural production had reached the 1913 level. The taxation of agricultural homesteads was progressive.

On the other hand, the officially sponsored idea of collective farming did not make much headway. Only 0.7 percent of the arable land belonged to farm collectives in 1925.[9] At the same time, the growth of commercial production in agriculture slowly but inexorably led to social differentiation, which was anathema to Party doctrinaires. It was just a matter of time before the Communist Party would start revolutionizing the situation in the rural area.

THE PARTY AND NATIONAL COMMUNISM

Bolshevism in Belarus, from its beginnings in the early 1900s until 1917, was an urban and military phenomenon and had a Russian orientation, indifferent or hostile to the Belarusan national movement. The rural areas were dominated by the Socialist Revolutionaries. The Belarusan intelligentsia supported the Belarusan Socialist Union (Hramada), which Lenin categorized as "national petty bourgeois party of left populist orientation."[10]

Until January 1918, when Lenin signed a decree instituting the Belarusan National Commissariat, the Bolshevik organizations in Belarus were regional units of the Russian Social-Democratic Labor Party and did not even use the term Belarus in their official names. The party itself was small. In 1922 it had 6,157 members, of whom 72 percent were Russians.

Only in 1928 did Belarusans make up more than half (54. 3 percent) of the 31,713 members, whereas Jews stood at 23.7 percent, Russians at 14.0, and others at 8.0.[11] As S. Krushinsky points out, however, "Among the Belarusans there were no Communists from the pre-revolutionary period. A majority of Belarusans joined the Communist Party after 1920."[12]

During the 1920s the Communist Party gained acceptance largely through its liberal economic and cultural policies. Even many opponents of Bolshevism, those who worked and fought for the Belarusan Democratic Republic (including most of the members of the government in exile) came from Lithuania, Czechoslovakia, Germany, and Poland in the second half of the 1920s to join in building the "Belarusan National Home."

Improvements were particularly visible in the field of education, if one considers that under the tsars not even a single institution of higher learning existed in Belarus. In the territorially truncated BSSR, by contrast, the Belarusan State University was opened in 1921, followed by the Belarusan Institute of Culture in 1922 (transformed in 1926 into the Academy of Sciences), the Veterinarian Institute in 1924, the Agricultural Academy in 1925, and fifteen community pedagogical colleges in 1928.

By 1926 the level of literacy in the republic had risen to 53 percent.[13] And in 1931 when compulsory seven-year education was introduced, the republic had 32 institutions of higher learning with 11,000 students, and 104 professional schools with 20,000 students.[14] Earlier, during the period 1922–1926, a majority of primary schools had switched to instruction in Belarusan. The native language was also being gradually introduced into institutions of higher education.

In accordance with the decree of 1924, which established equal rights for the four principal languages of the republic (Belarusan, Russian, Yiddish, and Polish), national minority schools were opened. According to the census of December 15, 1927, the languages were distributed as indicated in Table 3.2.

The Jewish and Polish teachers were prepared by the departments at the Belarusan State University and by one Polish and three Jewish teachers' schools. In 1927, for every twenty books in Belarusan, ten would be published in Russian, two in Yiddish, and one in Polish.[15] And out of the twenty newspapers and fifteen magazines appearing in 1925, eleven newspapers and ten magazines were in Belarusan.

Life under the Soviets during the 1920s, before the Stalinists began their onslaught in 1930, entailed political surveillance and censorship—and, hence, resistance. At the same time, the growth of education promoted development of the national idea, of a culture that would reflect and epitomize national originality and the free spirit of the artist. The liberal economic policy of the time was accompanied by artistic pluralism and

TABLE 3.2   Principal Languages in the Schools of the Belarusan SSR

Four-Year Schools

Language	No. of Schools	No. of Teachers	No. of Pupils
Belarusan	4,363	6,153	296,182
Yiddish	146	445	11,212
Polish	129	162	6,159
Russian	118	289	11,299
Mixed Belarusan & Russian	362	646	29,746
Other	45	76	2,060
Total	5,163	7,771	356,658

Seven-Year Schools

Language	No. of Schools	No. of Teachers	No. of Pupils
Belarusan	176	2,193	66,563
Yiddish	53	733	13,778
Polish	12	145	2,627
Russian	18	305	7,910
Mixed Belarusan & Russian	40	600	15,988
Other	9	180	4,078
Total	308	4,156	110,944

Source: H. Niamiha, "Education in Belorussia Before the Rout of 'National Democracy': 1917–1930," Institute for the Study of the USSR, *Belorussian Review*, No. 1 (Munich, 1955), p. 53.

creative diversity. The vibrant literary scene was represented by competing clubs and societies. The most remarkable of these was the nationally oriented *Uzvyšša* (Excelsior) Club of talented young poets and prose writers. In early 1927, the club published its "Theses on the Formation of Excelsior." Contrasting the didactic literature (which was expected though not yet demanded by the Communist Party) with artistic aims, these young writers issued a summons to create their own art "based on a rich cultural heritage and on the study of contemporary life" and thus to reach for "excelsior heights that will be seen by centuries and nations."[16]

ON THE POLISH SIDE:
CURTAILED POSSIBILITIES

Polish political aspirations on the eastern borderlands in 1918–1921 were under the spell of past glories when Poland was a mighty state in union with the Grand Duchy of Lithuania and Ruś. Polish politicians debated during 1919 how much of those eastern territories should be included in the new Poland that was being resurrected. Of the two opposing camps, federalists and unionists, the latter prevailed. The unionists flagrantly rejected President Woodrow Wilson's stipulation regarding peace settlement in Europe (in one of his Fourteen Points) that an independent Poland "should include the territories inhabited by indisputably Polish populations."[17]

British Prime Minister David Lloyd George, one of the Big Four of the Versailles Peace Conference, who had an intimate knowledge of Polish diplomats, observed:

> Drunk with the new wine of liberty supplied to her [Poland] by the Allies, she fancied herself once more the restless mistress of Central Europe. Self-determination did not suit her ambitions. She coveted Galicia, the Ukraine, Lithuania, and parts of Belorussia. A vote of the inhabitants would have emphatically repudiated her dominion. So the right of all peoples to select their nationhood was promptly thrown over by her leaders.[18]

The most eloquent advocate of such a course of action was Roman Dmowski, the leader of the Polish National Democracy Party. Dmowski represented "a tendency," says Juliusz Bardach, "based on the national-democratic ideology ... a notion formulated by S. Balicki, i. e., so-called national egoism."[19] Dmowski's "national egoism" called for a Poland of 35 to 40 million people extending as far into Lithuanian, Belarusan, and Ukrainian territories as could be practically assimilated.[20]

Józef Piłsudski, the Polish commander-in-chief whose army occupied Belarus in 1919–1920, subscribed to federalist ideas; but his federalism was of a tactical nature, "a suitable slogan in the war for the eastern territories."[21] At a meeting in Vilnia in February 1920, Piłsudski admitted: "I am in favor of some significant concessions to the Belarusans in the field of their cultural development, but I do not wish to make any political concessions favoring a Belarusan fiction."[22] But even in the realm of culture there was no consistency, as Józef Lewandowski admits: "The matters of Belarusan culture were treated unevenly, depending on the changing political circumstances. The approach was dominated by a sickening, National-Democratic, myopic attitude of unrelenting suppression of everything that was Belarusan and peasant."[23]

BELARUSAN COMPLAINTS IN THE POLISH DIET

The Poland of 1921–1939 had an eastern frontier much like the one in 1793, before the second partition of the Commonwealth. The new Polish state of 150,000 square miles and a total population of 35 million (in 1939) included 40,000 square miles of Belarusan ethnographic territory and a total population of more than 4.4 million in 1931.[24] The national minorities in Poland between the two World Wars constituted about one-third of the state's population. The number of Belarusans stood at about 3.5 million.[25]

Demographic statistics inevitably vary according to who is counting. Polish authorities, for example, conducted their own census in 1921, when the number of Belarusans in West Belarus was reduced to slightly over 1 million, and in 1931, when the number was lowered to 890,000. The census-takers arrived at these figures by counting every Roman Catholic as a Pole even if the person did not know the Polish language.[26]

The initial policies of the Polish government toward national minorities had been shaped along the lines of Pilsudski's "significant concessions" in the field of culture. In its tug-of-war with Lithuania over the Vilnia region, before the League of Nations, Warsaw made an effort to prove that it was treating its national minorities fairly. And, indeed, the facts supported Poland's claims. Immediately after the Riga Treaty of 1921, more than 400 Belarusan primary schools, seven high schools, and three teachers' colleges were opened. The government financially supported some Belarusan cultural activities and even subsidized the Belarusan press. As a result of this relaxed atmosphere, Belarusans were able to send to the Diet three senators and eleven deputies in the 1922 elections. But the democratic experiment with the minorities lasted no longer than Warsaw's brief altercation with Lithuania and Germany over the border settlement. By 1924 Polish authorities felt ready to start pressure on the "Eastern Provinces," trying to make them linguistically Polish by closing non-Polish schools, banning non-Polish publications, and settling Polish colonizers. Speeches by the Belarusan and Ukrainian deputies in the Diet, as well as petitions to them from their constituents in the mid-1920s, catalog a long litany of complaints about abuses and atrocities at the hands of the authorities at all levels. Speaking before the Diet in July 1924, Deputy Branislaŭ Taraškievič, the president of the Belarusan Parliamentary Club, accused the government of violating its own constitution, which on paper guaranteed free cultural development for the minorities. "The government closed 400 Belarusan achools," complained Taraškievič. "Instead of land reform, we have [Polish] settlers, and the Ministry for Land Reforms is nothing other than a Ministry for Colonization and Settlements."[27] West Belarus, with its large rural population (85 percent of the total) was an agricultural appendix to the more industrialized Poland. Of the 4.6 million inhabitants of West Belarus, only 38,000 were engaged in industry.[28]

The land was distributed very unevenly. The 3,400 landlords, who made up fewer than 1 percent of all landholders, possessed more than 50 percent of the privately owned properties. Each of their holdings totaled 1,250 acres on the average, while the other 99 percent of the landholders had to satisfy themselves with 17. But many peasants had even less land; some had none at all.[29] The system of taxation heavily favored the big landed estates in the hands of Polish lords and military settlers. Moreover, peasants had to perform a number of corvée assignments entailing road construction, transportation, and so on.

At the beginning of the 1930s, unemployment in rural areas was rampant. Between 1925 and 1938, 78,000 people in search of work emigrated from West Belarus to France, Latin America, and other countries.[30]

THE BELARUSAN PEASANT-AND-WORKERS' UNION

In view of the injustice and persecution besetting West Belarus,[31] some of the Belarusan deputies in the Diet decided to take a more radical course of action. Influenced by the Communist Party of West Belarus and the Independent Peasants' Party, the Belarusan Peasant-and-Workers' Union (BPWU) mobilized the masses for a political action in the summer of 1925. Led by the eloquent and energetic Branislaŭ Taraškievč, the BPWU met with a phenomenal response all over West Belarus. In less than two years the Union's membership had grown to well over 125,000. The Union had more than 200 chapters, held several regional conferences, published several newspapers and calendars, and exerted a decisive influence on cultural and commercial institutions.[32] Along with the BPWU a wide range of cultural activities were conducted by the Belarusan School Society, which demanded the release of all political prisoners and the reopening of Belarusan schools.

Other parties and organizations were active as well, including the Belarusan Christian Democracy, the Belarusan Peasant Union, the Belarusan Scientific Society, the Belarusan Institute of Economy and Culture, and the Belarusan Student Union.

Meanwhile, Marshal Józef Pilsudski, the war hero who was supported by the military and rightist parties against the squabbling legislature but who resigned as head of state in 1922, carried out a coup d'état in May 1926. He was immediately denounced in the Diet by leftist deputies. "Who does not know," said Taraškievč in July 1926, "that in fact all power is in the hand of the dictator Pilsudski, that the Diet has been diminished, and that deputies have been voting submissively, accompanied by the swishing of a dictatorial whip?"[33]

The leader of the BPWU saw the new course of the Polish regime as "more frightening to Ukrainians and Belarusans than the course of former governments."[34]

Events soon proved him right. Disturbed not only by the BPWU's massive size but also by the Communist influence on it, the Polish government cracked down on the Union. In disregard of parliamentary immunity, five Diet deputies were arrested in January 1927 along with dozens of other activists. In a widely publicized "Trial of the 56," they were all sentenced to various terms of imprisonment. The BPWU went underground. Part of its activity was taken over by the Belarusan School Society, which numbered about 15,000 members in 1928.

THE 1930s IN POLAND: AUTHORITARIANISM

The Polish government in the 1930s grew more authoritarian and aggressive in its policy of Polonizing West Belarus or, to use the current official phrase, the "Eastern Provinces." Oppression, more pervasive than ever because of the economic crisis affecting all countries, was felt with particular acuteness in West Belarus because of its economic backwardness and semi-colonial status.

In August 1930 Marshal Pilsudski dissolved the Diet. A month later, leaders of the center-left opposition were arrested and election results were tampered with. Liquidation of Belarusan cultural institutions continued unabated. By mid-1931 more than 200 chapters of the Belarusan School Society had been closed down by order of the authorities. The new constitution, approved by the Diet in January 1934 (and proclaimed on April 23, 1935), had enough loopholes in it to allow the administration unchallenged acts of repression against the national minorities. For example, the freedoms of religion and speech were to be evaluated from the point of view of the "common good" and "public order and morals." Religious instruction could be given only in Polish. One hundred and forty Orthodox churches were closed. In the sixty-mile-wide swath of territory along the Soviet border, Orthodox inhabitants were forced into Catholicism under threat of deportation. And nationally conscious Belarusan Catholic priests and monks were forced to leave their native land.[35]

On September 13, 1935, Poland canceled the treaty on ethnic minorities at the League of Nations, claiming that its Polish laws were "adequate."[36] In December of the same year, a concentration camp was set up at Bereza Kartuska to hold opposition leaders and "socially dangerous elements" detained by an administrative decision. Many Belarusans found their way to Bereza Kartuska.

In the general elections of 1935, the Belarusans lost their last seat in the Polish parliament. In 1936–1937 many Belarusan cultural organizations were closed, including the Christian Democratic Movement and its organ *Bielaruskaja Krynica* (Belarusan wellspring), the Belarusan Institute of Economy and Culture, the Belarusan School Society, the Union of Belarusan Teachers, and the Belarusan National Committee.

The Act of 1925, which guaranteed the right of the natives to have their own schools, was repealed on November 15, 1938. The state then moved more deeply into matters of religion. The presidential decree of 1938, "On the Relation of the State to the Polish Autocephalous Orthodox Church," marked "a significant increase of government involvement in the internal affairs of the Polish Orthodox Church."[37] In particular, the Orthodox citizens of Poland were denied the right to acquire land.

IN THE USSR: GENOCIDE AND ETHNOCIDE

There is an ironic symmetry in the methods used by the Russian and Polish imperialisms (both of which claimed a part or the whole of Belarus) to combat Belarusan nationalism. Initially, during the second half of the nineteenth century and the first four decades of the twentieth, each side denounced "Belarusanness" as an "intrigue" of the other. In the second half of the 1920s and throughout the 1930s, the most frequent accusation leveled against Belarusan activists in Poland, however flimsy the grounds for such charges, was that of being involved in a Communist conspiracy. On the other side of the border, it was "Polish espionage" that provided the pretext for firing people from their jobs or executing the so-called Belarusan National Democrats. This tragic parallelism had a chronological aspect as well. The first rumblings of the coming storm on both sides of the border were heard in 1927. In Poland there were arrests of the leadership of the Belarusan Peasant-and-Workers' Union and massive trials in the following year; in the Belarusan SSR the head of the government, Jazep Adamovič, was demoted for promoting Belarusization and a "social campaign" against leading poets of the Excelsior Club. "The power of the GPU [secret police]," writes Anthony Adamovich, one of the *Excelsiorists*, began to be particularly felt in Belarusan literature in 1928."[38]

Of course, there were also striking dissimilarities, both ideological and physical, between the Polish and the Bolshevik methods of repression. The Poles denied the Belarusans any political concessions; they rejected the very idea of a Belarusan state or autonomy. For them, Belarusans were "raw ethnographic material" to be swallowed and digested.[39] Marshal Józef Piłsudski, the military architect of Polish independence in 1918, divided peoples into "historical" and "nonhistorical." The Belarusans he considered a "nonhistorical" entity.[40]

On the other hand, the Bolsheviks, having accepted the idea of a Belarusan national state, fought the people who wanted to give substance to the form and make out of the proletarian state a true "Belarusan National Home." As we now know, Bolshevik brutality occurred on a genocidal scale. The contrast between the Polish and Russian methods of suppression of political dissent is obvious. Suffering under a harsh regime in Polish prisons, Branislaŭ Taraškievič nevertheless had "a minimum of the rights that were due to a political prisoner;" he received certain books and was even able to make a translation of the long poem by Adam Mickiewicz, *Pan Tadeusz*, into Belarusan.[41] Nothing of the sort was possible for Taraškievič's counterparts in Soviet prisons. The very concept of the prisoner itself was different there. In the Soviet Union, opponents of the regime were not political prisoners but class enemies who had to be destroyed. Having been sent to the Soviet Union in a political prisoner exchange in 1933, Taraškievič himself was executed in 1938.[42]

The Great Terror in Soviet Belarus in the 1930s had a catastrophic impact on Belarusan culture. In three waves of arrests, in 1930, 1933, and 1937–1938, hundreds of thousands of people of all walks of life were eliminated. Particularly heavy losses were sustained among the intelligentsia. The genocidal campaign was conducted under the slogan of a struggle against the "National Democrats," who were accused of a sinister plot to tear Belarus away from the Soviet Union and sell it to capitalist imperialists. State security organs began preparing a show trial of the so-called Union for the Liberation of Belarus (ULB), concocted on the model, already in process, of the Union for Liberation of Ukraine. However, this design was frustrated when Janka Kupala, Belarus's foremost poet slated for the role of ULB leader, attempted suicide in November 1930. The next in line for the same infamous role could have been the president of the Belarusan Academy of Sciences, Usievalad Ihnatoŭski, but he committed suicide (in February 1931) after several interrogations by the GPU. The idea of holding a show trial was dropped, but the arrests continued unabated. The extent of the devastation is evident from the losses suffered by literature. In 1937, after 128 writers had been arrested, only one literary organization remained in the republic: the Writers' Union of Belarus, with 39 members, only 14 of whom wrote in Belarusan.[43] Of the 238 writers arrested during the years of repression, only about 20 survived and were released from captivity by the time of Stalin's death in March 1953.[44] The Institute of Belarusan Culture, established in 1922 and transformed into the Belarusan Academy of Sciences in 1928, lost "nearly ninety percent" of its members; "the vast majority of them were shot."[45]

Michail Bič, who has researched the effects of Stalinist crimes in Belarus, notes: "In the 1930s, almost the entire national intelligentsia, the majority of whom were educated during the Soviet period became victims of the Stalinist-Beria repressions."[46] This policy of mass destruction of the national intelligentsia was extended into West Belarus after its incorporation into the Soviet Union in September 1939. More than 200,000 people were deported from West Belarus in 1940 alone.[47]

Only in recent years has the horrifying magnitude of Communist crimes become clear. To the list of such names as Buchenwald and Auschwitz was added one more in 1988: Kurapaty, a forest near Miensk where victims were executed on a daily basis from 1937 to 1941. The site was uncovered by Zianon Paźniak and his co-workers. "The Soviet estimate of the bodies in mass graves in the area already examined was 102,000," reported the *National Review,* "but the chief investigator has just published an estimate of 250,000 to 300,000 for the whole site. And this for the capital of a minor Soviet republic—with five other sites around it still awaiting investigation, and others near the Byelorussian provincial capitals!"[48]

Quoted at a commemorative session in Miensk devoted to the memory of the victims of Stalinism was Barys Sačanka, a specialist in the subject of the 1930s repressions. Sačanka noted that, according to his calculations and those made by others, "the number of victims equals the number of those who perished during the Great Patriotic War."[49] The losses during that 1941–1945 war in Belarus are estimated at 2.2 million people.[50]

Such figures, however, are only one dimension of the tragedy. A concomitant aspect of the Communist genocide in Belarus was Russification. In 1933 a language reform was decreed, bringing Belarusan orthography and vocabulary closer to Russian at the expense of the natural character of the Belarusan language and its many specific features. The Belarusan language was banned from high official places and from higher education. Speaking Belarusan in formal gatherings became a sign of "bourgeois nationalism."

The history of Belarus was completely rewritten. Many of its outstanding personalities—including Francišak Skaryna and Kastuś Kalinoŭski—were denounced as reactionaries and condemned to oblivion. At the same time, Russian tsars, generals, and writers became models to be studied and emulated by Belarusan youth. The history of the Belarusan people was reduced to a single desire to be united with the Russians. Cultural activities, instead of concentrating on native themes and heritage, centered on so-called internationalism, with a heavy emphasis on everything Russian. The devastating effect of these genocidal and ethnocidal policies were admitted by even the most conservative Communists in the years of perestroika. As the main organ of the Communist Party of Belarus (CPB), *Kommunist Belorussii,* wrote in 1990: "The struggle with the so-called *natsdems* [National Democrats] and kulaks in 1929–1933 shifted to a liquidation of foreign agents in 1937. As a result, the process of the formation of a national intelligentsia was arrested for a long time."[51]

THE REUNION OF 1939–1941

On September 17, 1939, two-and-a-half weeks after Germany attacked Poland and occupied a considerable part of its territory, Soviet troops crossed the eastern Polish border "to protect the life and property of the population of West Ukraine and West Belarus."[52] The partition of Belarus by the Riga Treaty of 1921 was thus undone and the Belarusan people again found themselves in one state. The territory of the republic increased by nearly 39,000 square miles and the population by 4.5 million.

Soviet histories distort the truth when they say that the invasion of Poland by the Red Army was prompted by the "danger to West Belarus and West Ukraine of fascist subjugation."[53] There was no such immediate threat because Moscow's move was made in a climate of cooperation with Berlin and as a result of the then-secret Soviet-German *nonaggression* pact signed on August 23, 1939, just a week before Hitler attacked Poland.

Most Belarusans welcomed the Soviet soldiers because they knew much more about the persecution by Polish authorities than about the crimes of the Soviet regime. Indeed, the Soviet government made certain that people in West Belarus learned as little as possible about what was going on in the eastern part of the republic: The border between the two parts remained strictly guarded until it was swept away by German tanks on their way to Moscow in the summer of 1941.

West Belarus under the Soviets was swiftly incorporated into the USSR and BSSR. Less than three weeks after the Soviet regime was established, the authorities announced elections to a National Assembly of West Belarus. These elections were held on October 22, 1939, under the close supervision of the Communist Party. Of the 2,672,280 persons eligible to vote, 96.7 percent voted for the "national ticket." The National Assembly, consisting of 929 deputies (among them 621 Belarusans, 127 Poles, 72 Jews, 53 Ukrainians, 43 Russians, and 10 of other nationalities), was held on October 28–30, 1939, in the city of Bielastok (today Bialystok, Poland). It adopted a series of declarations, including requests that West Belarus be admitted into the Soviet Union and reunited with the Belarusan Soviet Socialist Republic. These requests were granted by both the Supreme Soviet of the USSR (on November 2, 1939) and the Supreme Soviet of the BSSR (on November 12, 1939).[54]

On November 1, 1939, Belarusans were astonished to discover that the Vilnia region (2,750 sqare miles in size, with a population of 457,500) had been transferred by the Soviet government from West Belarus to Lithuania in an agreement signed on October 10, 1939, but kept unpublished until the elections to the National Assembly of West Belarus and the Bielastok session had become history. The Soviet commissar of foreign affairs, Vyacheslav M. Molotov, speaking on November 2 before the Supreme Soviet of the USSR, gave the following explanation:

> The Vilna [Vilnia] territory belongs to Lithuania not by reason of population. No, we know that the majority of the population in that region is not Lithuanian. But the historical past and the aspirations of the Lithuanian nation have been intimately connected with the city of Vilna, and the Government of the USSR considered it necessary to honor these moral factors.[55]

If Molotov knew anything of the "historical past" of the Grand Duchy of Lithuania, it was most likely the official Russian version that disre-

western border of the Belarusan SSR, September 1939

Vilnia region, given to Lithuania on October 10, 1939

The Belarusan SSR in September 1939, one month before the Vilnia region was given to Lithuania.

garded the terminological discrepancies between the twentieth century and the medieval times discussed in Chapter 1. But even if he knew otherwise, Molotov was interested not so much in history as in the exchange of Vilnia for the right to establish military bases on Lithuanian territory.

Events soon showed that the "moral factors" of which the Soviet minister spoke were indeed of secondary importance. The Kremlin, having arrested the major Belarusan leaders (Anton Luckievič, Senator Viačaslaŭ Bahdanovič, poet Makar Kraŭcoŭ, journalist Janka Paźniak, Siarhiej Busiel, and others), ceded the Vilnia region to Lithuania in preparation for the bigger bite soon to come: In August 1940 the Soviet troops occupied the entire country along with the two other Baltic republics, Latvia and Estonia. West Belarus, meanwhile, was gradually being Sovietized and purged of "unreliable elements." The Polish settlers who were given land for their participation in the 1918–1920 campaign, policemen, and other functionaries and their families were deported to Siberia under inhumane conditions in the winter of 1939–1940. In August 1940 the rest of the Belarusan leaders and activists in Vilnia were arrested. The next waves of deportations of "class enemies" followed in February, May, and June 1941. These arrests swept away many former members of the Communist Party of West Belarus, which was disbanded by the Comintern along with the Polish Communist Party in 1938—allegedly because it was infiltrated by Polish police agents. About 300,000 persons were deported from West Belarus (including Vilnia) before the German attack on the Soviet Union on June 22, 1941. The losses of the population were replaced by an influx of personnel from the Soviet Union, most of whom were non-Belarusan (administrators, propagandists, police, Party functionaries, teachers, etc.). The total population of West Belarus in 1941 stood at approximately 5 million, of whom Belarusans made up 77 percent of the total; Jews, 12.8 percent; Russians, 5.1 percent; Lithuanians, 1.5 percent; Poles, 1.3 percent; Ukrainians, 1.3 percent; and others 1.0 percent.[56]

Soviet cultural policy in West Belarus was mild in comparison with the Russification drive in the eastern part of the republic, cordoned off by a strictly guarded border. Belarusan and other nationalities' schools and cultural clubs were opened; periodicals were subsidized. But all this activity was accompanied by ideological and political indoctrination, with lecturers and agitators sent in from across the border.

The economy exhibited the greatest change of all, not only because of the nationalization of industry, banks, and various enterprises but also because of the scarcity of consumer goods. Stores were empty within a few weeks. Whatever had been left in them was grabbed by Soviet soldiers at any price. Salt, soap, sugar, and other items of everyday consumption were now extremely hard to get. The goods imported from the Soviet Union were of demonstrably lower quality.

Peasants, including those who received land that had formerly belonged to big landlords, resisted the drive to collectivize them. On the eve of war with Germany, only 1,115 collective farms (involving 6.7 percent of the total number of farmers and 7.8 percent of tillable land) were organized.

NOTES

1. Ignat Abdiralovich, "Izvechnyi put'. Opyty belorusskogo mirovozzreniya," (The eternal path: An essay on the Belarusan Weltanschauung), *Nioman* (Neman), No. 11 (Minsk, 1990), p. 175 (emphasis in the original).

2. P. N. Olshansky, *Rizhski mir* (The Treaty of Riga) (Moscow: Nauka, 1969), p. 208.

3. U. M. Ihnatoŭski, *Karotki narys historyi Bielarusi* (A concise outline of the history of Belarus), 5th edition (Minsk: Bielaruś, 1991), p. 178.

4. Vilhelm Knoryn, quoted in Ivan S. Lubachko, *Belorussia Under Soviet Rule, 1917–1957* (Lexington: The University of Kentucky Press, 1972), p. 50.

5. Usievalad Ihnatoŭski, "Bielaruskaje nacyjanalnaje pytańnie i Kamunistyčnaja partyja. Tezisy" (The Belarusan national question and the Communist Party: Thesis), *Volny Ściah* (The free banner), No. 6 (8) (Minsk, December 25, 1921), pp. 38–40.

6. Academy of Sciences of the BSSR, *Bielaruskaja Savieckaja Encyklapiedyja* Vol. 12, (Minsk, 1975), p. 143.

7. H. I. Kaspiarovič, "Etnademahrafičnyja pracesy i mižnacyjanalnyja adnosiny ŭ BSSR," (Ethnodemographic processes and national relations in the BSSR), *Viesci AN BSSR. Sieryja hramadskich navuk* (Proceedings of the Academy of Sciences of the BSSR: Social sciences series), No. 5 (Minsk, 1990), p. 83.

8. N. P. Vakar, *Belorussia: The Making of a Nation* (Cambridge, Mass.: Harvard University Press, 1956), p. 256.

9. Academy of Sciences of the BSSR, *Istoriya Belorusskoy SSR* (Minsk: Nauka i tekhnika, 1977), p. 281–283.

10. V. I. Lenin, *Polnoye sobraniye sochineniy* (Complete works), Vol. 24, 5th ed. (Moscow: State Printers of Political Literature, 1961), p. 315.

11. Lubachko, *op. cit.*, p. 70.

12. S. Krushinsky, *Byelorussian Communism and Nationalism: Personal Recollections* (New York: Research Program on the USSR, 1953), Mimeographed Series No. 34, p. 17.

13. Academy of Sciences of the BSSR, *Istoriya Belorusskoy SSR,* pp. 288–291. For information regarding community pedagogical colleges, see *Bielaruskaja Savieckaja Encyklapiedyja,* Vol. 8 (Minsk, 1975), p. 365.

14. Lubachko, *op. cit.*, p. 89.

15. Vakar, *op. cit.*, p. 142.

16. Anthony Adamovich, *Opposition to Sovietization in Belorussian Literature (1917–1957)* (New York: Scarecrow Press, 1958), pp. 85–86.

17. Crane Brinton, John B. Christopher, and Robert Lee Wolff, *A History of Civilization,* Vol. 2, 3rd ed. (Englewood Cliffs, N.J.: Prentice-Hall 1967), p. 385.

18. David Lloyd George, quoted in Lubachko, *op. cit.*, p. 43.

19. Juliusz Bardach, *Studia z ustroju i prawa Wielkiego Ksiestwa Litewskiego XIV–XVII w.* (Studies on the government and laws of the Grand Duchy of Lithuania from the fourteenth to seventeenth centuries) (Warsaw: Panstwowe Wydawnictwo Naukowe, 1970), p. 14.

20. Józef Lewandowski, *Federalizm. Litwa i Bialoruś w polityce obozu belwederskiego* (Federalism: Lithuania and Belarus in the policy of the Józef Pilsudski camp) (Warsaw: Panstwowe Wydawnictwo Naukowe, 1962), pp. 31–32, 39–41.

21. *Ibid.*, p. 79.

22. *Ibid.*, p. 244.

23. *Ibid.*, p. 246.

24. Lubachko, *op. cit.*, p. 129. Vakar (*op. cit.*, p. 121) specifies 3.7 million Belarusans.

25. Mikola Volacič, in "The Population of Western Belorussia and Its Resettlement in Poland in the USSR," *Belorussian Review*, No. 3 (Munich: Institute for the Study of the USSR, 1956), p. 12, specifies 3,460,900 Belarusans in West Belarus in 1931, whereas Vakar, *op. cit.*, p. 121, specifies 3,700,000 in 1921.

26. Vakar, *op. cit.*, p. 121; Lubachko, *op. cit.*, p. 119.

27. Branislaŭ Taraškievič, *Vybranaje* (Selected) (Minsk: Mastackaja litaratura, 1991), pp. 161, 166. For details regarding the repression of Belarusans in West Belarus see Vakar, *op. cit.*, pp. 122–125. Deputy B. Taraškievič debunked Polish democratic laws as "nothing but a smoke screen" and, in his speech before the Diet on March 25, 1925, said that he had witnessed a police search operation in the Navahradak village of Krasnaje. "I have seen myself," he said, "how nails were torn out from the fingers by pincers, pins driven in, hair torn out, ribs crushed, how the breasts of women were crushed." See B. Taraškievič, *op. cit.*, p. 185.

28. Academy of Sciences of the BSSR, *Istoriya Belorusskoy SSR*, p. 343. The author has been unable to reconcile the discrepancy between numbers for West Belarus's population—"more than 4.4 million," mentioned at the beginning of this section, and "4.6 million."

29. Academy of Sciences of the BSSR, *Bielaruskaja Savieckaja Encyklapiedyja*, Vol. 4 (Minsk, 1971), p. 533.

30. Academy of Sciences of the BSSR, *Istoriya Belorusskoy SSR*, p. 345.

31. In April 1926 Deputy Taraškievič scolded Józef Pilsudski before the Diet, calling him "an ex-Socialist" who "promised federation" and who had been silent while "from five to six thousand political prisoners are rotting in prisons." See Taraškievič, *op. cit.*, pp. 224, 225.

32. Aleksandra Bergman, *Sprawy bialoruskie w II Rzeczypospolitej* (Belarusan affairs in the Second Republic) (Warsaw: Panstwowe Wydawnictwo Naukowe, 1984), pp. 34–36.

33. *Ibid.*, pp. 233–234.

34. *Ibid.*, p. 240.

35. Vakar, *op. cit.*, pp. 130, 131.

36. Iwo Pogonowski, *Poland: A Historical Atlas* (New York: Hippocrene Books, 1987), p. 29.

37. Thomas E. Bird, "Orthodoxy in Byelorussia: 1917–1980," *Zapisy* (Annals) of the Byelorussian Institute of Arts and Sciences, Vol. 17 (New York, 1983), pp. 158–159.

38. Anthony Adamovich, *op. cit.*, p. 21.

39. Leon Wasilewski, quoted in Lewandowski, *op. cit.*, p. 51.

40. Józef Pilsudski, quoted in Lewandowski, *op. cit.*, p. 43.

41. Taraškievič, *op. cit.*, pp. 40–41.

42. *Ibid.*, p. 41.

43. *Zviazda* (Star), Minsk, March 19, 1989. A concise account of the 1937 purge in the Communist Party of Belarus can be found in Zbigniew K. Brzezinski, *The Permanent Purge* (Cambridge, Mass.: Harvard University Press, 1956), pp. 180–184.

44. *Zviazda* (Star), Minsk, March 19, 1992.

45. Emanuil Jofie, *Litaratura i Mastactva* (Literature and art), Minsk, February 14, 1992.

46. Michail Bič, quoted in *Nastaŭnickaja hazieta* (Teachers' newspaper), Minsk, March 25, 1989.

47. Simon Kabysh, "The Belorussians," in Nikolai K. Deker and Andrei Lebed, eds., *Genocide in the USSR* (New York: Scarecrow Press, 1958), pp. 84, 85.

48. "Coming to Terms with the Past," *National Review*, New York, March 10, 1989, p. 15.

49. *Zviazda*, Minsk, March 19, 1989.

50. Academy of Sciences of the BSSR, *Bielaruskaja Savieckaja Encyklapiedyja*, Vol. 1 (Minsk, 1969), p. 217.

51. "V poiskakh utrachennogo vremeni" (In search of the lost time), *Kommunist Belorussii*, No. 1 (Minsk, 1990), p. 65.

52. Akademija nauk BSSR, *Istoriya Belorusskoy SSR*, p. 357.

53. *Ibid.*

54. *Ibid.*, p. 359.

55. Vyacheslav Molotov, quoted in Vakar, *op. cit.*, p. 159.

56. Mikola Volacič, "The Population of Western Belorussia and Its Resettlement in Poland and the USSR," *Belorussian Review*, No. 3 (Munich: Institute for the Study of the USSR, 1956), pp. 15–16.

FOUR

Destruction by War and Russification (1941–1985)

THE YEARS OF WAR, 1941–1944

The German attack against the Soviet Union on June 22, 1941, opened a four-year period of the most devastating losses in Belarus's history. As in previous East-West and West-East military conflicts—those of Ivan the Terrible, Napoleon, and Kaiser Wilhelm—the war path led directly through Belarus. Hitler's army group, "Center" (consisting of fifty divisions, including fifteen divisions of tanks), rolled over Belarus in the direction of Miensk, Smolensk, and Moscow. The thrust was intense and the advance was rapid—up to forty miles a day. Miensk was taken by the Germans on June 28. By the end of September all of Belarus lay west of the German-Soviet front. In a panicky retreat the Soviets managed to evacuate 1.5 million citizens and 674,000 head of cattle, and to remove more than 100 factories and other enterprises.[1] Uncounted numbers of political prisoners, unable to evacuate before the oncoming enemy, were summarily executed by the NKVD (security troops). And in Viciebsk, the city jail was burned, together with 200 inmates.[2]

No tears were shed over the fleeing Communist authorities. People were getting rid of one brutal regime without knowing what the new one had in store for them. Distant and relatively mild memories of the first German occupation of 1916–1918 combined with the hope that nothing could be worse than the NKVD terror and threat of deportation to Siberia. But disappointments for many were not long in coming.

The German scheme for Belarus envisioned it as one of the four ethnic areas (*Generalbezirk*) of *Ostland* (along with Lithuania, Latvia, and Estonia), whose territory would eventually be turned into German *Lebensraum*. Twenty-five percent of the Belarusans were to be Germanized and the rest destroyed or resettled to the east. In the spring of 1941, while planning his "Barbarossa Operation" against Russia, Hitler spoke of Ukraine,

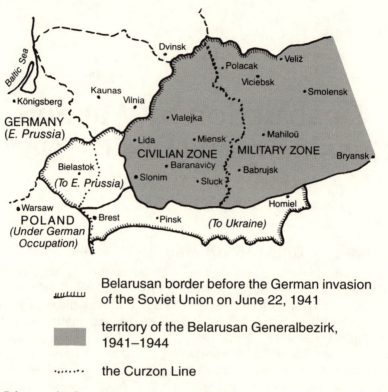

Belarusan border before the German invasion of the Soviet Union on June 22, 1941

territory of the Belarusan Generalbezirk, 1941–1944

········ the Curzon Line

Belarus under German occupation in World War II.

Belarus, and a federation of the Baltic lands as "buffer" states that, he said, "must be Socialist but without their own intelligentsia."[3]

Although when the Germans entered Belarus "none of the occupation authorities was instructed as to the projected political status" of the territory,[4] a general outline was there—"buffer states without their own intelligentsia." As Generalkommissar Wilhelm Kube is known to have said: "The White Ruthenians [Belarusans] shall become a 'nation' only to the extent that they shall be capable of forming a wall against Muscovy and the Eastern steppe."[5] In other words, Hitler wanted essentially what Stalin had almost achieved—an ethnic area fully subordinated to the central command. The German tyrant, however, was more reckless with Belarusan territory. The *Generalbezirk Weissruthenien* was established only on a quarter of the former BSSR, with the Vilnia region left within the Lithuanian *Generalbezirk*, the Bielastok area annexed to East Prussia, a southern swath of territory given to the *Reichkommissariat* of Ukraine, and the territory east of the Berezina River left under military rule. Eventually, though, the Belarusan "buffer" was to be increased territorially; according to the plan, it would stretch east to include the region and the city of Smolensk.

Life under German occupation was characterized by guerrilla warfare. One-third of the republic's territory is covered with forests and marshes, which gave the Soviet military an advantage in conducting diversionary hit-and-run operations against the enemy. The guerrilla warfare was slow to start, however, because of the local population's lack of support for the Soviet regime and the wait-and-see attitude vis-à-vis the Germans. "An overwhelming majority of the Belorussian population—including the misinformed Jews—continued to feel indifferent, if not outright friendly, toward the Germans for some length of time," notes historian Nicholas Vakar.[6] But the waiting period was not long. Toward the end of July 1941, along with POW camps around Miensk, a Jewish ghetto was set up in the city itself with more than 100,000 internees.[7] The executions of the Jewish people started in the fall of 1941.[8] Between October 1941 and February 1942, thousands of Jews were brought to Belarus from the West, including Hamburg, Germany.[9]

The local inhabitants were horrified by the brutality of the Germans. As Vakar writes: "With surprise a Nazi official reported that, in the eyes of the population, the Germans appeared as 'barbarians and hangmen, the Jew being held to be as much of a human being as the Belorussian.'"[10] "Though the Germans found their individual collaborators among the Byelorussians," according to the head of the Miensk ghetto, Yefim Stolerovitch, "these were the exception and not the rule. The dominant characteristic of the Byelorussian population was one of friendship and sympathy toward the Jews."[11]

The commiseration of the Belarusans for the Jews was bonded by the ruthlessness with which German troops burned villages where the Soviet guerrillas operated—in some cases, with all the inhabitants herded into the local church. The guerrilla leadership knew now how to replenish their ranks—they needed only to kill a German soldier near a village to have its dwellers flee into the woods.

Those Belarusans who lived in cities and towns under the German control had a hard choice to make. The nationalist leadership, aware of the tragedies under both the Communists and the Poles, gambled on the Germans, who allowed at least some rudiments of civil administration and cultural activities in the truncated Belarusan *Generalbezirk*.

Generalkommissar Wilhelm Kube (who arrived in Miensk in September 1941 and was assassinated on September 22, 1943) was mildly tolerant of Belarusan national aspirations and even patronized some cultural activities. By October 1941 the Belarusan Mutual Aid Society (*Narodnaja Samapomač*) had been set up. Primary and junior high schools were opened, along with some professional schools (but not high schools—"no intelligentsia!" said Hitler), and a civil administration was organized. By July 1942 "concessions" were extended to allow the recruitment of a "Belarusan Defense Corps" and the opening of military courses in Miensk. After all, Generalkommissar Kube wanted his *Generalbezirk* to be "a wall against Muscovy."

Belarusan cultural life in the zone of civil administration began to acquire a semblage of normalcy at the beginning of 1942. The front was far away. The outcome of the battle was not yet certain. The Belarusan intelligentsia used every opportunity to forge the spirit of reviving national values. Literary works and plays, forbidden by the Bolsheviks, were reprinted and staged. New ones were created. History was defalsified, though not without restrictions imposed by the new masters. Schools became hotbeds of patriotic upbringing of youth (which was the main reason the Communist guerrillas forbade attendance at schools above the primary level). At the beginning of September 1942, the All-Belarusan Orthodox Council proclaimed the autocephaly of the Belarusan Orthodox Church.[12] But all important political decisions and economic matters were completely and exclusively in the hands of the occupying authorities. Every undertaking was subordinated to the war effort and to racial theory. Peasants who had spontaneously parceled out collective farms were ordered to return to the collectivized ways of farming (to facilitate the authorities' collection of taxes). Young people were rounded up and deported to Germany as laborers. When in the summer of 1942 Belarusan leaders began protesting the German treatment of the civil population and prisoners of war, many protesters were arrested. "Belorussian committees that had assumed too strong a nationalist hue," notes Vakar, "were dissolved and their leaders arrested, some deported to Germany and some shot. Belorussian emblems and flags were removed from public buildings."[13]

Within less than a year the population of occupied Belarus changed its attitude toward the Germans—from friendliness or neutrality to hostility. Guerrilla activity increased. Thousands of POWs, who had worked as civil laborers or professionals and were left behind by the rapidly retreating Soviet armies, took to the woods. Capitalizing on these sentiments, the newspaper *Pravda*, on November 14, 1942, declared that the Soviet leadership had decided "to engage in the armed struggle wide strata of the population, reinforcing the guerrilla formations."[14] "Reinforcement" came by means of various tactics, including parachuting organizers and political commissars from Russia, provoking Germans into reprisals by committing various acts of sabotage near villages, and forcible induction of villagers into guerrilla units.

By May 1943 more than 75,000 Soviet guerrillas were operating in occupied Belarus.[15] The Germans tried belatedly to remedy the situation in the summer of 1943. They decreed the private ownership of land by peasants,[16] created an advisory body (the Council of Men of Confidence) made up of Belarusans, and allowed the establishment of the Union of Belarusan Youth.[17] But the hour was already late. In the fall of 1943, following the assassination of Generalkommissar Kube, his replacement, General Von Gottberg, tried to combine brutal repressions with further concessions to Belarusan nationalism. In December 1943 the Belarusan Central Council (BCC) was formed as a self-governing auxiliary body whose main task was "to mobilize all the forces of the Belarusan people to destroy Bolshevism."[18] The BCC was empowered to call about 100,000 troops into the Belarusan Land Defense (BLD) in March 1944. The mobilization took place throughout the *Generalbezirk* with the exception of the Lida District, where the draft was conducted by the Polish Land Army (Armia Krajowa, or AK) in cooperation with the German authorities. However, the Germans were reluctant to arm the BLD fully. Only on June 15, 1944, when the front was already rumbling a short distance away, did a military school for junior officers of the BLD begin functioning in Miensk.

The last political move, laden more with symbolism than with practicality, was the convocation by the BCC of the All-Belarusan Congress in Miensk—a convocation fully approved by the German authorities. On June 27, 1944, 1,039 delegates—904 men and 135 women—came to Miensk for a one-day session. The delegates had been chosen by various organizations and professional groups and came from all parts of the Belarusan ethnic territories, including those under the German, Lithuanian, and Latvian administrations; some represented Belarusans deported to Germany.[19] Having condemned the Bolshevik regime for the annihilation of "1,800,000 of the best sons of our people," the assembly voted a laconic resolution. Without speaking of the future of the Belarusan people, and without mentioning Germany, the convention confirmed the Act of Independence of the Belarusan Democratic Republic of March 25, 1918, denounced all treaties signed for Belarus by both Russia and Poland, and announced that "the only legal representation of the Belarusan People and its land today is the Belarusan Central Council headed by President Radaslaŭ Astroŭski." At Astroŭski's suggestion, a telegram was dispatched to Hitler assuring him that the "Belarusan people will unfalteringly fight along with the German soldier against our common enemy, Bolshevism."[20]

It was the last hurrah of Belarusan nationalism under the German occupation. In the next few days, most of the participants of the Second All-Belarusan Congress, all of the members of the Belarusan Central Council, several Belarusan military units, and many activists from civic and cul-

Miensk in July 1944, ruined by the war. Courtesy of the Belarusan Institute of Arts and Sciences in New York.

tural life in the occupied territories braced themselves and scrambled for evacuation to the West. Within six days after the All-Belarusan Congress, on July 3, 1944, the battered city of Miensk was taken over by the Red Army.

From today's vantage point, the three-year German occupation period produced a demographic-political effect, unforeseen at the time—namely, the émigrés who left Belarus along with the Germans in 1944 and those who, after having worked in Germany as laborers, decided not to return to the Soviet Union. Most of these individuals emigrated in the late 1940s and early 1950s to the United States, Canada, and Australia. In these new countries of settlement they and their children established Belarusan organizations, churches, and national homes, and became professionals. They readily respond now to the invitations of various groups in Belarus to cooperate and share their Western experience in support of Belarus's newly proclaimed independence and, one hopes, democracy as well.

WAR DAMAGES AND EAST-WEST RESETTLEMENTS

By the time the war was over in May 1945, Belarus had lost more than 2.2 million inhabitants (including the nearly 380,000 who had been deported to Germany as laborers). Two hundred and nine cities and townships and 9,200 villages (1.2 million buildings) had been burned or destroyed. And the republic had lost 61 percent of its horses, 69 percent of its cattle, 89 percent of its pigs, and 78 percent of its sheep.[21] The material losses were estimated (in state prices of 1941) at 75 billion rubles.[22] An American observer who traveled for six months from one end of the republic to the other, two years after the war, found Belarus to be "the most devastated territory in the world," with principal cities such as Miensk, Viciebsk, and others 80 to 95 percent in ruins.[23]

One assessment of the population losses of the Belarusan SSR covers the period from 1939 to 1959. At the beginning of 1939 the republic (within the borders of 1959) had 9,344,000 inhabitants, whereas the 1959 census found the population to be 8,055,000. According to Andrej Bahrovič of the Belarusan Institute of Arts and Sciences in New York,

> The twenty years demographic deficit of the republic is 6,045,000. One-third of that, 2,000,000, are direct or indirect World War II losses. Two-thirds, or 4,000,000, are direct or indirect consequences of political terror, mass deportations, and forcible resettlements to the remote, mostly Asian, lands of the Soviet empire.[24]

One result of the war was the change in Belarus's border with Poland. Currently it runs along the line established in September 1939 (when West Belarus was incorporated into the Soviet Union), minus the Bielastok region and some other modifications favoring Poland. The border issue was settled by Stalin, Churchill, and Roosevelt at the conferences in Teheran, Moscow, and Yalta, respectively. At each of these conferences, the Soviet delegation argued successfully that the USSR's western border with Poland should run along the so-called Curzon Line. Associated with the name of Lord Curzon, a British foreign secretary, the Curzon Line dates back to 1919, when it was drawn by the Supreme Allied Council to delineate the ethnic territories of Poland and Soviet Belarus. A year later, it was confirmed by the Western Allies with the intention of settling the Russo-Polish War of 1920. The Poles, however, refused to accept the Curzon Line as a basis for settlement; their memories of the 1772 border were simply too strong. As a result, the eventual peace treaty, signed in 1921 in Riga, established Poland's eastern border far to the east of what the Supreme Allied Council had in mind. Twenty-five years later, the issue surfaced again; this time, Stalin and Molotov convinced Churchill and Roosevelt that the Soviet claim to the territory east of the Curzon Line was, in Churchill's words, "one not founded on force but upon right."[25] The Polish delegation participating in the Moscow Conference (October 9–22, 1944) officially agreed to accept the Curzon Line as Poland's eastern frontier.[26]

The Republic of Belarus in 1993.

These territorial changes were accompanied by a program of resettlement of Poles to the west and Belarusans to the east. In particular, Poles and Jews who were citizens of the prewar Polish state and who found themselves on the Soviet side were moved to the new Poland. Thousands of Belarusans, especially Catholics, seized upon this opportunity to escape the Soviets, of whom they had seen quite enough in 1939–1941. By 1947, when the crest of the exodus had passed, a total of 120,000 Poles, 85,000 Jews, and 469,000 Belarusans had resettled from Belarusan territories to the west of the Curzon Line.[27]

In the opposite direction, migration was of much smaller proportions. In spite of Polish efforts at forcible deportation of Belarusans from the Bielastok district, most refused to leave the land they looked upon as their patrimony. According to an official Polish source of May 2, 1947, only about 30,000 Belarusans left Poland for the USSR.[28] The total number of ethnic Belarusans who remained under Polish rule in the Bielastok region, including those who settled in the territories reclaimed from Germany, is controversial. Official Polish statistics purposely ignore the issue because of the pretense that the state is "ethnically uniform." Scholarly estimates, on the other hand, vary from about 150,000[29] to 500,000.[30]

The three-year German occupation of Belarus, which suffered devastations but demonstrated much stamina in fighting the enemy, added an unexpected dimension to the status of the republic—namely, its membership, along with Soviet Ukraine, in the United Nations. This move in no way altered the puppet character of the Belarusan and Ukrainian governments or dramatically changed in Moscow's favor the balance in that international body. But it certainly flattered the national ego of the Belarusans and Ukrainians, who saw some of their national values and prestige rehabilitated as a result of the war and the German occupation. Stalin insisted on the inclusion of these two republics in the new world body, ostensibly because of the devastation they suffered and because of their input into the victory over Nazi Germany. Prime Minister Churchill accepted Stalin's argument at the Yalta Conference. "My heart goes out to White Russia [Belarus]," he said, "bleeding from her wounds while beating down the tyrants."[31]

President Roosevelt originally opposed the idea of two extra votes for Moscow, but "Churchill talked him around."[32] Belarus and Ukraine were invited to take part in the San Francisco Conference on April 25, 1945, and thus became founding members of the United Nations. Stalin's insistence on the UN seats for these republics seems to have had more to do with placating the Ukrainian and Belarusan nationalism that had demonstrated itself on the German side of the front than with rewarding Ukraine and Belarus for their role in fighting the enemy.

PURGES AND RUSSIFICATION

Although Stalin outwardly displayed an appreciation of the fighting spirit of the Belarusan and Ukrainian peoples for having resisted the enemy, they were inescapably stigmatized by the mere fact of having lived for three years under an anti-Bolshevik regime, having been exposed to anti-Bolshevik arguments and evidence, and having participated in one form or another in anti-Bolshevik activities. The stain of "collaboration" extended even to those who had been forced to become cooks or cleaning personnel for the Germans, let alone primary school teachers, scribes in local offices, and members of the nationalist youth organization. Those who had lived in German POW camps or had been deported to Germany as laborers were equally blacklisted and in most cases deported once again, this time to the far north or Siberia. As soon as Belarus was retaken by the Soviet Army, the state security organs went to work ferreting out the "unreliable elements."

Belarusan nationalism, or any other non-Russian nationalism for that matter, was viewed in the light of Stalin's famous toast to the Russian people on May 24, 1945, when the victorious dictator proclaimed:

I drink above all to the health of the Russian people because it is the most outstanding nation of all nations of the Soviet Union. I propose a toast to the health of the Russian people because it has merited in this war a general recognition as the guiding force of the Soviet Union among all the peoples of our country.[33]

In the first few years after the Soviet Army took Belarus, there was armed resistance by the nationalist forces, as was also occurring in neighboring Ukraine and Lithuania. In the virgin forest of Bielavieža in the Bielastok region, the nationalist guerrilla army of General Kastuś Vituška fought the Communists.[34] Peasants throughout West Belarus fiercely opposed collectivization. "Armed bands," notes one Soviet historian, "committed beastly executions of Party, Soviet, and Komsomol officials and activists. ... With the active support by the local population, the administrative organs had liquidated on the territory of the western districts 814 anti-Soviet groups and armed bands."[35]

For their part, the rulers in the Kremlin trusted no one, including Party members. Official Soviet sources indicate that by the middle of 1946, "ninety percent of the district Party secretaries, ninety-six percent of district and city administrative officials, and eighty-two percent of the collective farm chairmen" had been removed from their posts in Belarus.[36] "The thesis that Soviet totalitarianism is a system of permanent purge, varying in intensity," concludes Zbigniew Brzezinski, "thus finds further vindication in the Ukraine and Byelorussia during the postwar years 1946 to 1952."[37] Removal from a position in most cases entailed banishment or, worse, imprisonment.

As a rule, the purge included the substitution of local functionaries by outsiders, predominantly Russians, sent in from other republics. By the end of 1948, according to I. S. Lubachko, "all top Belorussian Communists had been purged and replaced by Russians."[38] This decimation at the top of the Party was also reflected in the republic's government. In 1951 the government of the BSSR was composed of "twenty-two Russians, one Georgian, one Jew, and nine Belorussians."[39]

The policy of distrust of local cadres bred resentment. When Stalin died in March 1953, his closest henchman, Lavrenti P. Beria, chief of security forces, tried to exploit the prevailing political mood in the outlying republics by wagering on the nationalism of the non-Russians. The drama in Belarus was staged in the Party headquarters in Miensk. As ordered by the "leading troika," Beria, Georgi M. Malenkov, and Nikita S. Khrushchev, a plenum of the republican Party Central Committee was held in June 1953.

The plenum was instructed by the Center to replace first secretary of the Communist Party of Belarus, Nikolai S. Patolichev (a Russian), with his Belarusan deputy, Second Secretary Mikhail V. Zimianin. Zimianin was the key speaker at the plenum. Illustrating "criticism by the CC of the CPSU of fundamental shortcomings and mistakes" in the realm of "Leninist nationality policies," he gave, among others, the following examples:

> In the "apparatus" of the Party organs of the republic the representatives of Belarusan nationality make up only 62.2 percent [in the republic's population Belarusans constituted 81 percent at that time]. Among the 1,408 officials of the Party oblast (provincial) committees in the western parts of the republic, only 114 were of local origin; and among the 321 officials of the city executive committee, only 25 were local Belarusans.

Zimianin complained that "the work by the Central Committee of the CP of Belarus and the Council of Ministers of the BSSR, local Party and Soviet organs, and even the organs of the People's Education is being conducted in Russian." He went on to say: "Lectures for the population are given almost everywhere not in the Belarusan language." The speaker also urged the plenum to adopt a resolution calling on the republic's party and government, as well as the local Party and Soviet organs, to transact all their affairs in the native language of the Belarusan people.[40]

Nikolai S. Patolichev, who had headed the Communist Party of Belarus for the last three years, survived the attempt to replace him. Although he took part of the blame for shortcomings in the area of nationality policies, he pointed out that "the paperwork in the governmental offices was switched to Russian many years ago. ... Some say it was in 1936, others in 1937."[41]

The "leading troika's" political flirtation with pro-nationalities sentiments did not survive its chief plotter, Beria, who was shot several months into the struggle, on December 23, 1953. Russification continued unabated. The "thaw" that followed Stalin's death and Khrushchev's condemnation of the dead tyrant's crimes at the Twentieth Congress of the Party in February 1956 did not touch upon the ethnocidal policies of the Kremlin. On the contrary. The widespread public discussions about the best methods of teaching Russian in the non-Russian republics ended with a general inter-republican conference in Tashkent, Uzbekistan, in August 1956. The conference concluded that the Russian language had become "a second mother tongue" for all Soviet peoples and was a means of "enriching" the dictionaries of the national languages.[42]

As in the early 1930s, a campaign was launched not only to "enrich" the national vocabularies with Russian words but to switch the entire cultural life to Russian. This policy evoked an outcry on the part of the various national intelligentsias, who, in the aftermath of the Twentieth Party Congress, became more outspoken.

The Belarusan periodicals of 1956–1957 are filled with criticism of Sovietization and Russification (although these terms are never actually used) and with demands for concessions to national values. A member of the former *Excelsior* literary club, Maksim Lužanin, pretty much summed up those demands when he wrote in the writers and artists weekly in March 1957:

> The further development of our culture is intimately linked with the dissemination of the Belorussian language. … One wants to hear the Belorussian language not only in cultural organizations, but also in offices, secondary schools and colleges, to see it on a cigarette pack, a tractor and a work bench.[43]

These sentiments were shared to a degree by some Belarusan Communists. In April 1957 the Central Committee of the CPB, headed since mid-1956 by Kiryl Mazuraŭ, the first Belarusan to lead the republic's Party organization,[44] criticized in a resolution the fact that "in many primary and secondary schools all subjects, except the Belarusan language and literature, are conducted in Russian, although students are using Belarusan-language textbooks," and that "in some schools willfulness is tolerated in freeing the students from studying the Belarusan language."[45]

This attempt at defending the native language was consistent with the personal views of First Secretary Mazuraŭ, who, in his criticism of Patolichev at the Party plenum in 1953, maintained (ironically, quoting Stalin from 1921) that "the culture of the Belarusan people can be elevated only in its native language."[46] Mazuraŭ soon found out that ethnocide was not included among the Stalinist crimes denounced at the Twentieth Party Congress. On the contrary, Russification was to continue. That became clear in January 1959, when Khrushchev came to Miensk to participate in the celebration of the fortieth anniversary of the Belarusan SSR and its Party organization. The occasion was marked by a gala ceremony at which First Secretary Mazuraŭ delivered a speech. Did Mazuraŭ know that his Belarusan language would anger his high-powered guest from Moscow? That's certainly what happened. Here is what Belarusan People's Poet Pimien Pančanka remembers of that political episode:

> The leader of the CPB K. T. Mazuraŭ made a speech in Belarusan (as was a habit then). An intermission was announced. Hardly had the audience left the hall (I sat not far away from the dais), when Khrushchev, here on the dais, began swearing at Mazuraŭ: why didn't he make his report in Russian: *"Ni cherta nye ponyatno"* (I couldn't understand a damned thing).[47]

On the steps of the Belarusan State University in Miensk, Khrushchev further declared: "The sooner we all start speaking Russian, the faster we

TABLE 4.1   Decline of Belarusan-language Publications in the Belarusan SSR

Year	1960	1970	1975	1980	1985
Total titles	1,602	2,174	2,941	3,009	3,431
Titles in Belarusan	425	428	475	370	381
Total copies (in millions)	14.2	25.2	34.4	38.3	53.3
Copies in Belarusan	7.2	9.4	11.0	8.2	4.9

Source: Central Board of Statistics of the Belarusan SSR, *Natodnoye Khozyaystvo Belorusskoy SSR v 1985 g. Statisticheskiy ezhegodnik* (The national economy of the Belarusan SSR: Statistical yearbook) (Minsk: Belarus, 1986), p. 162.

shall build Communism." Citing this pronouncement, Moscow University M. Vsevolodova wrote in *Pravda*:

> To what consequences led the zealous efforts of the official local authorities to fulfill this directive, illiterate in every regard, and at the same time to "accelerate" in such an easy way the construction of Communism, is known: in Belarus there remained no schools with instruction in the native language. [48]

In the mid-1960s, after Piotr Mašeraŭ (Masherov) replaced Mazuraŭ as first secretary of the CPB, there came a time of "epidemic of liberation from the Belarusan language." Students were readily excused from studying Belarusan in schools. And the republic was slated to become a showcase of the Soviet nationality policies aimed at creating a new "historic community—the Soviet People."

The "epidemic" spread to other areas of culture, too: printing, theater, choirs, lecture circuits, the cinema. When some defenders of Belarusan values criticized the studio *Belarusfilm* for the absence of national characteristics in its films, their criticism was denounced in February 1967 by B. Paŭlonak, chairman of the State Committee for Cinematography, as "something that smells of nationalism."[49]

One indicator of the denationalization process during the postwar years was the dwindling proportion of Belarusan-language publications in relation to the total output, as shown in Table 4.1. (almost all of the remainder were in Russian). The category of books and pamphlets can be taken as representative of publishing as a whole.

The quantitative side, however, is not the entire story by any means. A Belarusan-language publication is not necessarily filled with Belarusan spirit, with truth about the people's past or their aspirations. In this land of total literacy, the Belarusan nation (and all the other non-Russian republics, for that matter) grew woefully illiterate about its history and culture. Belarus was Russified to a greater extent than the other republics for three basic geopolitical and cultural reasons: (1) its geographic location (a natural crossroads from West to East), (2) its topographic physiognomy (one-third of the territory forested, convenient for emplacing arms), and

— Вось мы і ўз'ядналіся.

"Finally—we are united!" says the big (smiling) fish to the
smaller (mournful) one in this 1980 cartoon, published in the
Miensk weekly *Litaratura i Mastactva* as a commentary on
Moscow's way of merging the nations of the USSR into "one
Soviet People." Courtesy of the Belarusan Institute of Arts
and Sciences in New York.

(3) its linguistic proximity to Russia. "Ideological saboteurs, in their plans
for a 'crusade' against the first land of socialism," wrote Savielij Paŭlaŭ,
the chief republican ideologue, in *Polymia*, "assign an important role to Soviet Belarus. They have in mind first of all Belarus's geographical location.
The republic is the western gate to our land [i.e., the USSR]."[50] With this in
mind, the Communists transformed the two westernmost provinces of the
republic, Grodno and Brest (Hrodnia and Bieraście), into a *cordon sanitaire*
where the principal newspapers were in Russian only and the institutions
were thoroughly Russified.

NATIONALIST RESISTANCE

Belarus has been widely referred to, both in the Western and the Soviet
press, as a "docile" republic with a weak sense of national consciousness.
Obviously, the sense of nationhood among the Belarusans is not as pronounced as in neighboring Poland, Lithuania, Ukraine, or Russia; each nation develops according to the inner characteristics of its people and is
conditioned by external physical and political factors. It should be emphasized, however, that as far as the defense of national values goes, there
have been protests and there have been martyrs. The reason the world
heard much less about Belarus's resistance than about that of some other
Soviet republics has to do with the specificity of reaction by the republican
authorities to manifestations of dissent. Apparently, one of the principal
rules at the Miensk party headquarters and the KGB was avoidance of arrests through early firings, quiet banishments, and various forms of ha-

rassment at the slightest sign of protest. This method of combating dissent could have been associated with the desire of the central and local Party leadership to have an exemplary republic as a model for others; or it might have been dictated by geopolitical considerations. A lack of information also played a role in the creation of this image of the "docility" of Belarus.

Now, thanks to openness (*glasnost*), we know much more about what was going on in the republic during the postwar decades when the crime of ethnocide was being committed in Belarus. Thus, for example, we have only recently learned of the repression of all those who in 1957–1958 supported the published demand by then-young student Barys Sačanka for switching instruction in all of the republic's schools from Russian to Belarusan. Not only the editor of the weekly *Litaratura i Mastactva* (Literature and art) but "all those who prepared my article" lost their jobs. "Dossiers were initiated on those who wrote to the newspaper in support of my article. Many totally innocent people, especially students, found themselves in various places outside of Belarus."[51]

Historical scholarship became an arena for revisionism of official dogmas about Belarus's Russianized past. In the opinion of historian Mikola Praškovič, for example, had the religious Union with the Vatican (1596) not been liquidated in 1839, it could have had a beneficial effect on Belarus because it would "firstly, have freed Belarusans and Ukrainians from the Byzantine despotism and, secondly, would have reduced the animosity with which people of the Orthodox faith viewed all that was 'Latin,' including not only religion, but mainly progressive European science and culture."[52] Another historian, Mikola Aleksiutovič, has debunked the key Soviet dogma, which claimed that the Bolshevik Revolution gave Belarusans their statehood for the first time in history. A *socialist* statehood, yes, said Aleksiutovič—but not statehood in general, for there had been many nonsocialist states in history, of which one was enjoyed by the Belarusan people. He went on to argue that the Grand Duchy of Lithuania and Ruś "in its ethnographic composition, its territory and culture was predominantly Belarusan."[53] After the ouster of Khrushchev in October 1964 such views were decidedly out of sync with the Brezhnev leadership.

The two most celebrated Belarusan dissidents are Vasil Bykaǔ (Bykov), "a very courageous and uncompromising writer, rather of the Solzhenitsyn stamp,"[54] and Michael Kukabaka (Kukobaka), who spent seventeen years in concentration camps and psychiatric prison for denouncing the Soviet invasion of Czechoslovakia in 1968 and otherwise criticizing the Communist regime. In a recent personal account of his ordeal, Kukabaka recalled that during his trial in the city of Babrujsk in 1979 he had the full right to state that "Communism of the Soviet brand is a system of complete suppression and destruction of the individual, and the Soviet Union is nothing other than a boundless concentration camp."[55]

Vasil Bykaŭ has only recently told his readers about the price he had to pay for having written his war novella "The Dead Feel No Pain" in the mid-1960s:

> The situation of ostracism was a long one. It lasted not months—years. Living at that time in the provincial city of Grodno, the author had also [in addition to attacks in the All-Union press] a full measure of local persecution and harassment at work, smashing of windows in his house, attacks by hoodlums on the street—at the instigation of the local organs of the KGB.[56]

Bykaŭ, whose novella exposed the paralyzing hold on the Soviet Army of the security forces during World War II, resisted intense pressure from the KGB to write another "documentary novella about the Chekists of the war period, naturally, as they understood it and with their approval."[57] In addition, both Bykaŭ and Kukabaka defended the right of Belarusans to full-fledged use of their national language in all spheres of science and public life.

The decade between the mid-1960s and mid-1970s was a time of political ferment among students in Miensk. In 1970 numerous students at the Belarusan State University were accused of nationalism for petitioning the authorities to switch instruction to Belarusan. Some of the students were expelled or dispersed to other provincial schools.[58] Another campaign was conducted at the same time against Belarusan "nationalists," whose only crime was the "stubborn use of the Belarusan language, predominant subscription to Belarusan newspapers, and criticism by some individuals of the CPSU's nationality policy," resulting in their expulsion from work and in a "blacklisting" that prevented them from finding new employment.[59]

In 1973 a conference on the ethnogenesis of the Belarusans (prepared for at the Academy of Sciences) was banned and its organizers reprimanded. The following spring, at a Party plenum in Miensk, First Secretary Mašeraŭ denounced a group of scholars, including M. Praškovič, S. Misko, A. Kaŭrus, M. Čarniaŭski, V. Rabkievič, and P. Dziadziula, for the nationalistic character of some of their conceptions. The members of the Praškovič "conspiracy" were dismissed from their jobs. They averted being brought to trial through the intercession of some senior writers. Praškovič soon died, under unexplained circumstances—as did his predecessor in dissent, historian Mikola Aleksiutovič.[60]

The absence of mass arrests in Belarus is explained today by the observation that those in power saw no real danger that nationalism would take root in Belarusan society. Denationalization was considered to be an

"Watch yourself!" A Miensk satirical magazine in the summer of 1988 sees bureaucrats still looking back at the Kremlin to avoid misstep. Courtesy of *Bielarus*.

accomplished fact. Obviously, it was not. Now, says Uladzimir Arloŭ, "those who decided the fate of the free-thinkers, including Paźniak [the future leader of the Belarusan Popular Front] and other well-known individuals, are kicking themselves in the butt: Shucks! We should have jailed them!"[61]

The Helsinki movement in the 1970s and 1980s did not materialize in Belarus, as it had done in the neighboring republics. The remnants of the nationally conscious intelligentsia had been numbed by the Stalinist repressions. Moreover, the majority of intellectuals chose to work with or within the system, inasmuch as they saw no chance to challenge it successfully. Those who dared to confront it, as did writers Vasil Bykaŭ and Uladzimir Damaševič or historians Mikola Aleksiutovič and Mikola Praškovič, paid a price others were not ready to. The widely used Aesopian language in literary works had a limited effect because of the artificially small circulation of Belarusan-language publications. The only known dissident who openly denounced the criminality of the Soviet regime—and did so with political maturity, inasmuch as he provided references to fundamental international documents—was Michael Kukabaka.

The suppression of even the slightest manifestation of dissent was accompanied by noisy propaganda glorifying the achievements of the republic. Some of this propaganda effectively catered to the sense of national pride, as was the case with sports. Belarus had been allowed to develop a high-quality school of gymnastics, with spectacular results. For example, at the Twentieth Olympic Games in Munich (1972), where Belarusan gymnast Olga Korbut had burst into tears—and into world fame—athletes from Belarus won nineteen medals, including eleven gold ones, out of the USSR's total of ninety-nine. Although the Soviet athletes participated as a single delegation, the republican media belabored the glory of the Belarusan contingent.[62] (The republic's membership in the United Nations was constantly played upon as a proof of the independent international standing of "sovereign" Belarus.)

While the national language was being squeezed out of all official places, it was at the same time propagandized on a grand scale as a flourishing cultural asset of the Belarusan socialist nation. In 1975 one of the early Soviet astronauts, Belarusan Piotr Klimuk, took along on his maiden flight with Vitaly Sevastyanov, a Russian, a collection of verse by Belarusan classical poet Jakub Kolas. While in flight, he read it to his fellow astronaut. Upon his return Klimuk donated the book to the Kolas Museum.[63]

The episode with the Kolas book is an example of the crafty duplicity of Soviet nationality policy. Klimuk's devotion to his native language was displayed on a cosmic scale, but the monument honoring him in his place of birth bears an inscription in Russian only.

As far as is known, Klimuk's poetry reading in space was a historic first and, as such, deserves to be entered in the *Guinness Book of Records.*

ECONOMIC RECOVERY

In the wake of the devastation left by the German occupation and war—more than 2.2 million dead, cities ruined, villages burned, libraries and archives plundered, and nearly 3 million people left homeless—economic recovery was slow and painful. The bombastic assertions of official

The best-known export item of the republic, the tractor *Bielaruś,* also marketed in the United States. Courtesy of the F. Skaryna National Research and Educational Center in Miensk.

Soviet histories cover up much misery and suffering. Thus, despite the claim in one academic publication that "in 1949 resettlement of rural inhabitants from dug-outs into their own homes was already successfully accomplished,"[64] we learn from Aleksandr Lukashuk that "ten years after the expulsion of the Fascists, people still huddled in dug-outs, lacking the most essential items."[65]

Conflicts in West Belarus over the forcible collectivization, deportations to Siberia of the "collaborationists" under Stalin, massive recruitment of youth to cultivate the "Virgin Lands" in Kazakhstan under Khrushchev, and generally poor living conditions—it was for these reasons that the republic did not regain its prewar population of 9.1 million until 1971. At the same time, no one can deny the heroic efforts that led to successful reconstruction of the republic from the ruins of war. Along with the development of military underground airfields and rocket bases in forested areas of Belarus, civil construction continued at a rather rapid pace. Between November 1946 and December 1952 machine-building and consumer-goods-producing factories began operations in Viciebsk, Miensk, Mahiloŭ, Skidal, and other cities. Schools, institutes, theaters, and hospitals were built and started up. The first segment of a street-car line was

A thermo-electrical power plant near Miensk spewing pollution (1992). Photo by Michail Žylinski. Courtesy of *Narodnaja hazieta* (People's newspaper).

opened in Miensk in February 1953. And in January 1956 the Miensk Television Center began transmissions.[66]

Belarus's GNP in 1969 was structured as follows: industry, 45.7 percent; construction, 9.9 percent; agriculture, 29.8 percent; transportation, 4.0 percent; and commerce, supply and other forms of material production, 11.3 percent.[67] In the 1970s, in fact, Belarus was well on its way to becoming a major industrial region of the Soviet Union, specializing in the production of tractors, trucks, machine tools, precision instruments, computers, synthetic fibers, plastics, petrochemical products, mineral fertilizers, and various products of the light and food industries. In 1973 the republic produced every sixth Soviet tractor, every seventh metal-cutting lathe, almost half of the output of potassium fertilizers, and 16 percent of synthetic fibers. Belarusan agriculture in the same year, though predominantly taken up with livestock farming, accounted for about 17 percent of the Soviet Union's potatoes and almost 25 percent of its flax.[68]

By 1975 Belarus had acquired 9,442 schools of general education, with a total of 1,804,000 pupils. In its 30 institutions of higher learning, 153,000 students were enrolled. The number of specialists graduating from universities, colleges, and professional schools at the secondary level increased from 27, 000 in 1959 to 65,500 in 1974. And 33 research-and-development institutes of the republican Academy of Sciences employed 4,400 specialists.[69]

Yet the economic growth of the republic was achieved at a considerable price: Both environmental requirements and social needs were neglected. In the cities, construction of highrise apartment buildings, factories, and plants failed to take into account the necessary ratio of social service and transportation facilities. Inconveniences affecting everyday life became as unavoidable as the constant harangues to fulfill the Five-Year Plan.

The method of central planning underlying the economic development of the Soviet Union was linked with the Kremlin's nationality policy by two factors. The first of these concerned the destruction of ancient monuments and buildings (both religious and civic), in order to obliterate outward national characteristics and eradicate historical memory. According to Zianon Paźniak, the leader of the democratic opposition in the Belarusan parliament and one of the defenders of historical landmarks in Miensk:

> What had been bombed could very well have been restored. However, dozens of absolutely untouched houses were demolished in the name of the stupid idea of developing a grand Stalin Boulevard. The architects had been given this task and in the short span of two months in 1944 (!) they drafted a blueprint of the idea. ... Thus began the disappearance of dozens of houses—monuments.[70]

The other element of central planning dictated by nationality policy was the intertwining of the republic's economies in such a manner as to speed up the amalgamation of the peoples of the USSR and thus reinforce the empire. In short, economic rationality was subordinated to political aims. For example, it is widely accepted among Belarusan economists that building gigantic tractor and automobile plants in Miensk was devoid of any common sense because all raw materials and component parts had to be imported. The republic provided only the engineering and labor force. At the same time, agricultural technologies were woefully underdeveloped. Belarus prided itself on the production of huge trucks and tractors but was forced to send its cattle to meat plants in the neighboring Baltic countries. In addition, the republic continued to lose hundreds of tons of fruits and vegetables every year because it lacked the necessary food-processing facilities.

Now that the economic ties of the former Soviet Union have been sundered, the Belarusan government is facing additional difficulties in keeping its gigantic plants operational: Almost all raw materials and component parts have to be brought in from outside. Restructuring for an independent Belarus—as for any other Soviet republic, undoubtedly—

means first of all refocusing the entire economy on the strengths of its own resources and the needs of its people.

Nevertheless, by Soviet standards Belarus fared well. The republic has a skilled and disciplined workforce. Indeed, both labor productivity and the standard of living have been above average for the USSR. With the onset of perestroika in 1986, the Communist *nomenklatura*, anxious to preserve its power, pointed to the republic's relatively stable economy as a strong argument to proceed slowly with changes. Belarus's political conservatism is thus paradoxically rooted in both the destruction of public self-awareness and relative economic success.

NOTES

1. Academy of Sciences of the BSSR, *Istoriya Belorusskoy SSR* (Minsk: Nauka i tekhnika, 1977), p. 375.

2. Nicholas P. Vakar, *Belorussia: The Making of a Nation* (Cambridge, Mass.: Harvard University Press, 1956), p. 171.

3. Jerzy Turonek, *Bialoruś pod okupacja niemiecka* (Belarus under the German occupation), (Warsaw and Wroclaw: Wers, 1989), pp. 37–38.

4. *Ibid.*, p. 40.

5. Alexander Dallin, *German rule in Russia, 1941–1945: A Study of Occupation Policies* (London: Macmillan, 1957), p. 204.

6. Vakar, *op. cit.*, p. 184.

7. Academy of Sciences of the BSSR, *Historyja Minska*, edited by N. V. Kamienskaja et al. (Minsk: Navuka i technika, 1967), p. 440.

8. Ivan S. Lubachko, *Belorussia Under Soviet Rule, 1917–1957* (Lexington: University of Kentucky Press, 1972), p. 153.

9. Dallin, *op. cit.*, p. 208.

10. Vakar, *op. cit.*, p. 186.

11. Yuri Suhl, ed., *They Fought Back: The Story of the Jewish Resistance in Nazi Europe* (New York: Crown Publishers, 1967), p. 234.

12. T. E. Bird, "Orthodoxy in Byelorussia: 1917–1980," *Zapisy Bielaruskaha Instytutu Navuki i Mastactva* (Annals of the Byelorussian Institute of Arts and Sciences), Vol. 17 (New York, 1983), pp. 155–166.

13. Vakar, *op. cit.*, p. 190.

14. Academy of Sciences of the BSSR, *Istoriya Belorusskoy SSR*, p. 393.

15. Academy of Sciences of the BSSR, *Bielaruskaja Savieckaja Encyklapiedyja*, Vol. 8 (Minsk, 1975), p. 263.

16. Vakar, *op. cit.*, p. 202.

17. Dallin, *op. cit.*, p. 219.

18. R. Astroŭski, ed., *Druhi Usiebielaruski Kanhres. Matarjaly* (Second All-Belarusan Congress: Materials) (Belarusan Central Council, 1954), p. 78.

19. *Ibid.*, p. 8. A breakdown of the delegates according to the localities represented can be found in the minutes of the convention. See Leanid Halak, *Uspaminy* (Memoirs), Part 1 (New York: Letapis, 1982), pp. 221–223.

20. Halak, *op. cit.*, p. 241.

21. Lubachko, *op. cit.*, p. 166.

22. Academy of Sciences of the BSSR, *Bielaruskaja Savieckaja Encyklapiedyja*, Vol. 1 pp. 213, 217.

23. Vakar, *op. cit.*, p. 209.

24. Andrej Bahrovič, *Žycharstva Bielaruskaje SSR u śviatle pierapisu 1959 hodu* (The population of the Belarusan SSR in the light of the 1959 census) (New York: P. Kreceŭski Foundation, 1962), p. 7.

25. Winston Churchill, quoted in: Lubachko, *op. cit.*, p. 180.

26. M. Volacič, "The Curzon Line and Territorial Changes in Eastern Europe,"*Belorussian Review*, No. 2 (Munich: Institute for the Study of the USSR, 1956), p. 70.

27. Mikola Volacič, "The Population of Western Belorussia and Its Resettlement in Poland and the USSR," *Belorussian Review*, No. 3 (Munich: Institute for the Study of the USSR, 1956), p. 26.

28. *Ibid.*, p. 28.

29. Jerzy Tomaszewski, *Mniejszosci narodowe w Polsce XX wieku* (National minorities in twentieth-century Poland) (Warszawa: Editions Spotkania, 1991), p. 45.

30. H. I. Kaspiarovič, "Etnademahrafičnyja pracesy i mižnacyjanalnyja adnosiny ŭ BSSR" (Ethnodemographic processes and international relations in the BSSR), *Viesci AN BSSR. Sieryja hramadskich navuk* (Proceedings of the Academy of Sciences of the BSSR: Social sciences series), No. 5 (Minsk, 1990), p. 79.

31. Winston Churchill, quoted in Lubachko, *op. cit.*, p. 183.

32. C. L. Sulzberger, "Two Chinas with One Voice," *New York Times*, October 8, 1971.

33. Joseph Stalin, quoted in Lubachko, *op. cit.*, p. 171.

34. Volacič, "The Population of Western Belorussia," pp. 27, 28.

35. Academy of Sciences of the BSSR, *Historyja Bielaruskaj SSR*, Vol. 5 (Minsk: Navuka i technika, 1975), pp. 77–78.

36. Zbigniew K. Brzezinski, *The Permanent Purge: Politics in Soviet Totalitarianism* (Cambridge, Mass.: Harvard University Press, 1956), p. 139. See also Lubachko, *op. cit.*, p. 170.

37. Brzezinski, *op. cit.*, pp. 140–141.

38. Lubachko, *op. cit.*, p. 175.

39. Vakar, *op. cit.*, p. 215.

40. Aleksandr Lukashuk, "Zharkoye leto 53-go. Zametki na polyakh stenogramy iyun'skogo (1953 g.) plenuma TsK KP Belorussii" (The hot summer of 1953: Notes in the margin of the Verbatim Report on the June 1953 Plenum of the CC of the CP of Belarus), *Kommunist Belorussii*, No. 7 (Minsk, 1990), pp. 69–71.

41. Nikolai S. Patolichev, quoted in Lukashuk, "Zharkoye leto 53-go," *Kommunist Belorussii*, No. 8 (Minsk, 1990), pp. 74, 75.

42. P. Urban, "The Twentieth Party Congress and the National Question," *Belorussian Review*, No. 4 (Munich: Institute for the Study of the USSR, 1957), p. 93.

43. Maksim Lužanin, quoted in Urban, "Belorussian Opposition to the Soviet Regime," *Belorussian Review*, No. 6 (Munich, 1958), p. 38.

44. Discounted here is Vasil Šaranhovič, a Belarusan, who was first secretary of the CPB for a brief period in 1937 before his execution as a Bukharinite in 1938.

45. Institute of Party History at the CC of the CPB, *Kommunisticheskaya Partiya Belorusii v rezolutsiyakh i resheniyakh syezdov i plenumov TsK* (The Communist Party of Belarus: Resolutions and decisions of congresses and plenums of the Central Committee) (Minsk: Bielarus, 1986), pp. 42, 43.

46. Lukashuk, "Zharkoye leto 53-go," *Kommunist Belorussii*, No. 8 (Minsk, 1990), p. 77.

47. *Litaratura i Mastactva* (Literature and art), Minsk, April 7, 1989.

48. *Pravda*, March 6, 1989. Soviet statistics provide no data on the ratio of national-language schools to those in which instruction was in Russian.

49. Jan Zaprudnik, "Developments in Belorussia Since 1964," in George W. Simmons, ed., *Nationalism in the USSR and Eastern Europe in the Era of Brezhnev and Kosygin* (Detroit, Mich.: The University of Detroit Press, 1977), p. 110.

50. *Polymia* (Flame), No. 8 (Minsk, 1970), p. 162.

51. *Litaratura i Mastactva*, Minsk, September 13, 1991.

52. Mikola Praškovič, "Slova pra Afanasija Filipoviča" (A word about Afanasij Filipovič," *Polymia*, No. 12 (Minsk, 1965), p. 177.

53. Mikola Aleksiutovič, "A dzie-ž iscina abjektyŭnaja?" (And where is the objective truth?), *Polymia*, No. 5 (Minsk, 1966), p. 179. For more information on this subject, see Jan Zaprudnik, "Dziaržaŭnaść Bielarusi u dasavieckuju paru" (The statehood of Belarus in the pre-Soviet period), *Zapisy* (Annals) of the Byelorussian Institute of Arts and Sciences, Vol. 15 (New York, 1977), pp. 3–22.

54. Michael Glenny, "Writing in Belorussia," *Partisan Review*, Vol. 34, No. 2 (Spring 1972), p. 255.

55. Alaksandr Ulicionak, *Inšadumcy. Hutarki z tymi, kaho jašče ŭčora klejmavali 'demahohami'* (Dissidents: Interviews of those who only yesterday were branded "demagogues") (Minsk: Bielarus, 1991), p. 234.

56. Vasil Bykov, "Myortvym—nye bolno, bolno zhivym" (The dead feel no pain, but those living do), *Nioman* (Nemen), No. 1 (Minsk, 1992), pp. 144–145.

57. *Ibid.*, p. 145.

58. For more information on the subject of dissent, see Jan Zaprudnik, "Inakodumstvo v Bilorusi" (Dissent in Belarus), *Sučasnist* (Modern times), No. 7–8 (Munich, 1979), pp. 158–169.

59. *Litaratura i Mastactva*, Minsk, April 12, 1991.

60. *Ibid.* See also, *Litaratura i Mastactva*, May 10, 1991.

61. Ulicionak, *op. cit.*, p. 169.

62. *Zviazda* (Star), September 15, 1972.

63. M. Bazarevič, "Slova Kolasa natchniala Klimuka," (The works of Kolas inspired Klimuk) *Litaratura i Mastactva*, Minsk, October 24, 1975.

64. Academy of Sciences of the BSSR, *Historyja Bielaruskaj SSR*, Vol. 5, p. 87.

65. Lukashuk, "Zharkoye leto 53-go," *Kommunist Belorussii*, No. 7 (Minsk, 1990), p. 71.

66. Academy of Sciences of the Belarusan SSR., *Historyja Bielaruskaj SSR*, Vol. 5, pp. 732–734.

67. F. S. Marcinkievič, "Ekanamičnaje razviccio Bielarusi u sastavie SSSR" (Economic development of Belarus within the USSR), *Viesci AN BSSR. Sieryja*

hramadskich navuk (Proceedings of the Academy of Sciences of the BSSR: Social sciences series), No. 6 (Minsk, 1972), p. 25.

68. Press release from the Mission to the UN of the Byelorussian SSR, 1973, Annex, p. 9 of Annex.

69. Academy of Sciences of the BSSR, *Bielaruskaja Savieckaja Encyklapiedyja*, Vol. 12 (Minsk, 1975), p. 189.

70. Ulicionak, *op. cit.*, p. 307.

FIVE

Confrontation Between the National Intelligentsia and the Communists (1985–1992)

MAJOR DEVELOPMENTS IN BELARUS (1986–1992)

The direction and the character of developments in Belarus since Gorbachev's election to the post of General Secretary of the Communist Party on March 11, 1985, have been shaped and influenced by the following major events:

April 26, 1986	Chernobyl disaster
June 3, 1988	Revelation of the Kurapaty mass graves near Miensk, where up to 300,000 victims of Stalinists' crimes were unearthed
October 30, 1988	Violent clash between massive group of demonstrators and troops in Miensk
June 24–25, 1989	Establishment of the Belarusan Popular Front in Vilnia
January 26, 1990	Law making Belarusan the official language of the state
July 27, 1990	Declaration of Sovereignty of the Republic of Belarus
August 25, 1991	Declaration of Belarusan Independence, following the unsuccessful Moscow putsch
December 8, 1991	Establishment of the Commonwealth of Independent States and, three days later, denunciation by the Belarusan Supreme Council of the 1922 treaty on the formation of the Soviet Union.
January 1992	Campaign of the democratic parliamentary opposition launched; referendum of no-confidence in the govern-

ment aims to dissolve the Supreme Council and to hold parliamentary elections in the fall of 1992.

THE SPIRITUAL AND CULTURAL BASES OF NATIONAL RECONSTRUCTION

Today, Belarus is facing not only enormous economic hurdles but also spiritual and cultural obstacles of no lesser dimensions. Intractable and often mysterious, the deepening economic problems call for increasing psychological endurance. In such crises, as President Franklin D. Roosevelt phrased it, the important thing is not to be fearful of fear itself—but such equanimity requires highly developed spiritual qualities. In his international column, "My Partner, the Pope," Mikhail Gorbachev has said this about the people in his former realm: "Everything that can serve to strengthen man's consciousness and spirit is today of much greater importance than ever before."[1]

Spirit is the Great Mover. One hundred years ago, Belarusan Populists faced a somewhat similar situation regarding the strategy of national rebirth. Pondering over the poor, uneducated people of the country, they concluded that it is not a low level of culture that leads to subjection, "but on the contrary, subjection causes stagnation" (see Chapter 2). This interrelationship between the state of national consciousness and the level of material well-being of a nation was pointedly acknowledged by the contemporary Belarusan intelligentsia in the context of the Chernobyl nuclear calamity. It is an established fact that, because of the northern direction of the winds, 70 percent of the Chernobyl nuclear fallout landed on Belarusan territory. This horrendous fact, however, was hidden from the people of Belarus for three-and-a-half years by Moscow's bureaucrats in Miensk. When the facts about the Chernobyl radiation finally came to light under the pressure of glasnost, the daily *Sovetskaya Belorussiya* wrote: "The Chernobyl tragedy has demonstrated that the Belarusan people needs indispensably to raise its self-awareness. If our leadership had high national self-awareness, this would not have happened."[2] In other words, a nationally conscious leadership in Miensk would not have waited for permission from Moscow but, rather, would have acted in defense of its nation. But the latter did not happen, some are convinced, because Russification paralyzed the nation's ability to stand up for itself, destroyed its instinct of self-defense. Moreover, this paralysis resulted as much from political as from cultural developments in Belarus. Culture and politics here go hand in hand, one bolstering the other. And the roots of this organic interrelationship reach further into the past than the Bolshevik Revolution of 1917. Demographer U. P. Cieraškovič, while discussing the re-

With perestroika came religious revival: An Orthodox procession in the city of Navahradak in 1992. Photo by Siarhiej Hryc. Courtesy of *Narodnaja hazieta* (People's newspaper).

sults of the 1897 census in Belarus and the assimilation of local officials, Orthodox clergy, intelligentsia, and city bourgeoisie, observed incisively: "They considered their adaptation to the dominating [i. e., Russian] culture to be a demonstration of their loyalty to the policies of tsarism."[3]

"Adaptation to the dominating culture" was a sign of loyalty to the policies of Moscow during the Soviet period (except during the 1920s). For virtually the entire Soviet period, the order of the day was the so-called amalgamation of nations. After all, it was Lenin who wrote in his "Critical Notes on the Nationality Question": "Marxism is irreconcilable with nationalism, be it the most 'just,' 'pure,' refined, and civilized. Instead of any nationalism, Marxism advances internationalism, amalgamation of all nations in a higher unity."[4]

LETTER TO A RUSSIAN FRIEND

The results of the Leninist nationality policy in Belarus prompted an anonymous Belarusan author[5] in 1976 to write a "Letter to a Russian Friend" in which the "equality" of the Belarusan and Russian languages was compared to that of Little Red Riding Hood and the Wolf. Khrushchev's pronouncement in Miensk—that Communism will be built ever so much faster the sooner Belarusans learn to speak Russian—was implemented by Party bureaucrats with great zeal. The author of the "Letter" described the depth and thoroughness of the denationalization of Belarus, where learning of the native language was almost totally eliminated from the schools and other subjects (such as art, music, choreography, etc.) were being Russianized. The anonymous dissident painted a dreadful picture of spiritual destruction:

> Paintings, sculpture, graphic arts, poster art, music, cinema, choreography, in short the whole state of Belarusan culture, cannot be understood without reference to the problem of the Belarusan language. Here we must understand by language not so much its communicative function, but above all the spirit and ability of people to express themselves in all areas of activity. Without much risk of being mistaken one can assert that at the present time Belarusan culture, with certain exception of the literary field, has a large number of specialists, cadres with higher education, but disgracefully few real Belarusan intellectuals.[6]

Gorbachev's program of restructuring (perestroika) was launched in April 1985. It soon became clear that the program would have tough going in Belarus with its Russified leadership. Because Russification was an organic outgrowth of Stalinist policies, it became an additional psychological barrier to change. "Change" now meant return to, or at least tolerance of, Belarusan culture; but this culture was alien to the Russified bureaucracy. The bureaucrats of local stock hated the very idea of Belarusization because it reminded them of their cultural treason, as it were—of their abandonment of values that now were being proclaimed lofty. They felt morally indicted by the call to return to the Belarusan language they had abandoned, and this feeling provoked a profound revulsion to perestroika in most members of the New Class. Their wrath was displayed in a situation involving students of an art school, who exhibited a most innocent way of demonstrating attachment to national values.

On April 20, 1986, two artists, Alaksiej Marackin and Mikola Kupava, organized a celebration of the ancient folkloric tradition of Spring Calling (hukańnie viasny). Their younger friends—art students—were dressed in popular costumes and just about to start a procession carrying symbols of nature reawakening. Unexpectedly, they were attacked, beaten, and dispersed by a band of Communist thugs (members of the Komsomol), who were instigated by the Party organization of the city of Miensk.[7] Other similar incidents prompted Moscow-based Belarusan writer Aleś Adamovič to brand Miensk as "Vendée of perestroika," a label that firmly stuck with Miensk officials.

A PROGRAM FOR PERESTROIKA

What began as individual shots against the state of the national culture and the offensive neglect of the language had culminated by the end of 1986 in a comprehensive document that could be considered the program for a rebirth of the Belarusan nation. A flood of writings, a series of demonstrations, and a string of laws that ensued in the following years amounted to fulfillment of that program. The document itself took the form of a petition to General Secretary Gorbachev and was signed by twenty-eight intellectuals: fourteen writers, four historians, four artists, two actresses, one composer, one journalist, one linguist, and one educator.

In a brief introduction to this "Letter of the Twenty-Eight," the authors touched on the gist of the matter—the native language. "Language," they wrote, "is the soul of a nation, the supreme manifestation of its cultural identity, the foundation of its true spiritual life. A nation lives and flourishes in history while its language lives. With the decline of the language, culture withers and atrophies, the nation ceases to exist as a historical organism; it is no longer an invaluable component of cilvilization on Earth."[8]

Of course, what these authors said about the correlation of language and the historical existence of a nation is not universally true—there are, for example, flourishing English-language and Spanish-language nations other than England and Spain. But in the historical context of Eastern Europe, language and national existence are almost tantamount. And the national-language situation in the Belarusan SSR has indeed indicated that the titular nationality of that state was being swept out of existence.

The authors of the petition gave a concise account of this slow death:

From the middle of the 1950s, in the period of "voluntarism" [i.e., the years during which Khrushchev was in power], Belarusan schools in cities were closed on a grand scale, a number of Belarusan periodical publications shifted over to Russian, our language was squeezed out of almost all spheres of life.

In the last two decades this process has accelerated. The position of Belarusan schools in rural areas has become significantly worse. Very often they are Belarusan in nothing but name, because most subjects, especially in the senior classes, are taught in Russian. Hundreds of rural schools have already been officially transformed into schools using Russian as the medium of instruction. The decline in numbers of pupils in Belarusan schools is catastrophic. For example: judging by the number of copies printed of the Belarusan alphabet primer, 44,000 pupils entered the first grade of

Belarusan-language schools in 1983. In 1986 the figure was 34,000. This is no more than 25 percent of all first-graders; i.e., in the current year only one quarter of all first-graders in the republic entered school with Belarusan primers.

There is moreover no continuity of teaching in Belarusan in the public education system. Pre-school education in the native language is in a deplorably neglected state. There are no higher educational institutions, technical or vocational colleges which use Belarusan. For several decades now the pedagogical colleges of the republic have not been preparing teachers to work in Belarusan-language schools.

The status of Belarusan in the BSSR is quite clearly shown by the republic's book-publishing policy. Suffice it to say that the proportion of belle lettres published in the republic in Russian (expressed in terms of printed sheets) rose from 89.9 percent in 1981 to 95.3 percent (!) in 1984. Virtually no films are produced in Belarusan. There are about fifteen theaters in the republic; only three are Belarusan. Belarusan is almost never used as a working language either in official correspondence in Party organizations, or in local and national government.[9]

To avert what the authors called the "spiritual extinction" of the Belarusan people, they suggested the following measures:

- First, introduce Belarusan as a working language in Party, state, and local government bodies, particularly in the Ministry of Education, the Ministry of Higher and Secondary Specialized Education, the Ministries of Culture and Communication, the State Committee on Publishing, the Academy of Sciences, the book trade, cinema, television, and radio.
- Second, make the examination in Belarusan language and literature compulsory for graduation from secondary schools, and the examination in the Belarusan language compulsory for graduation from eight-year incomplete secondary schools, irrespective of the language of instruction in these schools.
- Third, introduce an examination in Belarusan language and literature that is compulsory for entry into all institutions of higher learning (students coming from outside the republic and from foreign countries would be exempt), and an examination in the Belarusan language that is compulsory for entry into the technical colleges of the republic.[10]

The four-page petition was accompanied by a seven-page Appendix detailing "Proposals for a Radical Improvement in the Position of the Belarusan Language, Culture, and Patriotic Education in the BSSR." The Appendix contains specific suggestions for policy changes in the areas of ideological upbringing, science, education, book publishing, culture, art, and the mass media.

The signatories of the petition reminded Gorbachev that discrimination against the Belarusan language had evoked in the republic "a noticeable growth of national awareness," which, in turn, "provokes a hostile reaction from the bureaucracy." They also expressed to the secretary general their "certainty" and "hope" "that the problems here set forth will meet with your understanding and that you will personally support and assist us in solving them."[11]

It was a vain hope. Moscow sent a commission to Miensk before which, one by one, all the signatories of the petition were brought to be roasted by Savielij Paŭlaŭ, the chief republic ideologue who wanted to hear an explanation of this "misguided" action and insisted that each signatory recant. None of the twenty-eight intellectuals withdrew his or her signature, but each paid a price. As Ms. Valentyna Parchomienka, a folk singer and one of the signatories, told this author, every endorser of the petition had to endure demotion, harassment, or loss of job. The findings of the commission were neither published nor even communicated to the petitioners. Soon, however, an indirect answer was given. The new Party boss, Jafrem Sakaloŭ, at a plenary session of the CPB's Central Committee on March 25, 1987, without mentioning the Letter of the Twenty-Eight, flatly denied claims that "spiritual extinction" threatened the Belarusan nation. Sakaloŭ insisted that "all the necessary conditions have been created for the development of Belarusan national culture in general." By way of illustration, he adduced some statistics representing the existing proportion of Belarusan-language books and newspapers, and named such publications as the *Belarusan Soviet Encyclopedia* (twelve volumes), *Belarusan Folklore* (thirty-five volumes), and, of course, the *Selected Works of Lenin* (ten volumes).[12] Sakaloŭ, whose linguistic abilities do not include Belarusan, exclaimed: "Is this neglect of the native language and culture!" Thence came the warning: "Whoever errs concerning these issues," said First Secretary Sakaloŭ, "should be helped to see clearly. Whoever wants to dramatize them should know that this would not help perestroika and the cause of upbringing."[13]

Activists on behalf of the national cause made one more attempt at gaining a sympathetic ear for their grievances from Gorbachev. This time they sent him an open letter with 134 signatories from people of all walks of life, including 16 workers; copies were sent to the Party daily, *Pravda*, and to the leadership of the Presidium of the BSSR. The letter, dated June 4, 1987, refuted Sakaloŭ's statistical assertions about the "flourishing" of Belarusan culture by quoting official sources showing that more than 83 percent of Belarusans remained faithful to their native language and that the "freedom of language choice" in education and literature, of which

Sakaloŭ spoke, was "more often than not a free coercion to use Russian." The open letter contended that the state must become involved in caring for the native language of the Belarusans and other national languages in the republic by passing appropriate legislation and guaranteeing its practical implementation. The approach of the Party leadership in Belarus to cultural matters was described as "not far-sighted" and contradictory to the spirit of perestroika. And a warning was sounded that this kind of approach was "pregnant with serious consequences both for culture and the cause of internationalism" in the Soviet Union. The letter postulated democracy as the surest means in the struggle "not only against manifestations of national egoism, but also against great power chauvinism."[14]

It is worth noting that on the day the Letter of the One Hundred Thirty-Four was dated, a plenary session of the Belarusan Writers' Union adopted a twelve-point resolution expressing essentially the same demands as those listed in the Letter of the Twenty-Eight.[15] Ultimately, however, as the reaction on the part of the authorities to both letters was official silence and harassment of the signatories, it became clear that the defense of national values would require other, more persuasive means than mere written complaints.

TAKING TO THE STREETS

The protests on paper soon found supporters in the streets of the capital. The first such demonstration took place on November 1, 1987, on which an unauthorized rally was scheduled to mark the traditional day of *Dziady* (analogous to All Saints' Day). About 300 demonstrators, mostly youth, came to Kupala Park, where speeches were being delivered denouncing the Stalinist genocidal policy in Belarus. Russification being the very reverse of Stalinist genocide, the rally became an open challenge to the current leadership in Miensk, stubborn in its pursuit of Russification. It was the first time that the word *genocide* was openly applied to the Soviet regime in Belarus. Anatoly Maysenya, a correspondent from *Sovetskaya Belorussiya* (the only newspaper that reported on the event—after a two-and-a-half-week delay), was left aghast by this accusation, which, until that moment, had been reserved for the policies of Adolf Hitler.[16]

Openness (glasnost) in public pronouncements and condemnation of abuses of power by the former rulers and their underlings gave rise to a new phenomenon—informal organizations of youth that spawned throughout the republic—that most dramatically signaled the disintegration of the Old Order. The Communist Party kept a vigilant eye on these groups and collected data. According to an internal report of the Party organization in Miensk dated November 1988, the membership of these

У акуліста.

Малюнак А. БРАНЦАВА.

Be more aware of the political groups, ignore the social problem groups, a Miensk satirical journal seems to be saying in January 1989. A policeman checks his (political) vision: He is expected to see clearly the first three groups, which are the Belarusan patriotic organizations. The rest of the names on the chart (in smaller and smaller letters): drunkard, thief, drug addict, and so on. Courtesy of the Belarusan Institute of Arts and Sciences in New York.

groups had increased several times over since August 1987. Miensk alone had 566 "amateur self-managing associations and clubs," with a grand total of more than 46,000 members. Although not as numerous, similar groups had sprung up in such other cities as Homiel, Hrodna, Viciebsk, Brest, and Lida. Sixty-five percent of the students surveyed at Belarusan State University were involved to varying degrees with informal groups, most of which had an apolitical orientation. And of the 566 groups in Miensk, 97 were found to have a "socio-political direction." These groups espoused, among other views, the idea of a Belarusan "Renewal" (*Adradžeńnie*).[17]

The aforementioned Party memo noted the tendency among the informal groups "to unite and consolidate with those who share their views." Indeed, this proclivity surfaced on December 26, 1987, when thirty independent groups sent delegates to Palačanka near Miensk for a two-day convention marking the occasion of their first General Diet (*Valny Sojm*). Representatives of democratic youth movements were invited from Lviv, Kaunas, Vilnia, Leningrad, and Moscow. Official press coverage of this unprecedented event was very skimpy and biased, however. Hienadź Buraŭkin, current Belarusan ambassador to the United Nations, who at the time had been minister in charge of the republic's information media and attended the Palačanka convention, remembered the event quite vividly. In an April 1992 interview with this author, Buraŭkin said:

> It was a very solemn occasion. The mood among the participants was serious. For the first time they felt empowered to decide important issues for themselves. Seeing in their midst representatives of the Academy of Sciences and the government, the young participants felt elated and good about themselves. The level of discourse was high and cultured. There was spirituality in the air and I saw light glimmering in the eyes of the young.

In July 1988 some of the results of the Palačanka convention circulated in a *samizdat* (unofficially published) document entitled, "An Appeal of the Initiating Group of the Confederation of Belarusan Associations to Belarusan Youth." Inspired by the example of their Baltic neighbors, the Initiating Group tried to arouse similar action in Belarus:

> The cause of self-determination of the Belarusan youth movement has ripened not only because of internal reasons. We are watched with hope and concern by the peoples of Estonia, Latvia, and Lithuania. They are waiting for us to join the formidable wave of national upsurge that is rolling over the Baltic region. In Belarus's joining this surge, there is the assurance of irreversibility of revolutionary changes in the Baltic republics as well as throughout the entire Soviet Union, which means that it is our international-

Erection of a wooden cross at Kurapaty near Miensk (1989) to mark the site of mass executions in 1937–1941. Photo by Anatol Klaščuk (given to this author by the photographer).

ist duty to do so [i.e., to support Gorbachev's perestroika by nourishing national revival].[18]

The Appeal set forth as its ultimate goal the formation of an organization uniting "all politically and nationally conscious youth," including "all Belarusan associations and societies that exist beyond the borders of the republic," who stand up "in support of the radical restructuring of Belarus."

KURAPATY: THE DEAD GALVANIZE THE LIVING

On June 3, 1988, a political bombshell exploded on the pages of the Writers' Union weekly, *Litaratura i Mastactva* (Literature and art), a description of the unearthing of mass graves in the environs of Miensk. The genocidal character of Stalinist crimes in Belarus was now painfully obvious.

After delays and stormy confrontations with his superiors in the Central Committee of the CPB, the newspaper's editor, Anatol Viarcinski, with the unanimous support of the editorial board, prevailed in publishing a documented account by Zianon Paźniak and Aŭhien Šmyhaloŭ of more than 500 mass graves in the Kurapaty forest near Miensk. Up to

300,000 victims were said to have been executed there by Stalin's henchmen during the years 1937–1941. The 300,000 figure, which had been mentioned in the galleys of the article, was omitted in the final version as a result of a compromise with the censors. Overnight the name of Kurapaty placed itself next to Khatyn, the symbol of German atrocities in Belarus during World War II. The disclosure of the Kurapaty murders stained the conservative leadership of the republic and precipitated a chain of events leading to the formation of the Belarusan Popular Front, which has since become the core of the democratic opposition.

Dissatisfaction with the work of the official commission that had been formed to investigate the shootings at Kurapaty prompted creation of a civic group called the "Martyrology of Belarus" (similar to Moscow's "Memorial") consisting of prominent citizens whose purpose was to inquire into Stalinist crimes. About 400 people attended the constituent meeting of Martyrology in the Miensk House of Cinema on October 19, 1988. At that meeting, writer Vasil Bykaŭ, a moral authority in contemporary Belarus, laid out the purpose of the group:

> We ought to compile a grand Martyrology of our losses and our martyrs. This would be laid as a cornerstone in the foundation of our national consciousness, would become an important element of our historical memory and a guarantee of the future of our people, who have been struggling with the determination of a condemned man through genocide, blood, and insults toward light, goodness, and justice.[19]

Zianon Paźniak was elected chairman of Martyrology's five-member Civic council. In addition to compiling a martyrology of Belarus, the organization spelled out its political aims:

> Martyrology promotes the development of the political, legal, and cultural-national consciousness of our citizens and youth in the spirit of rejection and condemnation of the political system of Stalinist excesses, of compulsory, violent, and undemocratic methods of solving social, political, and economic problems.[20]

THE BELARUSAN POPULAR FRONT

At the same meeting the first organizational step was taken toward establishing the Belarusan Popular Front for Restructuring, or "Renewal" (hereinafter abbreviated BPF). The rally elected a thirty-two-member organizational committee and adopted a draft program that postulated the roots of Belarusan nationhood:

The Belarusan people gained the right to sovereign nationhood by struggle and suffering throughout their entire history. The traditions of nationhood in the principalities of Polacak and Turaŭ; the sovereignty of Belarus and Lithuania embodied in the Grand Duchy of Lithuania, Ruś, and Samogitia; the traditions of struggling for a respectable existence of man and nation—the uprisings of [Tadeusz] Kościuszko and [Kastuś] Kalinoŭski, the revolutions of 1905–1907 and 1917—all this led logically to the proclamation of the independent Belarusan Democratic Republic on March 25, 1918, and then to the creation of the sovereign Soviet Socialist Republic of Belarus on January 1, 1919.[21]

CONSERVATIVES' COUNTERACTION

The Party nomenklatura, challenged by such diametrically opposing views of history (the official dogma maintained it was the October 1917 Revolution alone that brought Belarusans their statehood), staged a vitriolic attack against the BPF in the press, which was still largely under its control. A series of denunciatory articles appeared in republican and regional newspapers accusing the BPF's initiators of nationalism and political extremism, and of having damaged perestroika. But the split among the official publications deepened, even as these unsubstantiated charges mounted against the BPF. The Party daily *Zviazda*, for example, published in August 1988 a round-table discussion on the ethnic makeup and national identification of the Belarusans. In the course of this discussion the archconservative historian Adam Zaleski conceded that "the time has ripened to state openly the fact that as early as the fourteenth to sixteenth centuries Belarus had its statehood.[22]

One hundred years ago, Belarusan populists predicted the emergence of an intelligentsia who would build a full-fledged nation on the basis of the uncorrupted original culture preserved by the people. This prediction came true only partially, however. The Soviet regime had produced a mass of educated individuals who, because of their Russian-centered and Communist-ideologized education, can hardly be called a national intelligentsia. Belarusan People's Writer Vasil Bykaŭ—who, through suffering and moral rectitude, earned for himself the sobriquet "Conscience of the Nation"—characterized the Belarusan intelligentsia "in its mass" as "a typical embodiment of sycophantic conformism."[23]

"National nihilism" has become the theme of discussions among the intelligentsia on how to elevate and uphold the spirit of the nation under conditions of newly acquired independence. The group most actively pursuing this course has been organized around the weekly of the Union of Writers, *Litaratura i Mastactva*. Other Belarusan-language periodicals that have developed into forums of nationalist ideology include *Čyrvonaja zmiena* (Red generation), *Krynica* (Wellspring), *Maladość* (Youth), *Nastaŭnickaja hazieta* (Teachers' newspaper), and the monthly *Bielaruś*. By mid-1988 these newspapers and magazines had moved away from the conservative position stubbornly maintained by the Party leadership in Miensk. A number of *samizdat* periodicals also appeared, with clearly nationalist overtones.

It should be emphasized that the differentiation of the press between liberal and nationalist, on the one hand, and conservative, on the other, generally followed the language division: The Russian-language publications, with some exceptions, abandoned the old dogmas and stereotypes at a slower pace than did their Belarusan counterparts. The Russian language in Belarus has remained a carrier of imperial thinking, which, perforce, is tied up with political conservatism. Perestroika and glasnost opened the door to a plethora of new Russian-language publications throughout the republic, some of them openly reactionary and anti-Belarusan, such as the notorious *Politicheski sobesednik* (Political interlocutor), *Slavyanskiye vedomosti* (Slavic news), and *Vecherniy Minsk* (Evening Minsk).

By contrast, many Moscow publications—*Ogonyok, Literaturnaya gazeta, Izvestiya, Moscow News,* and occasionally even *Pravda* and the army newspaper *Krasnaya zvezda* (Red star)—came down on the side of those in Belarus who were branded nationalists and extremists by the conservative Minsk press.[24]

The war of words, and dynamic developments in the neighboring Baltic republics leading toward independence and secession, only radicalized the situation. A violent confrontation erupted on October 30, 1988, during a mass commemoration of the victims of Stalinist crimes. About 10,000 people had flocked to a cemetery on the outskirts of Miensk, not far from the site of the mass graves at Kurapaty, to observe the traditional *Dziady* (Remembrance of the dead). But what the participants found at the site of the meeting were water cannons and police with dogs and tear gas. Clashes and beatings ensued, and arrests were made. Part of the dispersed crowd marched to Kurapaty, where they held a rally. The incident received worldwide attention. In Washington the visiting Russian academician Andrei Sakharov referred to the violent breakup in Miensk as one of the reasons he felt "very great anxiety" over the course of perestroika.[25]

DEFENSE OF THE LANGUAGE

The October 30 incident turned out to be the political christening of the national democratic opposition movement in Belarus. The clash dramatically demonstrated the inability of the Party leadership in Miensk to moderate its administrative-command approach to the society's grievances and only reinforced the determination of the opposition groups.

On January 14–15, 1989, the second convention of self-managed youth organizations took place in Vilnia, Lithuania. The Miensk authorities prevented the organizers from staging the event in their own capital. Two hundred and forty-six delegates representing sixty-six organizations accepted the challenge with optimism. In their appeal they declared: "In spite of severe bureaucratic pressure, events have taken place during the last months proving that the Belarusan Renewal has a future."[26]

The city government of Miensk, facing criticism in press accounts of the Vilnia youth convention, finally decided to allow a mass meeting convoked by the Organizational Committee of the BPF and the Confederation of Belarusan Youth Societies. The rally, which drew 40,000 people, adopted a number of resolutions, including demands to repeal the leading role of the Communist Party and to form Belarusan national units in the armed forces. Such slogans as "Sovereignty for Belarus" and "Official Status for the Belarusan Language" expressed the mood of the crowd, above which many national white-red-white flags could be seen waving. According to an eye-witness report, "practically everyone voted for legalization of the BPF, while only one-fifth of the participants were members of the Front."[27] Piotr Kraŭčanka, secretary of the Party organization in Miensk, told Vadim Medvedev, chairman of the CPSU Ideological Commission (who had come to Miensk for a visit) that mistakes of previous years in the realm of national culture and language had led to "an emotional 'explosion' among the intelligentsia."[28]

In the March 1989 elections to the Congress of People's Deputies of the USSR, the BPF successfully supported a number of independent candidates on a platform that included renewal of the national culture. Among those who won with BPF backing were writer Vasil Bykaŭ; Stanislaŭ Šuškievič, future president of the Belarusan parliament; and Mikalaj Ihnatovič, future attorney general of independent Belarus. Encouraged by their success, the BPF activists convoked a constituent assembly to formalize the movement. The plan was to hold this assembly in Miensk. However, because of the intransigence of Party bureaucrats, the event had to be transferred to Vilnia, where Lithuanian sympathizers, embattled in their quest for freedom, were happy to accommodate political allies from the neighboring republic.

This founding congress of the BPF, held on June 24–25, 1989, was attended by more than 400 delegates. Zianon Paźniak, the architect of the Kurapaty crimes revelation, was elected president. The organizers of the BPF announced in a statute that they were launching a "mass socio-political movement for restructuring of society and renewal of the Belarusan nation on principles of democracy and humanism, development of culture of the indigenous people and of all national minorities in Belarus."[29] The assembly assured the authorities in Miensk and Moscow that the BPF would conduct its activities "within the framework of the Constitution of the BSSR" and would aim "at defending the interests of the working people, encouraging citizens to be socially active, developing their political, legal, and national consciousness, and guaranteeing the irreversibility of perestroika in the BSSR."[30]

Underlying the "irreversibility of perestroika" have been two powerful psychological factors strongly associated with the activities of the Belarusan Popular Front and its leader Zianon Paźniak. One such factor involved the exposure of Stalinist crimes, for which Kurapaty had become a grim symbol; the other pertained to the revelation of Chernobyl's devastating effects. More than three years passed before the authorities grudgingly acknowledged the very real damage to human beings and the environment caused by this nuclear disaster. Zianon Paźniak was one of the first to forcefully accuse the authorities for their criminal coverup.

RESCUE FROM THE SPIRITUAL CHERNOBYL

By 1992, three years after the collapse of Communist regimes in Eastern Europe, more and more analysts had arrived at the conclusion that the greatest damage done by the Old Order was to human nature. Communism has injured the mentality of men and women, sapped their work ethic, initiative, and self-reliance, and instilled in them a dependency on the state. In Belarus the ruinous effects of Communism have engulfed the Belarusan people's culture—including its central element, the language. The current phrase, "spiritual Chernobyl" refers to this moral devastation, considered by many to be the principal obstacle on the road to recovery. One recurrent theme in the Belarusan press has been the argument that, in Zianon Paźniak's words, "there does not exist in society any stronger consolidating element than national consciousness."[31]

Convinced that spirit is primary and matter secondary, Belarusan renewalists have been waging a campaign to infuse into society an appreciation of indigenous cultural values. Their rationale is the hopeful expectation that cultural ambitions will stimulate economic effort. Naturally, not everybody accepts this argument; among those who have lost the ability to speak Belarusan, for instance, many are either skeptical of or outrightly hostile to the idea of "Belarusization." This group, however, seems to be in the minority. A poll conducted in the spring of 1989 by *Sovetskaya Belorussiya*, a Russian-language newspaper largely critical of the Belarusan national movement, indicated that 65.6 percent of the respondents favored declaring Belarusan the official language of the republic.[32]

To urge the government toward this end, the Belarusan Language Society (BLS) was established on June 27, 1989, with the participation of 300 delegates representing the Writers' Union, the State Publishing Committee, the ministries of Education and Culture, and other official bodies. Nil Hilevič, a poet-scholar and long-time defender of the national language, was elected president. Republican Deputy Prime Minister Nina Mazaj told the gathering that a number of steps had already been taken toward implementation of the program adopted by the BLS. However, the republican Party leadership, consisting almost exclusively of Russified technocrats, remained mute on the subject of the national language.

Critics of the government who blamed the Party nomenklatura for the slowness of reforms, kept pointing to the Baltic republics where changes had developed at a faster pace. The explanation offered was that in Estonia, Latvia, and Lithuania, Communists did not differ from democrats in their attitude toward national culture and unanimously acknowledged the necessity of political independence, whereas the Russified Party apparatus in Miensk was immobilized by its view of the republic as a province of Moscow. Provincialism was the worst malady in Belarus, charged the critics, and it was there that both reactionary conservatism and foot-dragging in perestroika had their roots.

RELUCTANT SUPPORT OF BELARUSIZATION

Michael Urban, in his detailed study of Party elite circulation in Belarus in 1966–1986, concluded that the republican leadership of the early 1980s, in contrast to their predecessors within the so-called Partisan group (those who fought in the war), were devoid of "a political identity oriented to the concept of nation as the Partisans managed to do."[33] Nevertheless, the CPB, which in 1989 numbered nearly 700,000 (77.2 percent of whom were Belarusans),[34] was not without defenders of the national cause. After all, Belarusan Soviet statehood itself had survived and taken root through the efforts of many Belarusan Communists in the 1920s and 1930s. Moreover, about half the founders of the BPF were currently or previously Party members. Some of them initially had difficulty speaking Belarusan, but in terms of political persuasion they were patriots and even cultural nationalists. Granted, at higher echelons of the Party such individuals were rare; but they were by no means totally absent. With nationalist movements getting stronger every day throughout the republic, some "closet patriots" decided to come forth.

One early supporter of the rehabilitation of the Belarusan language was Miensk *gorkom* Secretary Piotr Kraŭčanka, who became minister of foreign affairs of Belarus in July 1990. A year earlier Kraŭčanka had expressed confidence that "the Belarusan language will have state status and we should get ready for that psychologically."[35]

The political fermentation that began eroding Party ranks forced the authorities to look for remedies; among these was the decision to improve the situation surrounding the Belarusan language. In particular, a state commission was formed to draft legislation concerning the official status of Belarusan, Russian, and other languages in the republic.[36] The clamor of the defenders of the native language evoked a negative response from various quarters of Russian-speaking officialdom, including the tacit disregard of Belarusan by Party higher-ups for whom any forsaking of Russian must have felt like abandonment of ideological purity. Some of the lower brass followed the lead of their bosses with open scorn. The secretary of the Lepel Party *raykom*, for example, forbade reporters of the regional newspaper to talk to him in his office in Belarusan.[37]

But the government could not ignore the general trend occurring throughout the non-Russian republics of the Soviet Union: Particularly in the neighboring Baltic area and Ukraine, national movements were much more advanced and did not go unnoticed in Belarus. Prodded by activists from the intelligentsia who had joined the ranks of the BPF and BLS, the authorities in Miensk grudgingly conceded. After months of meetings, rallies, conferences, and hundreds of articles on behalf of the native tongue, the Supreme Council voted on January 26, 1990, to make Belarusan the official language of the state. The "Law About Languages in the Belarusan SSR" opens with the following tenet:

> Language is not only a means of communication, but also the soul of a nation, the foundation and the most important part of its culture. As long as language lives, the people lives. Every language in its literary as well as local and historical varieties is a priceless treasure which belongs not only to a single people, but to humanity as a whole.
>
> It is an honor and duty of all of us to esteem the native language, to contribute to its development and flourishing, and to respect other peoples' languages.

The law also took under its protection the languages of the minorities, thus reverting to the policy of the 1920s. The official status of Belarusan, it held, "does not affect the constitutional rights of citizens of other nationalities to use Russian or other languages."[38] The law became effective as of September 1, 1990. From the very beginning, however, apparatchiks openly resisted the new law, balking at it under an array of pretexts. It was increasingly obvious that implementation of the law would not be achieved without further legislation. One of the nationalist champions of the native language even suggested a philosophical rationale for a forcible approach to the problem. "Philosophers, he argued, "say that between scorn and respect there cannot but be a zone of struggle and hatred. ... Now, if we want our language to be respected, we have to find the resolve within ourselves and stop evading the struggle by rejecting as false the condition that the implementation [of the law] should be voluntary."[39]

On September 20, 1990, the government approved "The National Program on the Development of the Belarusan Language and the Languages of Other Nationalities in the Belarusan SSR."[40] The document specified in detail what should be done by each branch of government and by public institutions to implement the language law. Because of the sensitivity of the issue, ample time was allowed for compliance. In some cases—in the field of education, for example—the deadline for full implementation of the law was set as far away as the year 2000.

Passing laws is easier, however, than changing reality. And the reality in Belarus is that the native language has long been relegated to a secondary place and stigmatized in the popular mind as an indicator of rural culture and mentality. Moreover, speaking Belarusan in formal settings has been perceived as a manifestation of nationalism and separatism. As a result, the "Law about Languages in the Belarusan SSR" has largely been ignored and even obstructed.

The intelligentsia, having long pressed the conservative bureaucracy to move on the language front, responded with a series of forums and other actions. On the eve of the last republican Party congress, a group of twenty-two writers, all Party members, published an open letter to the Central Committee of the CPB criticizing "leaders of the CPB and Party committees of various levels" for their "indifferent and nihilistic attitude toward the Belarusan language and culture." In particular, they noted that the CPB leadership "in their overwhelming majority are not using Belarusan, as they did not use it before, which, naturally, does not bring them honor."[41]

This letter evoked a response from newly elected First Secretary Anatol Malafiejeŭ (Malofeyev), who replaced Jafrem Sakaloŭ. In his speech at the congress Malafiejeŭ suggested "new approaches and forms of cooperation with the intelligentsia"—"that powerful force," as he put it. The only problem was that the new Party leader, as staunch a conservative as his predecessor, wanted an alliance with the intelligentsia to suit his own purposes—that is, for "a consolidation of forces that would be able to throttle the extremists."[42] According to the official definition, however, "extremists" were those who insisted on reinstalling the Belarusan language in national life. The longer the language controversy persisted, the clearer it became that the Party apparatus had been Russified at all its levels, almost beyond the point of return. Confrontation on the cultural front had indeed done its share to radicalize the mood of the public—on the eve, as it turned out, of a historic development. Before the August putsch brought down the Communist Party and precipitated the declaration of independence on August 25, 1991, the second convention of the Belarusan Language Society held in Miensk on June 14 and 15 reflected among some of the intelligentsia a political restlessness emanating from cultural grounds. In its resolution concerning the then-debated Union Treaty, the convention stated:

> The achievement by the Belarusan language of the real status of the state language in Belarus, its rescue and renewal, is possible only on the condition of the political independence of the Belarusan state. The convention urgently requests the Supreme Council of Belarus to give the Declaration on State Sovereignty of the BSSR constitutional status and to prevent Belarus from entering into a political Union and signing appropriate agreements before the Constitution of the sovereign Republic of Belarus is adopted. Only an independent and democratic Belarus, a guarantor of priority rights and historical perspective for the Belarusan language, will be able to defend and preserve its cultural uniqueness.[43]

Events since the summer of 1991 have been propitious for the native language's assumption of its normal place in the life of the Belarusan nation. The "Law About Culture" (passed on June 4, 1991), which stipulates that the language policy is determined by the "Law About Languages,"[44] was followed by the "Law About Education" (passed on October 29, 1991). This law defines the goal of education as, among other things,

- forming and restrengthening the national consciousness of the citizen of the Republic of Belarus as well as feelings of respect toward other countries and peoples of the world;
- securing knowledge of the state language as the principal means of communication among the citizens of the Republic of Belarus;
- preserving and multiplying intellectual property and cultural treasures of the Belarusan people and other national communities of the republic.[45]

Along with Belarusan, Russian and one other foreign language are now required subjects in all educational institutions of the republic.[46]

Of course, *full* restitution of the role of Belarusan is still to come. By their very nature, cultural changes are slow. In the face of inertia, and of political resentment, the culture persists in its unyielding adherence to old ways—above all, to the Russian language. Newspapers are filled with outcries from critics claiming that the "Law About Languages" does not work and that schools are Belarusan more in name than in fact. Other critics warn that Belarusan-language publications are losing ground in free-market competition. (In 1991, for example, the only Belarusan-language monthly for preschool children, *Viasiolka* (Rainbow), failed to appear the requisite number of times because of insufficient funds.) Moreover, various groups are demanding that the state become more active in fulfilling its role as defender of the national culture. In apparent reaction to this clamor, the Presidium of the Supreme Council adopted a resolution on February 10, 1992, directing the Council of Ministers to provide finances and technical assistance for Belarusan-language television and radio programs, newspapers and magazines, albums, post cards, calendars, maps, and so on. This resolution foresees subsidies for publishing houses if they encounter losses as a result of their Belarusan-language production. It also mentions financial assistance to "special broadcasts via state television and radio in languages of other national communities of the republic."[47]

Belarusization—which entails rebuilding the national consciousness of the Belarusan people, healing their spirit, and instilling self-esteem—is a generational process. It requires not only material means and political support but time as well. At a round-table discussion in January 1992, Deputy Minister of Education V. I. Stražaŭ stated that all teachers' colleges had now switched fully to the Belarusan language and that 55 percent of all first-graders in the republic were attending Belarusan-language schools. "In approximately ten years," he added, "the system of education will be fully in the Belarusan language."[48]

NOTES

1. *New York Times,* March 9, 1992.

2. *Sovetskaya Belorussiya,* January 20, 1990.

3. U. P. Cieraškovič, "Asnoŭnyja tendencyi razviccia bielaruskaha etnasu u epochu kapitalizmu" (The main tendencies in the development of the Belarusan ethnos during the period of capitalism), *Viesci AN BSSR. Sieryja hramadskich navuk* (Proceedings of the Academy of Sciences of the BSSR: Social sciences series), No. 5 (Minsk, 1986), p. 95.

4. V. I. Lenin, *Polnoye sobraniye sochineniy* (Collected works), Vol. 24, 5th ed. (Moscow: Political Literature Publishers, 1961), p. 131.

5. The letter is now known to have been written by Alaksiej Kaŭka, a cultural historian.

6. *Letter to a Russian Friend: A "Samizdat" Publication from Soviet Byelorussia* (London: The Association of Byelorussians in Great Britain, 1979), p. 24.

7. For a description of this incident, see *Bielarus,* No. 333. (New York, the Byelorussian-American Association) January-March 1987.

8. *Listy da Harbačova. Vydańnie druhoje, z pierakladam na anhielskuju movu* (Letters to Gorbachev: Second edition with original text and English translation) (London: The Association of Byelorussians in Great Britain, 1987), p. 19.

9. *Ibid.,* pp. 1–2.

10. *Ibid.*, p. 3.

11. *Ibid.*, pp. 21, 22.

12. Sakaloŭ chose not to mention the fact that, at the initiative of his predecessor, Mikalaj Śluńkoŭ, financing of the translation of Lenin's works into Belarusan was stopped "at the beginning of the 1980s." See Rostislav Platonov, "K novomu urovnyu issledovaniy" (Toward a new level of research), *Kommunist Belorussii*, No. 6 (1991), p. 75.

13. *Zviazda* (Star), March 27, 1987.

14. *Listy da Harbačova. Vydańnie druhoje, z pierakladam na anhielskuju movu*, pp. 1–5 *passim*.

15. *Litaratura i Mastactva* (Literature and art), Minsk, July 10, 1987.

16. *Sovetskaya Belorussiya*, Minsk, November 17, 1987.

17. "Some Current Questions of Ideological Work Under Contemporary Conditions," *Belorusskaya Tribuna*, No. 3, Samizdat, Minsk, December 18, 1988.

18. This document can be found in the archives of the newspaper *Bielarus* in New York.

19. *Press-hrupa "Navina paviedamlaje"* (Press-Group "News Release"), Minsk, Samizdat press release, n. d., pp. 2–3.

20. *Martyralogy*, No. 1, Samizdat (Minsk, 1989), p. 14.

21. *Naviny BNF* (News of the BPF), No. 3 (Miensk, 1989), p. 3.

22. *Zviazda*, Minsk, August 30, 1988.

23. *Litaratura i Mastactva*, June 14, 1991.

24. For a detailed account of the press controversy surrounding the BPF, see Jan Zaprudnik, "Belorussian Reawakening," *Problems of Communism*, Vol. 38, No. 4 (Washington, U.S. Information Agency [USIA], July–August 1989), pp. 44–46.

25. *Chicago Tribune*, November 9, 1988.

26. *Supolnasć*, No. 1 (Togetherness), Samizdat (Minsk), January 14–15, 1989, p. 1.

27. *Niva* (Soil), Bielastok, Poland, April 16, 1989.

28. *Selskaya gazeta* (Agricultural newspaper), Minsk, March 3, 1989.

29. *Prahramnyja dakumienty BNF "Adradžeńnie"* (The programmatic documents of the BPF "Renewal") (Minsk, 1989), p. 25.

30. Radio Liberty, Belarusan Service, June 29, 1989.

31. *Litaratura i Mastactva*, Minsk, July 7, 1989.

32. *Sovetskaya Belorussiya*, Minsk, April 26, 1989.

33. Michael E. Urban, *An Algebra of Soviet Power: Elite Circulation in the Belorussian Republic, 1966–1986* (Cambridge, England: Cambridge University Press, 1989), p. 133.

34. *Kommunist Belorussii*, "KPB v zerkale statistiki" (The CPB in the mirror of statistics), No. 5 (Minsk, 1990), p. 29.

35. *Nastaŭnickaja hazieta* (Teachers' newspaper), Minsk, March 22, 1989.

36. *Litaratura i Mastactva*, September 1, 1989.

37. See the interview with writer Vasil Yakovenko in *Kommunist Belorussii*, No. 12 (1989), p. 74.

38. *Litaratura i Mastactva*, February 16, 1990.

39. P. Bič, "Kab zakon zapracavaŭ" (So that the law may work) *Naša Slova. Biuleteń Tavarystva Bielaruskaj Movy* (Our language: The Bulletin of the Belarusan Language Society), No. 7 (Minsk, September 1990), p. 9.

40. For the full text of this program, see *Litaratura i Mastactva*, September 28, 1990.

41. *Litaratura i Mastactva*, October 5, 1990.

42. *Zviazda*, November 30, 1990.

43. *Nastaŭnickaja hazieta*, August 3, 1991.

44. *Viedamasci Viarchoŭnaha Savieta Bielaruskaj SSR* (Proceedings of the Supreme Soviet of the Belarusan SSR), No. 20 (Minsk: Supreme Council of the BSSR, 1991), p. 14.

45. *Viedamasci Viarchoŭnaha Savieta Respubliki Bielarus* (Proceedings of the Supreme Council of the Republic of Belarus), No. 33 (1991), p. 4.

46. *Ibid.*, p. 5.

47. *Litaratura i Mastactva*, March 6, 1992.

48. *Litaratura i Mastactva*, January 31, 1992.

SIX

Political Players
(1985–1992)

THE PROBLEM WITH
POLITICIZING PERESTROIKA

One of the major problems associated with perestroika is a lack of societal politicization. The result of this low level of political culture has been a dearth of the sort of sociopolitical energy that is critical to bringing about deep structural changes in any regime.

Stalinism was marked by the physical destruction of parts of society; Brezhnevism deepened that onslaught by destroying confidence in the political process itself. In Belarus today, behind some demonstrations in the streets and contentious debates in the parliament, there is a demonstrable lack of impetus for change, a deficiency of belief that reality can be transformed by the will of the people. Therein lies the reason not only for the afflicting paucity of membership in political parties but also for their insularity and organizational slackness. Hence the 15 empty seats in the 360-member Supreme Council (Soviet) of the republic elected in March 1990. In some electoral districts in Miensk, elections have been held five and more times without any result, because of the apathy of the electorate. And this in the city that has been most politically active since the beginning of perestroika.

Vasil Bykaŭ, foremost Belarusan novelist and an outspoken critic of the status quo, deplores this fundamental deficiency. In an interview with the forward-looking heading "In Search of an Optimistic Outcome," he noted that "the contemporary state of our Belarusan society gives reason to speak of it as an apolitical society. … A politicized society would not have erected half a thousand identical monuments to an alien leader [Lenin], and would understand without any discussion why they should be disposed of now. Finally, politicized citizens would take a different approach to the parliamentary elections themselves when more than eighty percent of those chosen were Communist nomenclaturists."[1]

The inertia of which Bykaŭ spoke is both pervasive and enduring. In some areas, changes are occurring at a glacial pace. For example, Belarusan official historians in the 1989–1990 period, when revolutionary changes in Central Europe unleashed by perestroika had crested, resulting in the dismantling of the Berlin Wall, Belarusan officials devoted almost two-thirds of their publications to subjects directly connected with the activities of the Communist Party.[2] This thematic devotion of academicians to a bankrupt ideology was but one example of a much wider phenomenon. In short, despite the fact that the Communist Party had been thoroughly discredited and had suspended its activities, its presence was felt almost everywhere. In December 1991 a Miensk newspaper expressed astonishment at the survival of "idiocy" in social sciences instruction in the city's schools. "As we have learned," wrote the newspaper editor, "in one Miensk technical school they intend to introduce a state examination on the history of ... the Communist Party of the Soviet Union."[3]

Decades of "inculcating Orthodox Bolshevism could not but result in impoverishment of the intellectual potential of the nation," said thirty-year-old Supreme Council Deputy Siarhiej Navumčyk. In his view, Communist brainwashing produced a citizen who "customarily faces any fresh, original idea with the greatest skepticism, or even hatred."[4]

For psychological and social reasons, the first "politicizers" of Belarusan society were the young scions of the Party aristocracy. (Here we see evidence of the familiar "Golden Youth" syndrome.) Living in the secure atmosphere of influential families, having wider access to information about life in the outside world, and being of an idealistic disposition, some of these young people (though certainly not a majority of them) felt more acutely the moral split that permeated Soviet society. The onset of perestroika enabled them to act on their feelings and hardened their stance in sometimes dramatic confrontations with their parents.[5]

Recall from Chapter 5 the "Appeal of the Initiating Group of the Confederation of Belarusan Associations to Belarusan Youth" of July 1988. This was a call for action to "all *politically* and nationally conscious youth." Thirteen pages in length, the document spelled out the goals and methods of this youth movement, which, in its initial stages, numbered nearly 3,000 activists.[6] In particular, it urged youth associations to concentrate on discussing the sovereignty of Belarus, its economy, democratization, ecology, and national culture. On the subject of sovereignty, for instance, it read as follows:

It ensues from the constitutions of the BSSR and the USSR that the Belarusan SSR is a sovereign state. In practice, however, this sovereignty does not exist. We believe that only factual sovereignty would guarantee a harmony of in-

Young enthusiasts, including soldiers, with still illegal Belarusan national flags, on their way to Vilnius, Lithuania, for a convention of Belarusan youth associations in January 1989. Courtesy of *Bielarus*.

terests of the BSSR and other republics constituting the USSR and would allow the implemention of political, economic, and cultural programs most suitable to the character of our republic without centralist patterns.[7]

The authors of this Appeal did more than just discuss these issues. Much like the twenty-eight signatories of the letter to Gorbachev in December 1986, they formulated guidelines for spelling out the status of Belarus's sovereignty; defining the rights and duties of a citizen of the republic; expanding Belarus's international representation and ties; restructuring the economy in the interests of the republic; enhancing political pluralism by doing away with the monopoly of power exercised by the CPSU; renewing the Belarusan territorial army; making Belarus a nuclear-free zone; and rebuilding the national culture as well as the cultures of other ethnic groups in Belarus.

With perspicacity, the document foreshadowed the scope of issues that have become the agenda of the Supreme Council of Belarus elected in March 1990. "In 1988, we were an army without officers," related author

Siarhiej Šupa, one of the early participants in the youth movement. "Today, there are captains and even generals."[8]

Indeed, the flat political landscape of Belarus has changed dramatically since mid-1988. Of course, much of the transformation occurred by default, as it were, as a result of dynamic developments in the Baltic area, Russia, and Ukraine. However, it would be a mistake to judge developments in Belarus by the standards of other republics. Although comparisons are natural, one should keep in mind that Belarus is unique and should be evaluated on its own terms.

THE BPF VERSUS THE COMMUNISTS

The politicized movement of the young emerged from a motley of clubs, associations, and societies to become the Confederation of Belarusan Associations. To older political activitsts, the initial success of the Confederation seemed a good pattern to follow. Thus, when the constituent congress of the Belarusan Popular Front convened in Vilnia in June 1989, it adopted the deportment not of a political party but, rather, of a *movement* that would permit both collective and individual participation. The Front described itself in its statute as a "mass socio-political movement for the transformation of society and the renewal of the Belarusan nation on principles of democracy and humanism."[9] At the time the front was formally constituted, some of its leaders had been or still were activists in the youth movement. The concept behind the Front's structure—which permitted informal membership and autonomy of local "support groups," including an invitation to the Communists to join the movement—enabled it to win a measure of popularity and moral support. A polling of 2,000 Miensk residents on the eve of the BPF constituent assembly indicated that three-fourths of the respondents held a positive attitude toward the Front.[10]

THE BELARUSAN SUPREME COUNCIL (SOVIET)

The first elections to the Supreme Council (Soviet) of the Belarusan SSR were held on March 4, 1990. In Miensk most of the seats were contested, with at least fifteen contenders in each of the city's forty-eight districts. But the cards were stacked heavily against the challengers of the status quo—primarily because the Communist-appointed electoral committees were in charge of screening candidates—a fact that was loudly protested by the opposition. On February 25, 1990, a pro-democratic rally of 100,000 took place in Miensk. Sponsored by the BPF, it claimed as its primary purpose the "Protest Against Violation of the Elections Law."[11] The mass me-

Belarusan Popular Front activists during the March 1990 election campaign display their sign, which reads: "Belarusans, Russians, Ukrainians, Poles, Jews, Tatars, and all others who live in the BSSR: a democratic, renewed Belarus is our native home." Courtesy of the Belarusan Popular Front.

dia, fully under the control of the nomenklatura, spared no smear against the opposition candidates; oversight of the electoral process in many places was poor or nonexistent, and fraud in some of the hotly contested districts in Miensk was quite obvious. After two run-off elections, in May 1990, only about 345 out of 360 seats in the Supreme Council were filled. And more than a year later at least 11 seats from the Miensk area remained unoccupied, for lack of involvement on the part of the constituents.

The new Supreme Council of Belarus consists of two kinds of representatives: those who were *elected* in the 310 territorial districts and those *delegated* by social organizations such as veterans groups, teachers groups, and Komsomol—all under the tight control of the Communist Party. As a result, 86 percent of the new Supreme Council consisted of Communists when it began its work in May 1990. Only 33 representatives did not belong to the Party. The outcome of the elections disappointed the opposition. Only about 25 deputies in the national parliament were members or clear supporters of the BPF. Things looked somewhat better in the Miensk city government, however. Out of 106 municipal deputies, 40 represented

Session of the Belarusan Parliament (1992). Photo by Michail Žylinski. Courtesy of *Narodnaja hazieta* (People's newspaper).

the Democratic bloc, 20 belonged to the Communist Party apparatus, and 46 were undecided.[12] Regarding the support of the BPF on the national level, Zianon Paźniak, the leader of the Front and the newly elected national deputy, said after the March elections: "According to our own estimates, over forty percent of the voters in Miensk were in support of the BPF, three to seven percent in support of the Communist Party and the nomenklatura, and the rest were undecided."[13]

On March 24, 1990, at the initiative of both Supreme Council and Miensk city deputies, the so-called Democratic Trend (*Demakratyčnaja plyń*) of twenty-three plus twenty-one lawmakers was established.[14] It was at this early meeting that Stanislaŭ Šuškievič, who was elected national deputy with the support of the BPF, revealed the skills that, in August 1991, following the unsuccessful coup d'état, brought him to the position of speaker of the Supreme Council. Other participants in the meeting called for a struggle in what seemed a nomenklatura-packed parliament; Šuškievič suggested a different approach. "We should pull over to our side those on whom we haven't counted," he said. "Namely, those 120 individuals who are considered to be apparatchiks and with whom you don't want to deal. We should display initiative. I am for this kind of approach."[15]

The new parliament began its work on May 15, 1990. Its 345 deputies coalesced into several groups: the 27-member BPF faction, agrarians and veterans ("The Union"), industrialists, and 160 Communists. At the initiative of the BPF, about 100 deputies agreed to set up the Democratic Club to oppose the conservative majority.

Part of the Democratic Club consisted of the BPF faction itself,[16] which formalized its existence at the end of the first session, on July 16, 1990. It declared its main goals to be the independence of Belarus, substitution of the totalitarian system by a democracy, a market economy, and aid for the Chernobyl victims in Belarus.

At the end of July, immediately following adoption of the Declaration of Belarusan State Sovereignty by the Supreme Council of the BSSR, the BPF faction formally established the Democratic Opposition in the Supreme Council. Although the faction represents only about 10 percent of the total number of legislators, its influence is considerably more pronounced than its numbers might suggest.

On the eve of the first session of the Supreme Council (May 11, 1990), the Diet of the BPF specified "the main goals of the movement": achievement of independence for Belarus and transition to a commonwealth of independent states; establishment in Belarus of a democratic republican government without any party monopoly or dominance of any ideology; rebuilding of a market economy in the Republic closely linked with the economies of the neighboring countries; and renewal of the Belarusan nation and culture and rebuilding in Belarus of a civil society."[17]

DECLARATION OF STATE SOVEREIGNTY

By the time the first session of the new parliament had concluded late in July, an important item on the BPF's agenda—independence for Belarus—had been realized, at least nominally. When the three immediate neighbors of Belarus—Lithuania, Russia, and Ukraine—proclaimed their independence earlier in 1990, the Communist majority in the Supreme Council of the BSSR had no choice but to accept the urgings of the Belarusan Popular Front deputies in favor of state sovereignty. However, there remained a major point of disagreement between the BPF and a majority of the Communists—namely, the question of a Union treaty. The Front categorically rejected such a treaty. Nevertheless, the BPF legislators and Communists found sufficient grounds for cooperation. When the session was over, the BPF faction even received a public accolade from an anonymous "group of Communist deputies," who stated: "In the deliberations on the Supreme Council's agenda at this session, the BPF substantially added to the range of views, enriched the approaches, and more than once was instrumental in adopting compromising solutions."[18]

On July 27, 1990, the Supreme Council of the BSSR turned itself into a separatist body by adopting the aforementioned Declaration of Belarusan State Sovereignty. The vote was neither unanimous nor even enthusiastic. In fact, of the 345 deputies, 115 abstained from the deliberations—out of ideological disgust, one might assume. However, a quorum was present, and a twelve-article document was finally thrashed out.[19]

Acting "in conformity with the principles of the Universal Declaration of Human Rights," the Supreme Council of the BSSR declared the following main precepts:

- "Any forcible action against the national statehood of the BSSR on the part of political parties, public associations or individuals shall be punishable by law." (Article 1) Theoretically, this measure rendered the Communist Party vulnerable to charges of obstructing national statehood.
- "The right to act in the name of all the people of the Republic shall be vested exclusively in the Supreme Council of the BSSR." (Article 2)
- "The land, its mineral wealth, [and] other natural resources on the territory of the BSSR ... shall be the property of the Belarusan people. ... The BSSR shall have the right ... to its share of the diamonds, currency funds and gold reserves of the USSR.

  "The BSSR shall establish the National Bank, accountable to the Supreme Council of the Republic, [and] shall ... have the right to establish its own monetary system." (Article 5)
- "All questions concerning borders shall be decided only on the basis of mutual consent of the BSSR and the adjacent sovereign states through concluding corresponding agreements subject to the ratification of the Supreme Council of the BSSR." (Article 6)
- "Within the territory of the BSSR the constitution of the BSSR and the laws of the BSSR shall be supreme." (Article 7)
- "The BSSR shall have the right to compensation for the damage incurred as a result of activities of All-Union organs.

  "The BSSR demands from the Government of the USSR an unconditional and urgent compensation for the damage connected with the elimination of the effects of the Chernobyl disaster." (Article 8)
- "The BSSR shall ensure the functioning of the Belarusan language in all spheres of social life, preservation of national traditions and historical symbols." (Article 9)

- "The BSSR shall have the right to its own armed forces, internal security forces, [and] organs of state and public security controlled by
the Supreme Council of the BSSR.

  "The BSSR sets the aim of making its territory a nuclear-free zone
and of becoming a neutral state." (Article 10)
- "The BSSR proposes to immediately commence the elaboration of
an agreement on a union of sovereign socialist states." (Article 11)

It was at this point in the course of debates regarding the declaration
that the Democratic Opposition deputies, led by Zianon Paźniak, left the
chamber in protest against any accession to a "union of sovereign socialist
states." Paźniak denounced such a union as a "noose around the neck of
the Belarusan people."[20] The Opposition's counterproposal of a declaration on sovereignty[21] garnered only 47 votes; but its basic ideas were incorporated into the final text, which was adopted. Asked what he thought
of the Declaration of Belarusan State Sovereignty, Paźniak said that "as of
today, it is an empty piece of paper, nothing more." At the same time,
however, he noted that "ninety-five percent of the document adopted is
based on ideas of the BPF that had been formulated one-and-a-half years
earlier." Now it was up to the Belarusan people, added the leader of the
BPF, "to fight for true realization of the republic's sovereignty."[22]

Writer Vasil Bykaŭ, another perceptive commentator on the Belarusan
scene, recognized the "purely theoretical" significance of the declaration
and ventured a rather pessimistic forecast: "There is not any real fulfillment of this sonorous declaration," he said, "and it is doubtful that with
such an obvious, to put it mildly, conservatism of the CPB and the Soviets,
sovereignty will be achievable in the near future."[23] Of course, nobody in
the summer of 1990 foresaw the putsch that would occur in Moscow a
year later, the failure of which gave a powerful boost to the cause of sovereignty.

COLLAPSE OF THE COMMUNIST PARTY

By mid-1990 Belarus's Communists were very much in disarray both
ideologically and politically. Yeltsin's abandonment of the Party in July
1990 and the summons in Ukraine to the Communists to turn in their
membership cards undoubtedly encouraged Belarusan Party members to
leave the Party as well. Some joined other budding political structures
without formally resigning from the Party. For example, in September
1990, two months before the convocation of the last CPB Congress, the
Party secretary of the huge automobile plant in Miensk complained that
"quite a few card-carrying individuals are propagating clearly nationalist,

anti-socialist views. The impression is given sometimes that some people intend to be members of several parties."[24]

Sensing the looming collapse of discipline among the rank-and-file, First Secretary Jafrem Sakaloŭ sounded an alarm at the Thirty-First CPB Congress in November 1990, warning that "chauvinism, nationalism, and separatism are on the rise" and that "the crisis could grow into a catastrophe."[25] Indications of a "catastrophe," from Sakaloŭ's standpoint, were indeed at hand. The 650,000-member Party continued to hemorrhage profusely. It was reported at the Congress that 44,500 members had left the organization within a ten-month period in 1990, whereas only 3,109 had joined it.[26] The Party's basic shortcomings, in the words of one delegate, were "an absence of flexibility and ability to work with all political forces of the Republic" and "an incapability to defend its convictions by political methods."[27]

"By our straightforwardness, our habit of dictating, and our tendency towards uniformity," said Viačaslaŭ Kiebič (Vyacheslav Kebich), chairman of the BSSR Council of Ministers, in his rather blunt speech before the Congress, "we have often driven the intelligentsia [which he considered to be the generator of ideas in a society], especially the humanistic one, away from Party policy. As a result the Communist Party of Belarus finds itself increasingly removed from the mainstream growth in the people's self-consciousness."[28]

Nor was the Party leadership happy with its troops in the Supreme Council. In December 1990 newly elected First Secretary of the CPB and Politburo member Anatol Malafiejeŭ, himself a deputy of the All-Union parliament, expressed disappointment with the 296 Communist members of the Belarusan legislature. "Eighty-six percent of all deputies are Communists," he complained at the CPB plenum, "but our influence is hardly felt. The opposition—one should give its due—with lesser numbers has demonstrated considerably more initiative."[29]

Thus Communists, both individually and collectively, were indoctrinated and driven into a condition whereby, when the rules of the game were altered, they found themselves devoid of initiative and of resistance to the "microbes of freedom" (not unlike the Martians in H. G. Wells' *The War of the Worlds* who were destroyed by microbes in the Earth's atmosphere). It finally began to dawn on them that they, who had boasted of being the "guiding force in society," had become shackled by the herd mentality and converted into a slothful mass. In his report to the Thirty-First Congress, First Secretary of the CPB Jafrem Sakaloŭ admitted to the real state of his Party organization when he said that "the Central Committee of the CPB, its Bureau, and together with them the republican government have not succeeded in resisting the *diktat* from the center, in acting independently, against the often inconsistent decisions and recommendations

Troops of the Ministry of the Interior and policemen trying to contain an anticommunist demonstration on November 7, 1990 (the anniversary of the October 1917 Revolution), in front of the Government Building in Miensk. Courtesy of *Bielarus.*

coming from there."[30] The ideology that preached collectivist uniformity was so successful that it destroyed itself along with the society it was supposed to lead and guide.

OTHER POLITICAL PARTIES

Society's political languor, of which Vasil Bykaŭ had spoken, manifested itself most visibly in the small membership of new parties, now in the embryonic stage of development. The majority of the people today remain passive; some fear a return to dictatorship, others are apathetic or disoriented. According to one report in February 1992, for example, 56 percent of Belarus's inhabitants "are not leaning to any of the political forces."[31] This wait-and-see attitude (which is more pronounced in Belarus than in the Baltic republics) is explained largely by history and geopolitics. Indeed, the Belarusan people—whose territory has been trampled so many times and divided by overwhelming forces from East and West and whose culture has been smothered by the influence of the two contending stronger neighbors, Russia and Poland—need time to regain their self-confidence and resilience. But since the early 1990s, Belarusans have apparently been following their historically derived maxim: *Siem raz mier i jašče nia vier* ("Measure seven times and still be doubtful"). This feature of the Belarusan character, which recently became the subject of lively debate, has an advantage on one level crucially important for the modern world: It guarantees other minorities in the republic full consideration of their rights. For example, in the new documents regarding citizenship of Belarus, there is no indication of nationality. As one observer has noted, "Legislators have endorsed a law that prohibits requests, in any form, for an indication of party or ethnic affiliation. This law is radically different from similar acts adopted in other sovereign states of the former Union."[32] Such an attitude is also reflected in the programs of various political parties as well as in other legislative acts of the Supreme Council of Belarus.

At the beginning of 1992, in the midst of a petition drive for both the dissolution of the republic's parliament and the holding of new elections, there existed at least twenty parties or politicized movements and groups. Eighteen of these formed a democratic bloc called "New Belarus" for the purposes of drafting alternative legislation, supporting the referendum on the viability of the Supreme Council, and pressing for the introduction of presidential power.[33] The most notable parties will be described shortly;[34] but first there is a point to be made about the Belarusan Popular Front. Is it a party in the strict sense of the word? No, says its leader, Supreme Council Deputy Zianon Paźniak. The Front is a *movement*, he maintains, open to any individual or party, including Communists—assuming that those who join share the Front's basic goal of a fully independent and democratic Belarus. Yes, insist the Front's critics, who point to the movement's goals of seizing political power, establishing a "shadow cabinet" (with Deputy Uladzimir Zablocki as "premier"), and being engaged in parliamentary politics.[35] Finally, by American standards, the BPF is a party because of its formally adopted program and its direct engagement in pressing for a referendum on dissolving the 1990 Supreme Council and holding new elections. The reason the BPF has shunned the word *party* seems more psychological than political in nature, given its negative connotation in the context of the Communist Party.

The following parties have been active as of January 1992:

The United Democratic Party of Belarus

Founded in November 1990 and registered (i.e., officially recognized) in March 1991, this is the earliest existing political party. *Membership:* about 1,500 total, consisting of technical intelligentsia, professionals, workers, peasants, and BPF members. *Headquarters:* in Miensk, with branches in all major cities and towns of the republic. *Leadership:* A. Dabravolski, president; S. Husak, M. Pliska, and Ul. Kacora, vice-presidents. *Goals:* Independence of Belarus; political democracy; freedom of national cultures; market economy, including foreign investments; liberalism.

The Belarusan Social-Democratic Union (Hramada)

Founded in March 1991; registered two months later. *Membership:* about 1,000 total, consisting of workers, peasants, students, military personnel, urban and rural intelligentsia. *Headquarters:* in Miensk, with branches in major cities. *Leadership:* Michaś Tkačoŭ, president (died on October 31, 1992), replaced by People's Deputy Aleh Trusaŭ; Mikalaj Kryžanoŭski and Ihar Čarniaŭski, vice-presidents. The Union also has a 12-member faction in the Supreme Council of Belarus. *Goals:* Independence of Belarus, not precluding membership in the Commonwealth of Independent States; market economy, but with regulatory powers of the state in such spheres as education, health, and finances. The Union cooperates with other parties and considers itself to be a part of the world social-democratic movement.

The Belarusan Peasant Party

Founded in February 1991; registered in April of that year. *Membership:* hundreds of members, all peasants. *Headquarters:* in Miensk, with branches in a majority of counties. *Leadership:* Jaŭhien Luhin, president; Ivan Nikitčanka and M. Antanienka, vice-presidents. Some members are deputies of local councils and the Supreme Council of the Republic. *Goals:* Privatization of land; free market; government for the people, not the other way around; renewal of national consciousness and culture; humanism; collaboration with other sociopolitical movements.

The Belarusan Peasant Union

Founded in November 1989; registered in August 1991. *Membership:* nearly 500 farmers. *Headquarters:* in Miensk. *Leadership:* Kastuś Jarmolenka, president. Some members of the Union are deputies in local governments, and about 7,000 peasant families in Belarus are willing to become independent farmers. Contacts are maintained with similar unions in Estonia, Latvia, and Lithuania. *Goals:* Defense of private farmers' interests; free commercial activities; independence of Belarus.

The Belarusan Christian-Democratic Association

Founded in June 1991 as a continuation of the Belarusan Christian-Democratic Party in West Belarus in the 1930s, disbanded by the Polish authorities; still waiting for registration as of November 1991. *Membership:* The core of the organization comprises the 102 delegates of the constituent conference, mainly from the intelligentsia. *Headquarters:* in Miensk, with branches in all major cities. *Leadership:* P. Silka (coordinator), I. Bahdanovič, M. Areškaŭ, E. Sabila, and F. Januškievič, co-presidents. *Goals:* Renewal of society on the basis of Christian values, especially non-violence, pluralism, private property, interethnic harmony.

The Belarusan Ecological Union

Founded in the spring of 1989; registered in July of that year. *Membership:* about 6,500 representatives of all strata. *Headquarters:* in Miensk, with chapters in various cities and towns. *Leadership:* B. Savicki, president, member of the Presidium of the Supreme Council of Belarus; Radzim Harecki, Ja. Piatrajeŭ, L. Tarasienka, vice-presidents. More than 20 members of the Union are legislators at various levels, including 6 in the Supreme Council. *Goals:* Defense of the environment and humanity in cooperation with all parties and movements, including the "Greens" in Eastern Europe and Scandinavia.

The National Democratic Party of Belarus

Founded in June 1990; registered in June 1991. *Membership:* about 300, some of whom are members of local governments. *Headquarters:* in Miensk. *Leadership:* A. Astapienka, V. Navumienka, and M. Jermalovič, co-presidents. *Goals:* national renewal of Belarus, democracy, private property, political and economic independence of the republic.

Other political actors were on the scene as well, as evidenced by a document uncovered after the August 1991 putsch. The Supreme Council Commission, charged with investigation of the republican government's complicity in the botched coup d'état, cited in its report to the Supreme Council a "Reference on the Socio-Political Situation and Disposition of Political Forces in Belarus" dated June 12, 1990, as well as a supplementary "Reference on Some Political Associations" dated July 5, 1990. The two documents, compiled by "one of the State Security offices" in Miensk, contain a roster of "destructive forces." The list includes the Belarusan Popular Front "Renewal," the Workers' Union of Belarus, the Vienna Committee (concerned with the Chernobyl disaster), the Civic Parliament for Defense of Democracy, the Social-Democratic Union, the Belarusan Democratic Party, the Independence Party of Belarus, the National Democratic Party of Belarus, the Democratic Party of Belarus, the Organizing Committee of the Republican Party of Belarus, the Union of Poles in Belarus, and the Christian-Democratic Union.[36]

The Belarusan Association of Servicemen

When the August coup d'état precipitated the declaration of Belarus's independence, the republic's military commanders, unlike those in Ukraine, continued to hold staunchly pro-Russian (imperial) positions. Significantly, among the officer corps of the Belarusan Military District at the time of the coup, only 20 percent were natives of Belarus, whereas more than 50 percent were Russians and more than 20 percent were Ukrainians, according to General Piotr Čavus.[37] This circumstance gave impetus to a group of Belarusan servicemen whose aim was to organize into a civic organization to promote the cause of a national army. Calls for such a force had been made part of the programs of the BPF and most other political parties. One of the most active along these lines was the Belarusan Social-Democratic Union (Hramada), which set up its military section in March 1991. Headed by the enthusiastic patriot Lieutenant-Colonel Mikalaj Statkievič, this section became the organizational core from which the Belarusan Association of Servicemen (BAS) was established. Its founding congress was held in Miensk on October 12–13, 1991, and was attended by more than 120 delegates representing Belarusan military clubs and societies from all over the Soviet Union. The goal of the Association, according to its statute, is to "assist in the establishment of a Belarusan army, defense of democracy and state sovereignty of Belarus, and defense of the rights of Belarusan servicemen."[38]

The task of building a national army turned out to be an arduous one. In an "Open Letter" to the chairman of the Belarusan Supreme Council, written soon after its founding, the BAS complained of harassment and persecution of its members by military authorities, warning that "in circumstances of a deepening crisis on the territory of the former Soviet Union, Belarus could find itself in a situation in which it had been in 1918"—that is, without its own armed forces.[39] One of the steps taken by the Supreme Council of the Republic to prevent such a recurrence was a vote on January 11, 1992, to subordinate all former Soviet troops on Belarusan territory to the republican authorities and to adopt a military oath for new draftees whose loyalty henceforth will be "to the Republic of Belarus and its people."[40]

The Party of Communists of Belarus

Diminished, compromised, and suspended in its activity after the August 1991 coup, with most of its assets confiscated or pilfered, the Communist Party of Belarus reemerged in the summer of 1992 under the slightly altered name of the Party of Communists of Belarus (PCB). Given the tremendous economic difficulties now facing Belarus (relative to which the pre-perestroika years look reasonably good to many citizens) and because of the lack of political energy in society to propel the other parties in their growth, the PCB could once again become a serious factor in the political arena of the republic. According to one report, a registration of former CPB members "has shown that the PCB pretends to be the most populous party." More than 15,000 individuals, including some young people who previously did not belong to any party, confirmed their readiness to join its ranks.[41] The Communist Party was given another lease on life on February 4, 1993, when the conservative majority in the Supreme Council prevailed in lifting the suspension of the Party's activities, although it failed to reclaim the Party's property. The latter remained confiscated in the hands of the state.

THE AUGUST PUTSCH

The first indication of the coup d'état in Moscow and Crimea came to Miensk early in the morning of August 19 in the form of a coded telegram from KGB chief V. A. Kryuchkov to the chairman of the republic's KGB, General Eduard Šyrkoŭski. It was an order to secure implementation of the new law "On an Emergency Situation." Šyrkoŭski's reaction to the telegram is known only from his own published account, at a time when everybody was trying to look innocent. The chief of the Belarusan KGB told *Narodnaja hazieta* ten days after the coup that he decided not to follow the order he had received from Kryuchkov by saying to himself: "It was not you who had confirmed me, but the Supreme Council of Belarus. I swore my allegiance to that body and it will I serve." Šyrkoŭski then made a telephone call to the Ministry of the Interior and, upon learning that Minister V. Yegorov was on vacation, got in touch with his deputy, Viktor A. Kovalyov—with whom, emphasized Šyrkoŭski, "our positions coincided in all principal matters." The KGB chief also communicated with the republic's prime minister Viačaslaŭ Kiebič, whose immediate reaction was unequivocal. The premier told him "not to accept any orders from Moscow, put the coded telegram aside, and secure order and legality on the entire territory of the Republic." Šyrkoŭski subsequently explained, "On me was laid the task to coordinate the efforts of all republican organs acting in this direction. And the work started."[42]

What kind of work it was can be learned from the report of the parliamentary Ad Hoc Commission, which investigated the role of the state organizations and of various individuals in the August putsch.[43] Although some of the military personnel and Party officials refused to cooperate in the investigation, thus demonstrating the ineffectiveness of the parliamentary authority, enough evidence was collected by the commission to indicate collusion between the putschists and the republic's governmental bodies, including the Ministry of Justice.

According to the commission's report, Justice Minister Leanid Dašuk ordered judges to forgo their vacations and to stand by for "securing immediate expediting of arrest cases" (p. 10); with the knowledge of CPB First Secretary Anatol Malafiejeŭ, the newspaper *Znamya yunosti* containing a condemnation of the putsch was barred from appearing on August 20; Aliaksandar Stalaroŭ, chairman of the State Committee on Tele-Radio, forbade broadcasting of the latest news from Moscow about President Yeltsin's stand (p. 11); and similar acts were repeated by local bureaucrats in many other regions and cities of the republic. Not a single Party organization condemned the coup (p. 17).

The leadership of the Belarusan Military District responded swiftly, although its chief commander, General Anatol Kastenka (Kostenko), claimed later in the Supreme Council of the Republic that "the Military Council displayed restraint and reasonableness in the appraisal of political events" (p. 20). The military preparations for a crackdown included systematic high-alert and emergency measures. For example, an order was passed along from the USSR Ministry of Defense to execute all the directives of the National Emergency Committee (putschists) and "not to pay any attention to this adventurer [i.e., Boris Yeltsin] waving his papers from a tank" (p. 37). All of the opposition activists were put under strict surveillance by the military, and the medical emergency service, including blood banks, stood ready for the possibility of massive repressions (pp. 43–48). Fortunately, the anti-coup mass demonstrations that were organized in Miensk on August 19, 20, and 21 by the BPF, the Social-Democratic Union, United Democratic Party, the National Democratic Party, and the Miensk Strike Committee took place without a clash with the military.[44]

The seven-member commission, chaired by Deputy Ihar Pyrch, concluded that Commander of the Belarusan Military District General Anatol Kastenka supported the putsch and recommended, among other things, a thorough reorganization of the KGB that would deprive it of its political surveillance capabilities and prohibit its employees' membership in any political party (p. 69).

The commission further decided to "consider impossible the continuation in their function" of thirteen officials, among them Deputy Minister of the Interior Viktar A. Kavaloŭ (Kovalyov). It is remarkable and quite telling that KGB chief General Eduard Šyrkoŭski's name was not mentioned a single time in the commission's report, despite the fact that his position in the putsch affair, as he himself said, "coincided on all principal matters with that of Kovalyov." Here is a classic case whereby silence speaks volumes.

Also recommended for dismissal for their role in the putsch were Generals Anatol Kastenka and Paval Kazloŭski (Kozlovski), Kastenka's chief of staff. But no such dismissal ever occurred. In April 1992 General Kazloŭski became defense minister of the Republic of Belarus and General Kastenka, whose Belarusan Military District was abolished, was made one of Minister Kazloŭski's deputies.

PROCLAMATION OF INDEPENDENCE

Ironically, the putschists' attempt to forestall the undoing of the Soviet Union (the coup was organized on the eve of the signing of a new Union treaty) precipitated its final formal disintegration and served as a coup de grâce for the moribund Communist Party. In a sense, one could say that the coup was a complete success—for its adversaries.

In Belarus, the days following this dramatic event saw a series of historic steps taken by the Supreme Council, with crowds of demonstrators noisily signaling their presence in front of the Government Building. There an extraordinary two-day session was held at the insistence of the BPF on August 24 and 25. Russian President Yeltsin's courageous stand in defense of constitutionality, President Gorbachev's resignation as leader of the Soviet Communist Party, his decree of August 24 calling for temporary suspension of the Party, and Ukraine's declaration of independence on August 24—all of these events enlarged and emboldened the democratic and nationalist opposition in the Belarusan parliament. The session ended with the following results:

1. Mikalaj Dziemianciej (Dementei), president of the Belarusan Supreme Council, was forced to resign because of his behavior during the coup.

2. The Declaration of State Sovereignty, passed on July 27, 1990, was given the force of constitutional law, and Belarus's political and economic independence was unanimously proclaimed on August 25. (Of all people, First Secretary of the CPB Anatol Malafiejeŭ, undoubtedly out of desperation, was the first to urge the independence vote by the Communist-dominated parliament.)

3. The Ministry of the Interior was transformed from an All-Union agency into a republican agency and was placed in charge of all troops of the former Interior Ministry on the territory of the republic.

4. "Departyization" of all organs of government, state enterprises and institutions was ordered, and the activities of the Communist Party were temporarily suspended.[45]

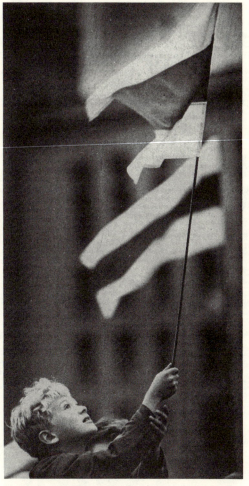

Young boy in the summer of 1991, hoisting national flag symbolizing the newly independent Republic of Belarus. Courtesy of *Narodnaja hazieta* (People's newspaper).

On August 28, 1991, Prime Minister Viačaslaŭ Kiebič published a statement to the effect that he and his entire cabinet had "suspended" their membership in the Communist Party and, in a change of heart, had condemned the attempted putsch and the solidarity of the Belarusan Party leadership with the putschists.

Then, at another extraordinary session, held on September 17–19, the Supreme Council elected Stanislaŭ Šuškievič as its chairman (president);

changed the name of the state from the Belarusan Soviet Socialist Republic (BSSR) to the Republic of Belarus (RB); and adopted as new state symbols the white-red-white flag (three stripes of equal width placed horizontally) of the Belarusan Democratic Republic of 1918 and a coat-of-arms in the form of "Pursuit" (a knight mounted on a racing horse). As the emblem of the Grand Duchy of Lithuania, Ruś, and Samogitia, the latter represents a link to a proud period in Belarusan history.

Referendum About a New Supreme Council

At the beginning of 1992, it was widely agreed in Belarus that the two-year old parliament had exhausted its intellectual ability and political will and had become bogged down along the road to a market economy and democracy. A steady decline in the standard of living had exacerbated the anger of the populace, which had already boiled over in April 1991. In that month, tens of thousands of striking factory workers had poured onto the streets of Miensk, Orsha, and other Belarusan cities. The unrest surprised the world, because it happened in what was believed to be a "quiet and docile" republic. It was then that N. Matukovski, the Belarusan commentator of *Izvestiya*, quoted V. Goncharik, a trade-union leader in Miensk, as having stated at the CPB Central Committee plenum that "the Belarusan SSR Supreme Council has become detached from the people. That is why the strikers are demanding its dissolution and the holding of new elections, under a new, more democratic electoral law."[46]

The BPF opposition in the parliament materialized that demand by means of a referendum. By law, such a ballot requires 350,000 signatures (5 percent of the electorate). Despite numerous obstacles created by the conservative majority in the Supreme Council and the government, about 1,200 enthusiasts throughout the republic collected within a two-month period nearly 450,000 signatures and submitted them on April 14, 1992, to the Central Electoral Committee.

The question asked of voters in the referendum was formulated as follows:

> Do you consider it necessary to hold in the fall of 1992 elections to the supreme organ of state power of the Republic of Belarus, on the basis of the Law on the Election of People's Deputies of Belarus, a draft of which had been submitted by the BPF Opposition in the Supreme Council, and therefore requiring an early dissolution of the current Supreme Council?[47]

The referendum was rejected by the Supreme Council on October 29, 1992. If it had taken place, it would have been the second in Belarus during the perestroika years. The first one, concerning the preservation of the Soviet Union, was held on March 17, 1991. At that time, 6,126,983 voters (83.3

percent of those eligible to vote) took part. Of that number, 82.7 percent chose to stay in the Union, whereas 16.1 percent favored a separation from the empire. The fact that 16.7 percent abstained from voting and 16.1 percent of those who voted preferred separation was interpreted by some commentators as indicating "an awakening of national consciousness among a considerable part of the nation, which has understood that the national interests of the Belarusans are not the same as those of the Communist Party of Belarus or the Communist Party of the Soviet Union or the Center or even Russia."[48]

The democratic opposition parties, led by the BPF, pressed for a second referendum on the dissolution of the Supreme Council and new elections in the fall of 1992, counting precisely on that "awakening of national consciousness." In these expectations they were encouraged by the fact that, over a period of two months, they were able to collect more than 442,000 signatures in support of the referendum. However, they underestimated the conservative mold of the majority of the Supreme Council, which itself was now encouraged by an electoral victory of former Communists in Lithuania as well as by the growing resistance to President Yeltsin's reforms in Russia. When the Belarusan Parliament met in October 1992, 202 deputies voted against the referendum, 35 voted for it, and another 35 abstained.[49]

In view of the fact that in May 1992 the Central Referendum Commission validated 384,318 of the 442,000 collected signatures (which well exceeded the 350,000 signatures required by law for holding a referendum), the BPF opposition—in a statement signed by 31 deputies—accused the Supreme Council's conservative majority of open violation of the constitution of the republic and of an attempt "to retain power by illegal means."[50] In this tug-of-war, however, the democratic oppposition won a small victory: The parliament agreed to shorten its five-year term by one year and scheduled the next elections for the spring of 1994.[51]

The Supreme Council decided to make adoption of a constitution its most urgent priority. With this in mind, it voted to install its Chairman, Stanislaŭ Šuškievič, as the head of the Constitutional Committee (in place of the former Speaker of the Supreme Council, Mikalaj Dziemianciej).[52]

KEY PERSONALITIES

Stanislaŭ Šuškievič (Stanislav Shushkevich)

Šuškievič was born in 1934 in Miensk, the son of a Belarusan poet. In the mid-1930s both of his parents were arrested and exiled as "enemies of the people." Their son, a physics major, graduated from the Belarusan

Stanislaŭ Šuškievič (Stanislav Shushkevich), speaker of the Supreme Council (Parliament).

State University in 1956. In 1969 he became an instructor at the same university, working his way up to full professor, doctor of sciences, author of several textbooks, and corresponding member of the Belarusan Academy of Sciences. Though a Party member for a number of years, he came to politics as late as 1986, in response to the Chernobyl disaster.

His election to the Belarusan Supreme Council in March 1990 was largely a result of his previous stance as People's Deputy of the USSR—on behalf of the victims of Chernobyl but also in defense of Belarusan cultural values against the Communist nomenklatura in the republic. The Belarusan Popular Front supported his candidacy but went its own way later, owing chiefly to disagreement over the issue of the Union (which Šuškievič very much wanted to preserve) and his pampering of the nomenklatura.

With his mild manners, remarkable patience, and a pronounced concern for all sides to be heard, Šuškievič epitomizes for some observers the qualities of his unassuming republic. At the same time, however, he says of himself: "I Differ from Gorbachev by One Thing—I Am a Man of Decision."[53] Some of Šuškievič's parliamentary critics do not doubt his decisiveness but perceive in it a misguided attempt to become de facto president of the republic. They see him "constantly maneuvering among the political groups," without holding to his own clear course.[54]

Šuškievič's name burst into the international media in connection with the so-called Miensk agreement on the Commonwealth of Independent States—what amounts to an understanding among the three top leaders

Prime Minister Viačaslaŭ Kiebič (Vyacheslav Kebich).

of Belarus, Russia, and Ukraine regarding termination of the Soviet Union. Whose idea was this agreement, and what was Šuškievič's role in it? "I brought both presidents together," said the Belarusan leader in the popular Moscow weekly *Argumenty i fakty*. "Long ago we had an agreement that Yeltsin would visit Miensk. … It seems to me that Gorbachev was very much against our meeting here. Because of him, first one such meeting was postponed and then another. Our Prime Minister [Kiebič] said: Perhaps Ukraine should also be invited? We got on the phone and agreed to meet on Friday [December 6, 1991], but Gorbachev scheduled a State Council meeting for that time (such meetings were never held on a Friday). Here I got mad [*ozverel*]. I thought: If it does not work on Friday, then we certainly will get together on Saturday."

Did Šuškievč have any idea what the result of their meeting on Saturday would be? Here is his answer:

> If someone had asked me the day before whether such a variant was possible, I would have answered: No, it's impossible. I was convinced that [President of Ukraine] Kravchuk would not join this commonwealth at any price. But if Ukraine is for it, then let's proceed to put it into shape [*davayte oformlyat'*]. All my energy was directed at keeping an open border between Belarus and Ukraine. We all became imbued with this idea—not to part without arriving at an agreement.[55]

Viačaslaŭ Kiebič (Vyacheslav Kebich)

Kiebič was born in 1936 into a peasant family. A graduate of the Miensk Polytechnic and of the Higher Party School (having joined the Communist Party in 1962), he majored in mechanical engineering. As of 1958 he worked in Miensk, advancing from engineer-technologist to plant direc-tor. In 1980 he was elected second secretary of the Miensk City Party orga-nization (gorkom). And in 1983 he took charge of the Heavy Industry De-partment of the CPB Central Committee, subsequently working as second secretary of the Miensk Regional Committee of the CPB.

In December 1985, Kiebič was appointed deputy premier and chairman of the State Planning Committee of the BSSR. In April 1990 he became prime minister of the republic and was elected to the Supreme Council of the USSR. Two months later he was reappointed as prime minister. He has received a number of high state awards, including the title of Distin-guished Machinebuilder of the BSSR.

Kiebič is a man of action, speaking resolutely on behalf of Belarus's in-dependence and devoting much effort to developing and maintaining bi-lateral economic ties with ex-Union republics as well as other states. His political opponents would concur with the description given him by Su-preme Council Deputy Uladzimir Hrybanaŭ: "He is an educated man, but he can not escape from the vise of yesterday, not simply from the ideologi-cal vise, no. For quite some time, if ever, he has not believed in the Com-munist idea. But besides ideas there are life, people, relationships. He is tied to the past through specific individuals."[56]

Zianon Paźniak (Zenon Poznyak)

Born in 1944 in West Belarus into a family with a tradition of Belarusan cultural work, Paźniak has been a singular moral and political force in the Belarusan democratic movement. Educated as an archeologist and art his-torian, and having spent many years leading resistance movements in Miensk against the annihilation of Belarusan cultural monuments, Paźniak gained national attention through his exposure of Stalinist crimes in Belarus. He became for Kurapaty what Alexander Solzhenitsyn is to the Gulag Archipelago. (Paźniak's grandfather, the editor of a Belarusan Christian Democratic newspaper in Vilnia under Poland, was executed by the Bolsheviks at Kurapaty.)

Elected in Miensk as a deputy of the Supreme Council of Belarus, Paźniak had been known as one of the founders and leaders of the Belarusan Popular Front, as a relentless and eloquent critic of Commu-nism, and as an ardent advocate of Belarusan independence, democracy, and free-market economy. Eventually he found himself at the helm of the parliamentary opposition, working selflessly to pull away the Commu-nist-dominated Supreme Council from its conservative underpinnings. In a vivid portrait of him, American author Hedrick Smith wrote: "Poznyak is a fighter, one of those dissenters who spring up miraculously under dic-tatorships: a moralist, daring, uncompromising, and forever challenging the authorities because his independent spirit will not be quelled."[57]

Leader of the Belarusan Popular Front Zianon Paźniak addresses a meeting at the Plaza of Independence in Miensk in 1990. Courtesy of the Belarusan Popular Front.

Paźniak is a rigorous maximalist who is seen by many as an extremist. But he is not undemocratic. It was Paźniak who spoke out against "witchhunting" for Communists and who called on the Communists themselves to join the BPF and work for the cause of democracy and national freedom. Many of the demands that he and the BPF pressed for, including Belarus's independence and the national emblems referred to earlier, have been adopted; indeed, these demands have gained the support of those who originally opposed them, thus justifying Vasil Bykaŭ's characterization of Paźniak as "an Apostle of the people's truth." As Anatol Kazlovič, a columnist, wrote: "The Belarusans need Zianon Paźniak as an indicator of their deeply hidden hopes and still unrealized aspirations for freedom."[58]

Archbishop Kazimir Sviontak

Born on October 21, 1914, Sviontak graduated from the Higher Theological Seminary in Pinsk in 1939. In January 1992 he was elevated to the rank of metropolitan-archbishop. He favors introduction of the Belarusan language into religious services, and has prohibited the display of Polish national symbols in Belarus's Catholic churches. Sviontak is currently metropolitan of the Miensk and Mahilou dioceses, apostolic administrator of the Pinsk diocese, and head of the Belarusan Catholics.

Ryhor Baradulin

Born on February 24, 1935, Baradulin graduated from the Belarusan State University in 1959. He has worked in various administrative and editorial positions in the publishing sphere and is author of many books of poetry and poetic translations. A strong supporter of the Belarusan Popular Front, he is also a member of its Diet. For his achievements in literature, Baradulin was awarded the title of People's Poet in September 1992.

Janka Bryl

Born on August 4, 1917, Bryl finished Polish primary school in West Belarus and, while working on his family farm, continued his self-education. He served in the Polish army, was a POW in Germany, and fought on the Soviet side against the Germans in 1942–1944. Author of numerous short stories, novels, and essays, he was awarded the title of People's Writer in 1981. Bryl is also a supporter of the Belarusan national cause.

Hienadź Buraŭkin

Born on August 28, 1936, Buraŭkin graduated from the Belarusan State University. He has worked on various periodicals and, as of 1968, was a correspondent for the central Soviet newspaper *Pravda*. In 1972 he became editor of the literary monthly *Maladość* (Youth) and has since authored several collections of poetry. In 1978 he was appointed chairman of the State Committee for Radio and Television. Buraŭkin was elected a member of the Supreme Council of the Belarusan SSR and since May 1990 has been chief representative of the Republic of Belarus to the United Nations.

Vasil Bykaŭ

Born on June 19, 1924, Bykaŭ studied sculpture at the Viciebsk Art School. He fought against the Germans in World War II. In fact, the war experience permeates his numerous novellas (translated into more than 100 languages), whose themes of humanity put him in conflict with the authorities in the pre-perestroika years. He was awarded the title of People's Writer in 1980, and his active support of Belarusan national revival earned him the sobriquet of "Conscience of the Nation." A member of the Diet of the Belarusan Popular Front, Bykaŭ was elected deputy of the People's Congress of the USSR in 1989.

Vasil Bykaŭ (Bykov), Belarus's best-known writer, whose civic and political activity earned him the sobriquet "Conscience of the Nation." Photo by Michail Žylinski. Courtesy of *Narondaja hazieta* (People's newspaper).

Radzim Harecki

Born on December 7, 1928, Harecki graduated from the Moscow Oil Institute. He has served as vice-president of the Belarusan Academy of Sciences; as director of the Institute of Geology, Geochemistry, and Geophysics of the Belarusan Academy of Sciences, and as a member of the Belarusan Language Society and the Association of Belarusans of the World.

Nil Hilevič

Born on September 30, 1931. Hilevič graduated in 1956 from the Belarusan State University, where he taught Belarusan literature for a number of years. A prolific writer and translator, he was awarded the title of People's Poet in 1991. During the 1980s he also served as first secretary of the republic's Writer's Union. Hilevič was elected in 1990 to the Supreme Council of the Republic, where he currently serves as chairman of the Committee on Education, Culture, and Preservation of Historical Heritage.

Anatol Hryckievič

Born on January 31, 1929, Hryckievič graduated from the Miensk Medical Institute in 1950, the Miensk Pedagogical Institute of Foreign Languages in 1955, and the Belarusan State University in 1958. He worked at the Institute of History of the Academy of Sciences of the Belarusan SSR from 1959 to 1975. And since 1975 he has served as head of the Department of History of Belarus and Foreign Countries at the Miensk Institute of Culture. Hryckievič has authored numerous works on the economy, politics, and religion of medieval Belarus. He is also one of the founders of the Belarusan Popular Front. In 1992 he was elected president of the Association of Belarusan Gentry.

Valeryjan Januškievič

Born on December 16, 1962, Januškievič graduated from the Belarusan State Institute of Drama and Art in 1987. A sculptor, he devotes much attention to figures and subjects of Belarusan history. He is also a member of the Belarusan Popular Front.

Valentyn Jelizarjeŭ

Born on October 30, 1947, Jelizarjeŭ graduated from the Leningrad Conservatory in 1972. In 1973 he was named chief choreographer of the State Ballet and Opera Theater in Miensk, and in 1979 he was awarded the title of People's Artist. Jelizarjeŭ studied ballet choreography in London, Paris, and Brussels. He also wrote numerous ballets that brought international acclaim to the Miensk ballet theater.

Mikola Jermalovič

Born on April 29, 1921, Jermalovič, graduated from the Philology Department of the Miensk Pedagogical Institute in 1947. Over the years he has worked as a high school and college teacher, published literary criticism, and studied Belarus's history. In 1975–1976 he published the underground bulletin *Hutarka* (Speech), which was devoted to Belarus's past. His major work, *Ancient Belarus: The Polacak and Novaharodak Periods* (1990), in which he took a revisionist approach, became quite popular among young readers.

Volha Ipatava

Born on January 1, 1945, Ipatava graduated from the Belarusan State University in 1967. She has worked in television and on literary journals in an editorial capacity. In her writings, prose, and poetry, she devotes much attention to historical subjects. She is also an active promoter of Belarusan cultural rebirth. Since 1991 Ipatava has served as chief editor of the weekly *Kultura,* published by the Ministry of Culture.

Uladzimir Konan

Born on April 23, 1934, Konan graduated from the Belarusan State University in 1959. Since 1966 he has worked at the Institute of Philosophy and Law of the Belarusan Academy of Sciences, where he was appointed head of the Department of Aesthetics and Social Psychology in 1984. Konan has authored several books on the history of aesthetics, folklore, and literary criticism in Belarus. He also actively supports national renewal.

Piotr Kraŭčanka

Born on August 13, 1950, Kraŭčanka graduated from the History Department of the Belarusan State University. From 1972 to 1979 he taught history there. And from 1985 to 1990 he was secretary of the Miensk city organization of the Communist Party of Belarus and continued teaching at the city's colleges. In March 1990 Kraŭčanka was elected to the Supreme Council of Belarus; in July of the same year he was appointed the republic's foreign minister.

Mikola Kupava

Born on January 31, 1946, Kupava graduated from the Belarusan Drama and Arts Institute in 1976. In his paintings and other graphics he devotes much attention to historical themes, especially to personalities of cultural history. Kupava is currently an active member of the Belarusan Popular Front.

Ihar Lučanok

Born on August 6, 1938, Lučanok graduated in 1961 from the Belarusan Conservatory, of which he was president in 1982–1985. In 1982 he was awarded the title of People's Artist. Earlier, in the 1970s, he was a participant and laureate of socialist international youth forums. He has written many songs, some of which survived the tide of ideological changes in the late 1980s because of their Belarusan patriotism and fine melodies. In 1980 Lučanok became president of the Composers' Union, and in 1985 he was elected to the Supreme Council of the BSSR.

Adam Maldzis

Born on August 7, 1932, Maldzis graduated from the Journalism Department of the Belarusan State University in 1956. A doctor of philosophy, he has authored twelve books on the history of Belarusan culture, has served as a member of the Diet of the Belarusan Popular Front and of the Belarusan Social Democratic Party, and is currently president of the F. Skaryna National Center and of the International Association of Belarusologists.

Alaksiej Marackin

Born on March 30, 1940, Marackin graduated from the Belarusan Academy of Arts in 1972. He serves as a member of the Diet of the Belarusan Popular Front, as president of the Association of Professional Artists and Art Critics, as chairman of the Department of Painting of the Belarusan Arts Academy, and as chairman of the History and Culture Committee of the Belarusan Popular Front. In 1992 he was awarded the F. Skaryna Medal.

Metropolitan Filaret

Born Kirill Varfalomeyevich Vakhromeyev on March 21, 1935, in Moscow, Filaret graduated in 1961 from the Moscow Theological Academy with a Master's degree. He now holds a doctorate *honoris causa* from several foreign divinity schools. In 1978 he was elevated to metropolitan of Miensk and Hrodna (Grodno). And in 1989 he was appointed exarch of the Moscow Patriarch in Belarus and president of the Synod of the Belarusan Orthodox Church. In 1992, owing to the increased number of dioceses in Belarus, his titles were changed to metropolitan of Miensk and Sluck, patriarchal exarch in Belarus, and president of the Synod of the Belarusan Orthodox Church.

Valantyna Parchomienka

Born on January 2, 1956, Parchomienka graduated from Homiel Musical College in 1975 and from Miensk Institute of Culture in 1987. From 1975 to 1980 she sang professionally and conducted a choir in Miensk. In 1985 she was awarded the titles of Distinguished Artist of the Belarusan

SSR and laureate of the International Song Festival in Moscow. And in 1986 she was gold medalist at the International Folklore Festival in Bratislava, Czechoslovakia. Since 1990, Parchomienka has resided in the United States.

Uladzimir Platonaŭ

Born on December 1, 1939, Platonaŭ graduated from the Belarusan State University in 1961. In 1977 he was named director of the Institute of Mathematics of the Academy of Sciences of the Belarusan SSR. Platonaŭ has authored numerous theoretical works in the field of algebra. He was elected president of the Belarusan Academy of Sciences in the mid-1980s and has been an active supporter of the Belarusan national cause. Since 1991 he has resided in the United States.

Stefanija Staniuta

Born on May 13, 1905, Staniuta graduated in 1926 from the Belarusan Drama Studio in Moscow. Since 1919 she has created many memorable characters on the theater stage and in cinema embodying wisdom, endurance, stamina, and strong attachment to her native land. Staniuta was awarded the title of People's Actress in 1957. Nearly thirty years later, in December 1986, she was one of the signatories of the Petition of 28 to Soviet leader Mikhail Gorbachev.

Mikalaj Statkievič

Born on August 12, 1956, Statkievič, graduated from the Higher Engineering Anti-Aircraft and Missile Defense School in 1978 and eventually attained the rank of lieutenant colonel. Since October 1991 he has served as president of the Belarusan Association of Servicemen. He is currently a member of the Belarusan Social-Democratic Union.

Michaś Tkačoŭ

Born on March 10, 1942, Tkačoŭ graduated from the Belarusan State University in 1964. After teaching for several years he started working in 1968 at the Institute of History at the Belarusan Academy of Sciences and eventually headed a project devoted to the six-volume Encyclopedia of Belarus's history. He also authored numerous books on Belarus's ancient and medieval history. Tkačoŭ was a political activist during the years of perestroika, one of the founders of the Belarusan Popular Front, and leader of the Belarusan Social-Democratic Union. He died on October 31, 1992.

Valancina Tryhubovič

Born on January 13, 1947, Tryhubovič graduated from the Belarusan State University in 1970. A journalist, she has served as manager of the Fine Arts Department of the monthly *Mastactva* (Art) and as chairperson of the Foreign Relations Committee of the Belarusan Popular Front.

Anatol Viarcinski

Born on November 18, 1931, Viarcinski graduated from the Belarusan State University in 1956. He has worked on various local newspapers as well as on the Miensk literary weekly *Litaratura i Mastactva* (Literature and art) which he edited during the 1980s. And from 1975 to 1982 he served as secretary of the republic's Writers' Union.

Uladzimir Zablocki

Born on December 17, 1939, Zablocki graduated from the Moscow Energy Institute. Until 1990 he worked at the Research Institute of Electronics in Miensk. Zablocki has served as a member of the Diet of the Belarusan Popular Front; as "prime minister" of the shadow government of the Democratic opposition in the Supreme Council, where he is its expert on economic matters; as deputy of the Supreme Council; and as deputy chairman of the Council's Committee on Science and Scientific-Technical Progress.

NOTES

1. *Litaratura i Mastactva* (Literature and art), Minsk, February 7, 1992.

2. See *Bielarusistyka. No. 10. Historyja* (Belarusan studies. No. 10. History) (Minsk: Department of Scientific Information on the Social Sciences of the Academy of Sciences of the BSSR, 1991), pp. 7–9 (Contents).

3. *Dobry viečar* (Good evening), Minsk, December 19, 1991.

4. Alaksandar Ulicionak, *Inšadumcy. Hutarki z tymi, kaho jašče ŭčora klejmavali "demahohami"* (Dissidents: Interviews with those who only yesterday were branded "demagogues") (Minsk: Bielarus, 1991), p. 191.

5. For an insight into this generational drama, see Siarhiej Navumčyk's story of moral revolt and intellectual liberation, in *ibid.*, pp. 178–188.

6. An informative sociological study of the youth movement in the second half of the 1980s has been published in Minsk. See S. A. Shavel and O. T. Manayev, eds., *Molodezh i demokratizatsiya sovetskogo obshchestva: sotsiologicheskiy analiz* (Youth and the democratization of Soviet society: A sociological analysis) (Minsk: Nauka i tekhnika, 1990), 133 pp.

7. This unpublished document can be found in the archives of the newspaper *Bielarus* (The Belarusan) in New York.

8. Siarhiej Šupa, in a personal interview with the present author (Summer 1992).

9. *Prahramnyja dakumienty BNF "Adradžeńnie"* (Programmatic documents of the BPF "Renewal") (Minsk, 1989), p. 25.

10. *Bielarus* (The Belarusan), No. 360 (New York, July 1989).

11. Art Turevich, "Elections in Byelorussia," *Byelorussian Review*, Vol. 2, No. 1 (Spring 1990), p. 6.

12. *Bielarus*, No. 369 (New York, April 1990).

13. Turevich, *op. cit.*, p. 7.

14. Michail Rasolka, "Deputackija hulni 'Viasna-90'" (Deputy games, "spring-90"), *Krynica* (Wellspring), No. 7 (Minsk, July 1990), p. 4.

15. Rasolka, *op. cit.*, p. 3.

16. See the interview with Zianon Paźniak in *Litaratura i Mastactva*, Minsk, August 10, 1990.

17. *Naviny BNF* (News of the BPF), Miensk, May 27, 1990.

18. *Zviazda* (Star), August 1, 1990.

19. For the text of this document, see *Zviazda*, July 29, 1990, and *Litaratura i Mastactva*, August 3, 1990. An English version was also issued in August 1990 in the form of a press release by the Belarusan Mission to the United Nations in New York.

20. *Bielarus*, No. 372 (New York, August 1990).

21. For the full text of this counterproposal, see *Bielarus*, No. 372 (New York, August 1990).

22. *Litaratura i Mastactva*, August 10, 1990.

23. *Litaratura i Mastactva*, August 3, 1990.

24. *Kommunist Belorussii*, No. 9 (Minsk, September 1990), p. 23.

25. *Zviazda*, Minsk, November 29, 1990.

26. *Zviazda*, November 29, 1990.

27. *Zviazda*, November 28, 1990.

28. *Sovetskaya Belorussiya*, December 2, 1990.

29. *Zviazda*, December 22, 1990.

30. *Zviazda*, November 29, 1990.

31. *Svaboda* (Liberty), No. 1 (Miensk, February 1991).

32. Moscow All-Union Radio First Program, October 22, 1991; text quoted in FBIS-SOV-91-203, October 23, 1991, p. 61.

33. *Belta-Tass*, February 3, 1992.

34. This information is based primarily, but not exclusively, on a report published by the newspaper *Naviny BNF* (News of the BPF), No. 7 (November 1991). Other data were taken from sources too numerous to list.

35. For elaboration of this latter view, see V. Fedorovich, "Vremya li delat' stavki? (Is it time to make bets?), *Chelovek i ekonomika* (Man and economy), No. 12 (Minsk, December 1991), pp. 20–21.

36. This list is contained in mimeographed booklet entitled *Otchetnyi doklad Vremennoy komissii Verkhovnogo Soveta Respubliki Belarus po otsenke deystviy chlenov GKChP i podderzhavshikh ikh obshchestvenno-politicheskikh obrazovaniy, organov gosudarstvennoy vlasti i upravleniya, dolzhnostnykh lits i grazhdan* (Report of the Temporary Commission of the Supreme Council of the Republic of Belarus on estimating actions related to the State Emergency Committee and the support of it by civic-

political structures, organs of government and administration, officials, and citizens) (Minsk, dated before December 17, 1991), p. 59.

37. *Zviazda*, January 10, 1992

38. *Naviny BNF* (News of the BPF), No. 7 (Miensk, November 1991).

39. *Sovetskaya Belorussiya*, November 27, 1991.

40. *Naviny BNF*, No. 2 (January 16, 1992).

41. Radio Liberty, "Kratkiye soobshcheniya ITAR-TASS" (Brief news of ITAR-TASS), *Russia and CIS Today*, May 11, 1992.

42. *Narodnaja hazieta* (People's newspaper), August 29, 1991.

43. *Otchetnyi doklad Vremennoy komissii Verkhovnogo Soveta Respubliki Belarus po otsenke deystviy chlenov GKChP i podderzhavshikh ikh obschestvenno-politicheskikh obrazovaniy, organov gosudarstvennoy vlasti i upravleniya, dolzhnostnykh lits i grazhdan*, 73 pp.

44. Alaksandar Mikalajčanka, "Epicentr, što pryvioŭ Bielaruś da svabody" (The epicenter that led Belarus to liberty), *Polacak*, No. 9 (Cleveland, 1991), pp. 4–8. This article contains a day-by-day account of the events that transpired in the central square of Miensk.

45. *Viedamasci Viarchoŭnaha Savieta Bielaruskaj SSR* (Proceedings of the Supreme Council of the Belarusan SSR), No. 28 (Minsk, 1991), pp. 4–15. For the text of the law concerning the Ministry of the Interior, see *Narodnaja hazieta*, August 27, 1991.

46. FBIS-SOV-91-073, April 16, 1991, p. 52.

47. *Zviazda*, February 15, 1992.

48. Uladzimir Starčanka, "Ci jość šanc pieramahčy?" (Is there a chance to prevail?) *Litaratura i Mastactva*, May 5, 1991.

49. *Litaratura i Mastactva*, November 6, 1992.

50. *Bielarus*, No. 395 (November 1992).

51. *Litaratura i Mastactva*, November 6, 1992.

52. *Ibid.*

53. This is the title of an interview with Šuškievič in *Zviazda*, September 3, 1991.

54. See the text of the speech by Deputy Dzmitry Bulachaŭ, chairman of the Legislative Committee, in *Dzieviataja siesija Viarchoŭnaha Savieta Respubliki Bielaruś dvanaccataha sklikannia* (Ninth session of the Twelfth Supreme Council of the Republic of Belarus), Bulletin No. 24 (April 7, 1992), pp. 45–48.

55. *Argumenty i fakty*, No. 1 (Moscow, 1991).

56. *Narodnaja hazieta*, January 17, 1992.

57. Hedrick Smith, *The New Russians* (New York: Random House, 1990), p. 122.

58. *Narodnaja hazieta*, November 7, 1991.

SEVEN

The Economy: A Measure of Perestroika's Success (1985–1992)

IN A "SICK SOCIETY"

Much of the political drama that has been unfolding in Belarus (and in the rest of the former Soviet Union, for that matter) is directly connected with the economy, from the standpoint both of professional analysts and of the populace. For the latter, the basic measure (if not the *only* measure) of perestroika's success is the level of income and the availability of goods. By this yardstick, perestroika has been an abysmal failure thus far, from which the political fallout takes the form of increasing nostalgia for pre-1985 times. The economy has not vindicated the rhetoric about "New Thinking" and the euphoria of national independence. On the contrary, Belarus now faces a multifaceted crisis caused by economic decline for which the only apparent consolation is the thought that in most other republics of the former empire the situation is even worse.

For the scholars of Russian history, what has befallen the old regime was inevitable. According to this view, the decision to support perestroika resulted from the realization that the Soviet Union, because of its politico-economic system, had hopelessly failed to keep up with the Western world's technological advancement.

An interesting study on this subject, entitled *Sick Science in a Sick Society*, was published in Miensk in 1990. According to its author, G. A. Nesvetaylov, the scientific-technological progress made in a sociopolitical system under a command administrative government is cyclical in nature. In fact, the phenomenon is statistically demonstrable. Consider, for instance, the rate of fundamental scientific invention in the USSR after World War II. During this period, when Soviet science was centered on nuclear energy, quantum electronics, and space technology, one discerns a closing cycle: In the 1950s, inventions stood at 34 percent of the total for the period; in the 1960s, at 46 percent, in the 1970s, at only 18 percent, and in the 1980s, at scarcely 2 percent.

The outside world, meanwhile, underwent a technological revolution in the areas of microelectronics, informatics, and biotechnology, says Nesvetaylov; but Soviet science, unable to escape its cycle, remained mired in the past. Deprived of stimulating interaction with the economy, it developed deformations and became "technicized," thus preventing redirection of the economy for the benefit of people, for solving ecological and health problems, and for increasing agricultural production.

Nesvetaylov sees not only a science paralyzed by the lack of a sound relationship with the economy but also the scientist (including, of course, the economist) as victim of the command administrative system:

> Command administrative relationships in the sphere of science have deformed the personality of the scientist making out of him a conformist devoid of initiative and personal opinion who has weakened the defensive reactions of science by developing an Acquired Immunodeficiency Syndrome in relation to outside administrative influence. During the years of stagnation, through this personality among scientists all the illnesses of society penetrated into science: bureaucratization, diminution of stimuli for work, lowering of the prestige of creative activity, bribery and pilferage, clannishness, sycophancy, etc.[1]

Bureaucratization of science drastically slowed the process of the application for inventions—another statistically demonstrable symptom of the Old Order's decay. Whereas the time elapsed between invention and its formal acceptance was six years in the 1961–1965 period, it grew to nine years in 1971–1975 and to more than fifteen years in 1981–1989.[2]

In the final analysis, the Soviet system produced "an economy unresponsive not only to the interests and needs of man, but also to scientific-technical progress."[3] Perestroika and its concomitant, glasnost, were thus inevitable. One of their by-products was the movement for real national independence with an underlying economic rationale.

ECONOMY AND THE IDEA OF INDEPENDENCE

When glasnost arrived in 1985, in the absence of full and reliable data (given the untrustworthy and incomplete statistics in support of Belarus's alleged success within the Soviet Union), it was inviting to argue for the independence of the republic on economic grounds. The economic argument has been used both by those who view independence primarily as a way to save the national culture and by those who object on a purely rational basis to the stifling centralism of the Muscovite bureaucracy in industry and agriculture.

The Belarusan Popular Front, which emerged first in the political arena to challenge the Old Order, expressed its position regarding the economy in its program adopted at the constituent convention of June 1989. The BPF called for "radical economic reforms" that would be based on the following principles:

1. The Supreme Council and local Councils (Soviets) of the republic are the only proprietors of all natural resources.
2. The basis of the regulated market economy are individual and collective shareholders, whose interests are equally defended by the state.
3. The central element of the economic system is an independent enterprise of shareholders.
4. Economic entities (enterprises, associations, etc.) are guided by national legislation and their mutual agreements.
5. The general guidance of economic life belongs to the government of the republic.
6. There are no obligatory provisions concerning All-Union funds; all agreements between the republic's economic subjects and the parties beyond its borders should be arrived at by consensus.
7. Enterprises have the right to direct economic ties with foreign countries.
8. Favorable conditions should be created for foreign investments.
9. The land belongs to the people and is handed over to local Councils for distribution. Farmers are responsible before the Councils for proper use of the land.
10. The main agricultural unit is a farm, which is received in perpetuity but cannot be sold. Farms are allowed to form cooperative associations for food processing and marketing.[4]

As the Soviet economy continued to disintegrate under the impact of free-for-all perestroika, economists looked for other models through which to restructure existing relationships. Inescapably, one primary question concerned the subordination of republican economies to the Moscow bureaucracy. "Look at the outside world!" exclaimed economist P. A. Kapitula at a round-table discussion in Miensk organized by *Kommunist Belorussii* in the spring of 1990. "The Ford factories are at work in dozens of countries on all continents. And who thinks of their subordination?" But in Belarus, said Kapitula, "the enterprises, as before, are enmeshed in a bureaucratic web."[5]

Belarus's neighbors, the Baltic states and Ukraine, were moving ener-getically to cut this bureaucratic web. The conservative Belarusan govern-ment, pressed by the small but vocal opposition in the streets and, after the March 1990 elections, in the parliament as well, could not help but fall in step. Newly elected Prime Minister Viačaslaŭ Kiebič, former director of a huge automobile plant, was convinced that economic ties to Russia re-mained a necessity for resource-hungry Belarus; yet he recognized the po-litical urgency of the issue of independence. In his maiden speech in the republican Supreme Council, he declared that "the only solution we have is the economic sovereignty of Belarus."[6]

Sovereignty it was, albeit still anchored to the idea of an undefined Union and ties with the Gorbachev-Ryzhkov government. The paradoxi-cal vote on July 27, 1990, for Belarus's state sovereignty by a parliament, 86 percent of whose members were Communists, is explained by a conflu-ence of economic, political, cultural, and moral motives. V. Samoilov, head of the economy section of the CPB's main publication *Kommunist Belorussii*, had it right when he summed up his journal's round-table dis-cussion on the state of the republic's economy as follows: "Today, the problems of the economy have become not only the most acute and vital to every member of our society, but they are in the full sense political and even moral problems."[7] Indeed, freedom is indivisible in all its aspects, as Sergei Naumchik (Siarhiej Navumčyk), an opposition activist and mem-ber of parliament, observed. Commenting on "the submissiveness" with which people had given up their "freedom of speech and freedom of spir-it," Naumchik mused: "Wasn't it because those freedoms were not based on economic freedom?"[8]

THE CHERNOBYL FACTOR

The discussion about economic independence resonated with a special intensity in Belarus in connection with the Chernobyl disaster which laid bare the immorality of subordination to a distant and alien authority. The painful dependency of the republic on the central bureaucracy remained poignantly relevant in the face of this overwhelming disaster. The main "theoretical and political" publication of the CPB, *Kommunist Belorussii*, began raising questions, thereby lessening the pro-Moscow orientation of the CPB. These questions, including the following, remain unanswered:

Whom are we to ask as to why we were forced to report in our Belarusan press about the problems of liquidating the effects of the [Chernobyl] acci-dent only with permission from the Interdepartmental Commission of the USSR Ministry of Atomic Energy? Why did the sharp and most truthful material have to be sent to Moscow (where it frequently disappeared) for approval?[9]

In relation to the drive for independence, the Chernobyl disaster was a two-edged sword. It also acted as an inhibitor. As demographer A. A. Rakov, participant in the *Kommunist Belorussii* discussion on the economy, was quoted as saying: "I believe that after 1986 there can be no talk of any independence. Now we are tied up by our misfortune with the entire state."[10] In August 1990, when the issue of an All-Union treaty was being hotly debated, Supreme Council Deputy Hienadź Hrušavy (Gennadi Grushevoy) told Radio Liberty: "People are convinced that if we leave the Soviet Union, no one is going to help us, and we will perish. This is a myth. It is a myth that has the entire nation by the throat."[11]

If the fear of independence was unfounded (according to some), the calamity itself remained staggering in magnitude. Premier Kiebič told the Belarusan parliament in June 1990 that "obvious losses of national wealth alone, according to current estimates, approximate 100 billion rubles, which exceeds eight annual budgets of the republic."[12] It was necessary to insist, Kiebič further indicated, that All-Union organs compensate Belarus for these losses. And, indeed, one month later, the republic expressed this idea in its Declaration of State Sovereignty: "The Belarusan SSR demands from the Government of the USSR unconditional and urgent compensation for the damage connected with the elimination of the effects of the Chernobyl disaster."

Soon, however, Belarusans realized that hopes pinned on Moscow were unrealistic. In September 1990 *Kommunist Belorussii,* commenting on the Twenty-Eighth CPSU Congress held in July of that year, bitterly admitted: "We are victims not only of Chernobyl itself, but also of the fact that until now, in spite of all the decisions, the national disaster has not been recognized, and that they are trying to get rid of us as though we were annoying flies. We are hostages to silence."[13]

Another example of Belarus's enduring and hurtful dependency on the old imperial center was brought up by Belarusan Foreign Minister Piotr Kraŭčanka at the United Nations in September 1991. The minister complained of Moscow's withholding badly needed hard cash for the Chernobyl relief. While the Belarusan republic, said Kraŭčanka, "does not possess a single child tomography machine for the early diagnosis of oncological diseases, ... the main culprit of the Chernobyl tragedy—the USSR Atomic Energy Ministry, which continues to exist as a powerful bureaucratic system—received 650 million dollars in 1991 from its energy exports, which are paid for in convertible currency. Of this astronomical sum, Belarus has not received a single kopeck."[14]

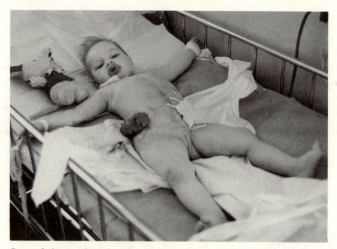

One of the multitude of young victims of Chernobyl radiation. Courtesy of the Belarusan Popular Front.

The situation did not change for the better after Boris Yeltsin put himself at the helm of the Russian government. Following President Yeltsin's visit to Miensk in January 1992, Belarusan Deputy Gennadi Karpenko wrote: "As far as the Chernobyl disaster and a helping hand are concerned, it was clearly stated at the meeting with Russia's President B. N. Yeltsin in the Belarusan parliament that Belarus would have to solve this disaster by itself."[15]

The prospects for the Chernobyl victims did improve somewhat, however, on the eve of the sixth anniversary of the accident. The Russian government adopted a resolution "About Measures of Implementing the Agreement Between the Republic of Belarus and the Russian Federation on Amounts and Ways of Financing in 1992 the Expenses for Liquidating Consequences of the Tragedy at the Chernobyl Atomic Electricity Plant." The agreement, signed by Russia's acting prime minister and chief economist, Yegor Gaidar, provided for quarterly payments by Russia of 4.6 billion rubles (in 1984 prices) into a special Chernobyl fund.[16] Belarus, nevertheless, remains the principal victim of Chernobyl, although—and this is particularly damaging—it is unacknowledged as such in the outside world. As David R. Marples of the University of Alberta, Canada, notes in his well-documented study, "one major reason for the slow progress of the republic has been the effects of the 1986 disaster at Chernobyl, a tragedy that struck Belarus much harder than any other region."[17]

THE ALL-UNION INDUSTRIAL OCTOPUS

The Soviet empire was held together by a multitude of integrative networks: administrative, cultural, military, and above all, economic. Raw materials, component parts, services, and goods—often contrary to principles of efficiency and even of common sense—were transferred from one end of the vast expanse to another in the name of forging a single economic organism with a single "new historic community," the Soviet People. When the empire crumbled under its own bulky weight, much of the ensuing economic hardship resulted from the previous integration and industrial assignments imposed on each of the republics. Belarus's problems during the perestroika years stemmed not only from the republic's overdependence on imports of raw materials and component parts for its machine-building industry but also from underdevelopment of its food-processing capabilities.

After the two declarations, that of "State Sovereignty" in July 1990 and of "Independence" in August 1991, and more than five years into *restructuring*, Supreme Council Deputy Siarhiej Papkoŭ doubted his government's ability to improve the economic situation because, as he said, "our Council of Ministers is managing only fifty percent of the economy. We do not have a single economy in the republic. ... The entire industrial intellect is engaged in enterprises of All-Union subordination."[18]

The command administrative system had developed a deeply rooted symbiosis of centrally managed economy and military industrial complex, which together siphoned off the choice resources of the republics' economies. Even as late as August 1991 the orthodox CPB publication, *Kommunist Belorussii*, admitted: "Until the very last moment, the military industrial complex mercilessly and recklessly skimmed and channelled into its insatiable belly all the cream of science."[19]

To bypass the nominally independent republics, this "skimming" was done through All-Union ministries that had full authority over a substantial part of production in each Union republic, but without any accountability to the republican governments. This semicolonial abnormality became subject to critical reviews when the Communist Party lost its monopoly of power and a new parliament of Belarus was elected on a multiparty basis. Opposition deputies immediately began questioning the fundamental relationship between the republic and the Center. Uladzimir Zablocki, a specialist in economic calculations for the BPF, was one of the first oppositionists to call attention to a significant inequity. "In our republic," he said, "fifty-four percent of all industrial output is of All-Union subordination. This is nonsense, because Belarus has a minimal benefit from these 'Muscovite' plants. While appropriating the lion's share of the profits, the central ministries and departments leave us only dirt and a devastated environment."[20]

In terms of everyday life the situation looked intolerable to the residents of the republic, thus lending support to the voices clamoring for independence primarily out of cultural concerns. Economist Uladzimir Kulažanka drove home his point by citing the example of a Miensk plant that manufactured refrigerators. Ninety-three percent of its production was exported, he wrote. Moscow received hard currency for the product while paying the republic with empty rubles not backed up with consumer goods, thus feeding inflation.[21]

One after another, examples of hard-currency robbery by the All-Union agencies were aired not only by the nationalist opposition groups but also by high-ranking nomenklatura members, including Prime Minister Kiebič himself, a core member of the old Communist guard. In December 1990 Kiebič, critical of Moscow's sudden steep price rise for raw materials that threatened to turn Belarus from a net exporter into a net importer, demanded the right for his republic to export its production independently. In an interview with *Rabochaya tribuna,* he cited a "discouraging example" of Belarus being swindled by the Center. While looking in far-away Thailand for new markets, Kiebič was surprised by a revelation concerning his republic. He learned from Thailanders that they would like to buy additional potash fertilizer, of which they could not import enough. The visitor from Miensk, whose republic is rich in potassium, was glad to hear the news. "I got interested in who sells fertilizer to Thailand," said Kiebič. "As it turned out, it was the Soviet Union. What a surprise! Our republic provides the Soviet Union with sixty percent of its potash fertilizer, which someone sells abroad, but Belarus has not received a single dollar. It's a paradox."[22]

INDUSTRIAL AND AGRICULTURAL POTENTIAL

Of Belarus's 9,942,000 inhabitants in 1985, 62 percent were urban, 38 percent were rural, 47 percent were men, and 53 percent were women. In that year, at the outset of perestroika, Belarus was a republic specializing mainly in machine-building industries and agricultural production. Because of the vast devastation inflicted by World War II, the republic's industrial base was of postwar vintage, enabling it to maintain a higher productivity of labor than that in many other areas of the Soviet Union burdened with older, prewar equipment. In 1985 industry in Belarus accounted for 60 percent of its GNP.[23]

Also in 1985, the Belarusan SSR produced each day of the year the following items, on average: 90,800,000 kw/hours of electricity; 16,400 tons of mineral fertilizers; 61 lathes; 263 tractors; 631 motorcycles; 2,117 bicy-

Abandoned village of Babčyn in the Chojniki county in southeastern Belarus near Chernobyl. Photo by Siarhiej Hryc. Courtesy of *Narodnaja hazieta* (People's newspaper).

cles; 518 tons of paper; 609 tons of cardboard; 1,800 refrigerators and freezers; 2,427 television sets; 1,951 radios; 26,400 watches and clocks; 375,000 pieces of knitwear; and 121,000 pairs of footwear.[24]

With 3.6 percent of the population of the Soviet Union, the republic contributed to the All-Union industrial output in 1987 as follows: 11.2 percent of lathes, 14.2 percent of tractors, 22.5 percent of motorcycles, 11.3 percent of refrigerators, 11.6 percent of television sets, 14.6 percent of watches and clocks, 7.8 percent of knitwear, 5.6 percent of footwear, 26.8 percent of synthetic fiber, and 18.2 percent of mineral fertilizers.[25]

As an agricultural area, Belarus cultivates wheat, barley, oats, buckwheat, potato, flax, and sugar beets, and specializes in animal husbandry (cattle, pigs, sheep, and poultry). Its productive potential, however, was severely reduced by the Chernobyl nuclear accident in April 1986, when 70 percent of the contaminants landed on Belarusan territory because of the direction of the winds. Before Chernobyl, Belarus possessed 9.7 million hectares (about 24 million acres) of farm lands. In speaking of the Chernobyl aftermath, Premier Viačaslaŭ Kiebič told the UN General Assembly in September 1990:

> Our republic suffered and is suffering enormous damage. Over 2.2 million people, i.e., every fifth resident of the republic, eighteen percent of the most productive farm land, and twenty percent of all woods have turned out to be in the zone of long-term action of radiation sources. ... The direct economic loss alone averaged ten annual budgets according to very modest estimates.[26]

In spite of Chernobyl, however, Belarus remains a major producer of food. In 1990 the republic's share in the All-Union food supplies accounted for 16 percent of the meat and meat products and 22 percent of the milk and milk products.

TABLE 7.1   Economic Ties Between Belarus and the Soviet Republics in 1990 (in millions of 1990 rubles)

Name of Republic	Importation to Belarus	Exportation from Belarus	Balance for Belarus
Russian Federation	10,402.8	11,152.3	+749.5
Ukraine	2,999.4	2971.5	−27.9
Uzbekistan	202.0	543.6	+341.6
Kazakhstan	326.4	815.3	+488.9
Georgia	248.7	289.9	+41.2
Azerbaijan	264.2	308.0	+43.8
Lithuania	512.8	597.9	+85.1
Moldova	310.8	398.6	+87.8
Latvia	373.0	453.0	+80.0
Kyrgyzstan	124.4	145.0	+20.6
Tajikistan	62.2	163.1	+100.9
Armenia	155.4	289.9	+134.5
Turkmenia	46.6	108.7	+62.1
Estonia	155.4	217.4	+62.0

Source: Gosudavstvennyi komitet Respubliki Belarus po statistike i analizu (State Committee of the Republic of Belarus for Statistics and Analyses), *Statisticheskiye dannyie ob ekonomike Respubliki Belarus v 1991 godu* (Statistical data on the economy of the Republic of Belarus in 1991) (Minsk, October 1991), p. 40.

Until 1990, while economic ties with other Soviet republics still existed under the Old Order, Belarus enjoyed net industrial and agricultural exportation within the Soviet Union (as shown in Table 7.1) thanks to high labor productivity. In 1990 the republic shipped out consumer goods for a total of 4.1 billion rubles and imported consumer goods for 2.1 billion rubles.

EXPORTS, IMPORTS, AND JOINT VENTURES

Belarus shipped the following industrial and agricultural items to other republics: trucks, tractors, tractor trailers, elevators, lathes, bearings, electric motors, computer equipment, synthetic yarns and fiber, tires, linoleum, flax fiber, textiles, carpets, potatoes, meat and dairy produce, and various consumer goods. At the same time, it imported oil, natural gas, coal, rolled ferrous metal, nonferrous metals, commercial lumber and sawed timber, chemical products, raw materials for the chemical industry, cement, cotton yarn, silk, machines and equipment, cars and buses, sewing and washing machines, paper, grain, fodder, cooking oil, sugar, tea, fish and fish products, vegetables, and consumer goods.[27]

In the food category, export-import figures for the interrepublican exchange in 1990 were 958 million rubles and 813 million rubles, respec-

TABLE 7.2   Economic Ties Between Belarus and the former Soviet republics in 1992 (in millions of 1992 rubles)

Name of Republic	Importation to Belarus	Exportation from Belarus	Balance for Belarus
Armenia	1,328	989	−339
Azerbaijan	2,691	6,123	+3,432
Estonia	1,089	3,105	+2,016
Georgia	1,110	1,736	+626
Kazakhstan	14,952	18,959	+4,007
Kyrgyzstan	1,218	1,553	+335
Latvia	5,065	8,120	+3,055
Lithuania	7,553	8,190	+637
Molodova	8,263	8,959	+2,696
Russia	269,705	211,593	−58,112
Tajikistan	933	1,527	+1,127
Turkmenia	1,986	3,113	+1,127
Ukraine	87,798	88,588	+790
Uzbekistan	7,368	12,409	+5,041

Source: *Zviazda* (Star), Minsk, February 5, 1993.

tively.[28] In the same year that exchange, plus trade with foreign countries, together amounted to 20.12 billion rubles in exports and 20.16 billion rubles in imports. In addition, Belarus exported goods worth 18.5 billion rubles and imported goods worth 16.2 billion rubles. The bulk of exports went to Russia (60 percent) and Ukraine (16 percent). From these two republics also came most of Belarus's imports: 64 percent from Russia and 19 percent from Ukraine. In 1990, Belarus exhibited a surplus with all the republics except Ukraine (Ukraine's exports to its northern neighbor exceeded imports from it by 28 million rubles).[29]

The overall export-import situation has worsened in the face of the economic disintegration of the former Soviet empire. In 1991, for example, Belarus exported 42 percent fewer goods than in the previous year. Exportation of trucks and television sets decreased by almost a half; of potash fertilizers, by 36.9 percent, of tractors, by 26.2 percent; and of refrigerators, by 14.1 percent. The republic exported 4.5 percent of its total production in 1990 but only 2.6 percent of that production in 1991.[30] And nobody knows the point at which this trend will bottom out. By 1993, with rampant inflation, the import-export balance worsened considerably for Belarus (as shown in Table 7.2). From a net exporter the republic became a net importer because of the trade imbalance with Russia whence Belarus imports a bulk of its raw material and oil, prices for which went markedly up.

In addition to interrepublican shipments, Belarus exported to and imported from other countries in 1991. During the first ten months of that year, exports equivalent to the total sum of 457.8 million convertible rubles went to Poland (17.7 percent), Bulgaria (10.5 percent), Hungary (5.6 percent), Germany (5.3 percent) Austria (5.2 percent), Yugoslavia (5.2 percent), the Netherlands (5.1 percent), Cuba (5.1 percent), Afghanistan (4. 9 percent), China (4.6 percent), and Egypt (4.0 percent). During the same period, Belarus imported goods equivalent to 239.5 million convertible rubles from Poland (28.7 percent), Germany (12.9 percent), Japan (10.2 percent), Yugoslavia (7.8 percent), the Netherlands (7.1 percent), Austria (6.2 percent), and Switzerland (5.5 percent).[31] A number of foreign companies have been trying to take advantage of Belarus's central location in Eastern Europe and its well-qualified workforce. By July 1991, 150 joint ventures had been registered: In 86 of them, partners came from capitalist countries; in 55, from former socialist states; and in 9, from the developing world. Among the most active joint enterprises were those connected with Poland (39 joint ventures), Germany (25), North America (19), and Austria (16). The bulk of exports from Belarus through these enterprises consisted of leather footwear (53.8 percent), peat (11.8 percent), transport services (7.6 percent), timber (7.7 percent), and furniture (4.8 percent).[32]

In November 1991 the Belarusan Supreme Council passed a law about foreign investments, specifying that "objects of foreign investments" can be "any enterprises and organizations engaged in activities not forbidden on the territory of the republic; buildings and construction, property of Belarusan juridical and physical persons; stock, bank deposits, insurance policies and other valuable papers and means; products of science and technology; rights to intellectual property." The law allows foreign investors either to form joint companies or to have their own exclusive companies for acquisition of real estate and other properties, including rights to use land and natural resources. In addition, companies willing to manufacture consumer goods are exempt from taxes during their first two years of operation. (On November 14, 1992, the Supreme Council directed the republican Council of Ministers to "secure revision of normative acts" that countered the above law as of February 1, 1992.)[33]

One advantage that Belarus enjoys in becoming involved in business ventures was noted at an international conference held in Miensk on May 17–19, 1991. "Among the most important conditions for the dynamic development of entrepreneurship in Belarus, including joint ventures," reported *Belorusskiy delovoy vestnik* (Belarusan business herald), "the participants of the conference noted a relatively stable politico-economic situation, not aggravated by any serious demonstrations of a nationalist nature, high qualifications and low (relative to other parts of the USSR) price of the labor force, and the convenient geographical location of the republic."[34]

Mountains of rock and dirt are the result of potash salt mining near the city of Salihorsk in southern Belarus, presenting a grave ecological problem. Photo by Siarhiej Hryc. Courtesy of *Narodnaja hazieta* (People's newspaper).

NATURAL RESOURCES: UNUSED POTENTIAL

One often hears that Belarus is a country poor in natural resources—a contention that not only reduces national self-assertiveness but, according to some, also translates into political weakness, making the republic vulnerable to outside economic pressures. Nationalists have debunked this contention as a myth born out of political dependency on imperial centers (namely, Poland in the distant past and Russia more recently) and a lack of development programs in the interests of the region. However, economic neglect of Belarus, notes Supreme Council Deputy Jaŭhien Cumaraŭ, does not mean the absence of natural resources. On the contrary, that neglect turned out to be a blessing in disguise, because the resources remained intact. Basing his information on data obtained from academician Radzim Harecki, director of the Institute of Geochemistry and Geophysics of the Belarusan Academy of Sciences, Cumaraŭ presented the following picture of what lies under the surface of his country:

Iron ores in amounts up to 1.5 billion tons; slates (fuel, construction material, and raw material for chemical industry)—up to 11 billion tons; coal (2.3 b. t.) and brown coal (3 b. t.); potash salt—up to 80 b. t.; gypsum and anhydrites—1 b. t.; phosphates—900 million t.; inexhaustible amount of rock-salt, enough to "feed" the entire world. Deposits of dawsonite, an extremely rare mineral unknown anywhere in the former USSR, have been uncovered; these deposits have been estimated at over 80 million tons. ... There are significant industrial deposits of mineral brines ("liquid ores"). This raw material yields iodine, bromide, lithium, strontium, and many other elements. Belarus can provide for itself and export granite, silicates, sapropels, dolomites, chalk, clay. ...

Research shows: the depths of our land have industrial deposits of diamonds, titanium, copper ore, lead, mercury, bauxites, nickel, vanadium, and amber.[35]

LEGISLATION ON THE ECONOMY

Two basic problems are impeding the economic revitalization of Belarus: (1) How can the importation of raw materials and component parts be secured so as to keep industry going? and (2) By what means can the interest of the population in a market economy be stimulated? The former problem is more pressing, but the latter is more fundamental and less manageable. "The readiness of working collectives for transformation, as experience shows, is not high," writes a government specialist. "The goals and ways to reach them are realized in the best of cases only by leaders. The majority of the members of a collective basically expects a pay raise from the innovations outlined."[36]

The sense of being lost before myriad problems, great and small, is not limited to factory "working collectives"; indeed, it also affects the highest-ranking and probably most confused collective, the 346-member parliament of the republic, in which 14 seats were still unfilled as of spring 1992. "Leaders we have," said Prime Minister Viačaslaŭ Kiebič on the eve of 1992, "but good economists so far are few."[37] The lack of competent economists and sound experts in civil society is especially manifest in the Supreme Council—a situation that only aggravates the squabbles that flow out of political differences. Here is a typical charge leveled by a Social Democratic deputy at the ex-Communist majority in the parliament:

The Supreme Council, whose majority consists of devoted members of the nomenklatura, is in no rush to pass a law on the privatization of state property and is not creating any mechanism to implement the right, to date only declared, to private land. Meanwhile, this entire nomenklatura and the mafia, which is tied to it, using various temporary and sublegal means, has been hurriedly conducting what is called "wild" privatization, openly plundering state property that was created by the nation.[38]

The government categorically refutes such charges, all the while blaming "conservatives and often the corrupted part of the local directing apparatus," which, however, remain invisible and always unspecified in official statements. Yet these refutations sound rather hollow coming from a government that has openly admitted (in a statement signed by twelve leaders of the executive branch) that "none of its members ... belongs to any party, or to any political movement."[39] Under the current circumstances, noninvolvement in any political movement is probably the strongest indication of an unacknowledged membership in what was yesterday the Communist Party of Belarus.

PRIVATIZATION: BARELY MOVING

At the beginning of 1992 the workforce of Belarus was above 5 million strong. Of this number, 72 percent worked for the state sector. Private enterprises, by contrast, employed 90,000 workers. During 1991 their share grew from 1.2 to 1.8 percent of the entire workforce.[40]

The litmus test of perestroika in Belarus is privatization of land, which has made little progress—despite the fact that 70 percent of the polled public spoke in favor of privatization in October 1991, when the question was debated in the Supreme Council.[41] The barriers impeding reforms are of three types: attitudinal, economic, and political. Consider an example from the first of these categories. Early polling of peasants indicated a lack of psychological preparedness among them to become private owners. At the same time, an average of 43.7 percent of collective and state farm peasants indicated their "total satisfaction" with the present system, 21.8 percent were "afraid of cheating on the part of various organs," 11.0 percent said they "lacked the experience to manage an individual farm," and 11.2 percent explained their negative attitude toward private farming in terms of the "lack of necessary agricultural tools."[42] Of course, attitudes change as the debate goes on. Land is needed not only for farmers but also for city dwellers, many of whom have ties to rural areas through their relatives. A poll conducted in October–November 1990 among the general population indicated that more than 87 percent of the respondents favored the private ownership of land.[43] Yet despite such support, land reform has been bogged down by local officials. The laws on the books are not being implemented. And some of the laws themselves are inadequate to begin with. "As a result of inflation," one Supreme Council deputy pointed out, "payment for a hectare of land is now equal to the price of a luncheon in the governmental dining room."[44]

Meanwhile, people are asking to be given smaller plots of land to cultivate. In local councils, notes Stanislaŭ Šuškievič, chairman of the Supreme
Council of Belarus, there are 380,000 applications to be processed.
(Šuškievič has since called on the government to speed them up.) The
number of farms is thus far dismally low, however. In parliament Premier
Kiebič noted that as of October 1991 there were merely 600 farms occupying 1,200 hectares of land,[45] out of a total of nearly 9 million hectares. Although the law allows an individual farm to take up as many as 50 hectares, the average farm is only 30 hectares in size.

According to Šuškievič, as of 1992 there are 600 more applicants for
farms (183 of whom are residents of urban areas, where there is a surplus
of labor); but the chances of their speedily obtaining property rights are
not very bright, as past experience shows. With a mildness typical of him,
Šuškievič indicated his understanding of the cause underlying this slowness: "The leaders of the collective farms have great difficulty parting
with the absolute power which they have acquired."[46] He said it hurt him
to realize that in Kyrgyzstan there were 11,000 individual farms whereas
Belarus had fewer than 900, a rather minute share in the collectivized agriculture of the republic. Leaders of the peasant parties have indicated that,
in order to create a viable alternative to the collective and state farms in
Belarus, 20,000 individual farmsteads are needed.[47] But that goal is still
distant. Chairman Šuškievič, speaking at the opening of a new session of
parliament, took a grim view of the situation. "Changes to a large extent
are being blocked by the former nomenklatura," he charged, "which is
able only to carry out orders coming from above and do that only out of
fear." As for the implementation of the law on private land, passed in September 1991, it was being "sabotaged," according to the Chairman, under
"the guise of demagogic pretexts that it was being done to prevent ruin-
ation of the collective farms."[48] Šuškievič—who, the opposition maintains, is one of the nomenklatura group interested in maintaining the status quo—limited himself to blaming local administrators for the slowness
of land privatization. The gist of this conflict was captured by a newspaper correspondent, Oleg Gruzdilovich: "The answer to the question of
why the land reform is being hampered lies on the surface: distribution of
land is a distribution of power. To share it with the people is something
none of the 'appanage princelets' wants."[49] Indeed, property and political
power go hand in hand regardless of political regimen. Money not only
"talks," as Americans well know; it also fights, as the Russians proved
during the August putsch. As Ben Slay and John Tedstrom have noted, "It
is instructive that the small but rapidly growing private sector in Moscow,
St. Petersburg, and other Russian cities played an important political and
financial role in opposing the coup attempt by Soviet hardliners in August
1991."[50]

AN ABSENCE OF MECHANISM

Three-fourths of the respondents in a poll taken in October–November 1990 favored the transfer of industrial enterprises to working collectives.[51] But the difficulties involved in bringing about this transfer are horrendous. Economic deterioration intensifies more rapidly than the government is able to anticipate, let alone prevent. Moreover, Belarus is tightly linked to the considerably larger economies of Russia and Ukraine, which are evolving under their own dynamics and in a direction not always favorable to Belarus. Overall, however, economic developments in Russia under the radical course set by President Yeltsin and his ministers have been speeding up the reformist activity of the Kiebič government in Miensk.

The mechanism of privatization itself is both complex and vague. What must be settled first is the division of property between All-Union and republican ministries. Second, republican and regional authorities must be empowered to proceed with concrete cases of privatization. Laws have to be devised and passed, enterprises for privatization selected, prices established, procedures designed, financing regulated, etc. And all these measures must be accompanied by enough publicity to inform—that is, educate—the ignorant and suspicious public in this intricate business of privatization. Publicity, however, has been rather scarce so far, thus providing fertile ground for sinister rumors of avarice and graft, which in turn have rendered the government vulnerable politically.

In combination with these factors, the absence of a comprehensive law on privatization has retarded the nation's progress toward a market economy. Moreover, officials have found it difficult to refute accusations about pilfering of state property. The group of responsible functionaries who countered such accusations in March 1992 had to admit to a dismal slowness in the processing of paperwork. Thus in 1991, out of 66 republican enterprises and 235 communal properties scheduled for privatization, only 19 and 33, respectively, had been privatized.[52] At the request of the government, furthermore, a German firm made an analysis of the proposed bill on privatization and concluded that if the bill became law, twenty years will pass before privatization is actually implemented.[53]

The issue of privatization is not only economic but profoundly political in nature. Members of the government and of the opposition in the Supreme Council know this full well. One of the opposition deputies, Jaŭhien Novikaŭ, hit the nail on the head when he said that "privatization in the conditions of a mixed economy secures sovereignty of the individual"[54] and that it is this "sovereignization of the individual" which the bureaucrats of yesteryear are trying to prevent by obstructing privatization.

TAXATION: A DENSE FOG

"Groping in the Dark" was the heading chosen by correspondent Ivan Rubin to describe the March 1992 session of the Supreme Council that wrestled with the issue of taxation. "Again a seditious thought crept in," confessed Rubin, "that nobody envisions and understands exactly and clearly such a very important economic lever as taxation. Suspicion grew stronger when [Premier] Kiebič said that at least four months are needed to arrive at certain conclusions. Perhaps the entire taxation system will have to be revamped again."[55]

Some very basic problems were being thrashed out at that session. What should be the taxation level of money and commodity markets? How high a price should be paid for privatized land? What should be taxed and what should be exempted to patch up so many holes in the budget? "Last year," remarked the skeptical correspondent, "the taxation laws were adopted by way of trial and error, and the same method continues today."

The 1992 budget (52.9 billion rubles in revenues and 56.4 billion rubles in expenditures, with a 3.5 billion rubles deficit) rested, therefore, on rather shaky ground. Its realization depended on a multitude of intangibles, including the following as specified by law: "forecasts of financial-economic activity of enterprises, associations, and organizations, the extent of changes of tax legislation, which goes into effect as of January 1, 1992, the transfer to the Republic of Belarus of enterprises, associations, organizations, and institutions of former All-Union subordination on the territory of the republic."[56] While all of these forecasts were being drawn up, the economy continued in its downward slide, making a mockery of the optimistic decision of the Supreme Council, adopted on January 15, 1992, to aim for a GNP of 103 percent relative to that of 1991.[57]

The newspaper *Birzhi i Banki* (Money markets and banks) published a biting commentary on the 1992 budget under the heading "New Taxes: A Deficit of the Budget or a Deficit of Brains?" The article contained the following point:

> One has to acknowledge rather that the kind of new Communist thinking manifesting itself in the current reforms will bring nothing good to the market structures. And it is doubtful that its proponents will last very long on the road to a market economy. The question now is: how to shorten their stay in power.[58]

In this context the business community had an interest in common with the Belarusan Popular Front, which spearheaded the drive for dissolution of the Supreme Council and resignation of the Kiebič government. At the same time, there were signs of tension between the government and the parliament. In a post script to the above-cited article, the newspaper noted that Prime Minister Kiebič had distanced himself from the new tax legislation, blaming the Supreme Council for botching it.

Whoever was responsible for the current budget, the overall economic picture presented by Premier Kiebič to the legislators in mid-March showed just how far off target they all were with their budgetary figures. The first two months of 1992 revealed a lowering of industrial activity by more than 12 percent, accompanied by a downward trend in agriculture. "Our economy is under the strong influence of processes going on in the economy of Russia," said Kiebič, having in mind Russia's price liberalization, the sharp decrease in Russian oil production, and the steep increase in the cost of energy.[59]

BELARUSAN MONEY

On November 16, 1991, the Supreme Council decided to introduce coupons into circulation along with money by January 1, 1992, with the purpose of protecting the local market from invasion by outsiders with rubles. The Supreme Council decreed that 60 percent of earnings and 100 percent of entitlements would be paid in coupons.[60] As with so many other decisions, the deadline was not met. But by April 1992 samples of Belarusan rubles in seven denominations, complementing the Soviet currency in use, had been advertized, and issuance by the National Bank of Belarus was scheduled for June 1992.[61] Then, on October 13, 1992, the Moscow news agency Interfax reported that, according to Supreme Council Chairman Šuškievič and Premier Kiebič, "the issue of introduction of national currency had already been solved." However, neither of the two was willing "to call even approximate terms of introduction of the currency into circulation." Interfax further noted that "according to the governmental sources, the Belarusan national currency is being printed in Germany already."[62]

COUNTERPROPOSAL ON THE ECONOMY

After two years of political combat, the BPF published in April 1992 its own "Conception of Economic Reform in the Republic of Belarus."[63] If parliamentary elections are held in the spring of 1994, as the Supreme Council decided on October 29, 1992, the Popular Front's program for economic reform would be the platform for opposition candidates.

The "Conception" foresees a full-fledged state with its own borders, custom, currency, and banking system as well as its own armed forces. In

Belarusan rubles. Issued on May 25, 1992, by the National Bank of the Republic of Belarus, these "bank notes" (*razlikovyja bilety*) in eight denominations (kopecks 50, rubles 1, 3, 5, 10, 25, 50, and 100) were made legal tender for all purchases and trans-

actions in Belarus. The value of the new currency was set officially at the ratio of 1 Belarusan ruble to 10 Russian rubles (*Zviazda*, May 23, 1992).

particular, it directs development toward a free-market economy with lands and housing privatized and nonstate enterprises enjoying "full freedom." It also encourages foreign investments. Although it views "mass bankruptcies" and unemployment as inevitable, the reform plan directs state-owned enterprises, during a "long" transitional period, to preserve their monopoly over the "main kinds of raw materials, jewelry, alcoholic products, and arms" in domestic and foreign trade. The state will use "administrative-planning methods" to "regulate the economy on a macroscopic level" during the period of transition.

Certain cumbersome features have already drawn criticism. Among these are recommendations for "monthly adjustments of taxes related to the socio-political situation," creation of an agency "which carries out a policy of prohibiting the importation of low quality goods and technologies," and "no less than once a year a referendum on confidence in the organs of state management of various levels."

FACING THE FUTURE

In the economic realm, as in that of politics, there is a dichotomy between legislation and fact, between the ideal and the real, between what republican authorities are aiming at and what is achievable given the psychology of the people. Countless obstacles, both internal and external, hinder improvement.

The inertia of old thinking is evident in the answers to this question in a poll conducted in 1990–1991: "Why wouldn't you like to work for a private company?" Replies included the following: "With a private employer a person feels debased, I want to be free." "I don't want to be a slave; this would be a return to capitalism." "I don't want to be exploited and dependent." And "I have been brought up in the spirit of socialism."[64] Furthermore, sociological studies show a strong dependency on the state in the event of a deepening budgetary crisis. Forty-two percent of those polled, whose average age was 41.3 years, said they expected the state to assist them instead of relying on their own initiative and hard work.[65]

The structure of the national economy inherited from the Soviet period is indeed out of joint. The restructuring and retooling of the republic's various industries, of which 40 percent have been geared to military production,[66] require not only much time but huge sums of money. The procurement of raw-material imports is burdened by the barter character of such deals. The labor force must be retrained. New markets must be found and the quality of goods improved. Finally, better management techniques have to be worked out and learned. Toward this end, Miensk has been very hospitable to Western specialists, including those representing the Belarusan diaspora.

NOTES

1. Akademija navuk Bielaruskaj SSR. Addziel navukovaj infarmacyi pa hramadskich navukach (Academy of Sciences of the Belarusan SSR: Department of Scientific Information on Social Sciences) *Referatyŭny zbornik. No. 9. Sieryja 7. Sacyjalohija* (Reference Book No. 9, Series 7: Sociology) (Minsk, 1991), pp. 23–25.

2. Yevgeniy Babosov, "Pochemu my okazalis na obochine NTR?" (Why have we found ourselves on the sidelines of the scientific revolution?) *Kommunist Belorussii*, No. 8 (Minsk, 1991), p. 37.

3. *Ibid.*, p. 36.

4. *Prahramnyja dakumienty BNF "Adradžeńnie"* (Programmatic documents of the BPF "Renewal") (Minsk, 1989), pp. 6–10.

5. *Kommunist Belorussii*, No. 4 (1990), pp. 36, 37.

6. *Čyrvonaja zmiena* (Red generation), Minsk, June 26, 1990.

7. *Kommunist Belorussii*, No. 4 (1990), p. 41.

8. Sergei Naumchik, quoted in Alaksandar Ulicionak, *Inšadumcy* (Dissidents) (Minsk: Bielaruś, 1991), p. 188.

9. A. Kryzhanovskiy. "Polyusa glasnosti" (The extremities of glasnost), *Kommunist Belorussii*, No. 1 (Minsk, 1990), p. 50.

10. "Kontseptsiya pod skalpelem nauki" (A conception under the scalpel of science), *Kommunist Belorussii*, No. 4 (1990), p. 37.

11. Kathleen Mihalisko, "Belorussia as a Sovereign State: An Interview with Henadz' Hrushavy," *Report on the USSR*, No. 35 (Radio Liberty, Munich, August 31, 1990), p. 14.

12. *Čyrvonaja zmiena*, June 26, 1990.

13. Anatoliy Yaroś, "Kakiye my—takoye vremya" (As we are, so are the times), *Kommunist Belorussii*, No. 9 (1990), p. 10.

14. Moscow Tass International Service, September 28, 1991, quoted in FBIS-SOV-91-190 (Washington: U.S. Government Publication, October 1, 1991), p. 60.

15. *Narodnaja hazieta* (People's newspaper), Minsk, January 11, 1992.

16. *Holas Radzimy* (Voice of homeland), No. 19 (Minsk, May 7, 1992).

17. David R. Marples, "Post-Soviet Belarus' and the Impact of Chernobyl'," *Post-Soviet Geography* (formerly *Soviet Geography*), Vol. 33, No. 7 (Silver Spring, MD, September 1992), p. 419.

18. *Niečarhovaja šostaja siesija Viarchoŭnaha Savieta BSSR Dvanaccataha sklikannia* (Sixth Extraordinary Session of the Twelfth Supreme Council of the BSSR), *Biuleteń*, No. 2 (Minsk: Supreme Council Publication, September 17, 1991), p. 71.

19. Babosov, *op. cit.*, p. 36.

20. *Litaratura i Mastactva* (Literature and art), Minsk, September 14, 1990.

21. *Litaratura i Mastactva*, October 5, 1990.

22. *Rabochaya tribuna* (Worker's tribune), Moscow, December 28, 1990.

23. V. F. Borushko, *Belorussiya: lyudi, sobytiya, fakty* (Belarus: People, events, and facts), 3rd ed. (Minsk: Bielarus, 1988), p. 105.

24. Tsentralnoye statisticheskoye upravleniye BSSR (Board of Statistics of the BSSR), *Narodnoye khozyaystvo Belorusskoy SSR v 1985 g.* (National economy of the BSSR in 1985) (Minsk: Bielarus, 1986), pp. 3, 4, 14.

25. Borushko, *op. cit.*, p. 104.

26. Byelorussian Soviet Socialist Republic, Mission to the United Nations, *Statement by H. E. Mr. Vyacheslav F. Kebich, Chairman of the Council of Ministers of the Byelorussian SSR in the General Debate at the 45th session of the UN General Assembly,* Press Release (New York, September 26, 1990), p. 8.

27. *Argumenty i fakty,* No. 45 (Moscow, November 1991).

28. *Argumenty i fakty,* No. 45 (November 1991); *Zviazda* (Star), Minsk, March 14, 1992.

29. Gosudarstvennyi komitet Respubliki Belarus po statistike i analizu (State Committee of the Republic of Belarus for Statistics and Analyses), *Statisticheskiye dannyie ob ekonomike Respubliki Belarus v 1991 godu* (Statistical data on the economy of the Republic of Belarus in 1991) (Minsk, October 1991), p. 39.

30. *Holas Radzimy* (Voice of homeland), No. 10 (Minsk, March 5, 1992).

31. Gosudarstvennyi komitet Respubliki Belarus po statistike i analizu (State Committee of the Republic of Belarus for Statistics and Analyses), *O rabote narodnogo khozyaystva Respubliki Belarus v yanvare-oktyabre 1991 g.* (On activity in the national economy of the Republic of Belarus from January to October 1991) (Minsk, 1991), p. 23.

32. *Byelorussian Business Herald,* Vol. 1, No. 2 (Safety Harbor, Florida, December 1991), p. 3.

33. *Zviazda* (Star), November 29, 1991.

34. *Belorusskiy delovoy vestnik* (Belarusan Business Herald), No. 2 (Minsk, 1991), p. 10.

35. *Zviazda,* November 14, 1991.

36. I. Lyakh, "Speshit' nel'zya i medlit' nevozmozhno" (Haste is not allowed and lingering is impossible), *Chelovek i ekonomika* (Man and the economy), No. 10 (Minsk, 1991), p. 2.

37. V. Kiebič, "Pa pryrodzie svajoj ja aptymist …" (By nature I am an optimist …), *Bielaruś,* No. 1 (Minsk, 1992), p. 23.

38. Mikalaj Kryžanoŭski, "Čamu nie palapšajecca stan našaj ekanomiki" (Why the state of our economy is not improving), *Mienski viesnik* (Minsk Herald), March 1992, p. 2.

39. *Zviazda,* November 19, 1991.

40. *Holas Radzimy,* No. 10 (Minsk, March 5, 1992).

41. *Zviazda,* October 2, 1991.

42. A. S. Krukovskiy, "Spetsifika sotsialnykh otnosheniy na sele v usloviyakh perekhoda k rynku" (The specificity of social relations in the countryside during transition to a market economy), *Belorusistika. No. 14. Gosudarstvennaya politika i rynochnaya ekonomika* (Belarusistics. No. 14. National policies and a market economy) (Minsk: Academy of Sciences of the BSSR, 1991), p. 132.

43. *Ibid.,* p. 177.

44. *Narodnaja hazieta,* March 13, 1992.

45. *Siomaja siesija Viarchoŭnaha Savieta Respubliki Bielarus Dvanaccataha sklikannia* (Seventh Session of the Twelfth Supreme Council of the Republic of Belarus), Bulletin No. 5 (Minsk: Supreme Council Publication, November 17, 1991), p. 8.

46. *Bielaruski čas* (Belarusan time), Minsk, March 30–April 6, 1992.

47. *Siomaja siesija Viarchoŭnaha Savieta Respubliki Bielarus Dvanaccataha sklikannia* (Seventh Session of the Twelfth Supreme Council of the Republic of Belarus), Bulletin No. 5 (Minsk: Supreme Council Publication, November 17, 1991), p. 43.

48. *Zviazda,* March 12, 1992.

49. *Znamya yunosti* (The banner of youth), Minsk, April 15, 1992.

50. Ben Slay and John Tedstrom, "Privatization in the Postcommunist Economies: An Overview," *RFE/RL Research Report,* Vol. 1, No. 17 (Munich: RFE/RL Research Institute, April 24, 1992), p. 2.

51. *Ibid.,* p. 177.

52. *Narodnaja hazieta,* March 11, 1992.

53. Radio Liberty, *Materyjaly Bielaruskaha Manitorynhu* (Materials of Belarusan monitoring), No. 229/66 (Munich, March 2, 1992).

54. *Litaratura i Mastactva,* Minsk, June 14, 1991.

55. *Narodnaja hazieta,* March 16, 1992.

56. *Narodnaja hazieta,* February 15, 1992.

57. *Ibid.*

58. *Birzhi i banki* (Money markets and banks), No. 1 (Minsk, January 28–February 4, 1992).

59. *Narodnaja hazieta,* March 13, 1992.

60. *Narodnaja hazieta,* February 15, 1992.

61. *Svaboda* (Liberty), No. 4 (Miensk, April 1992).

62. FBIS-SOV-92-199, October 14, 1992.

63. *Narodnaja hazieta,* April 16, 1992.

64. R. A. Smirnova, "Izmeneniye otnosheniy naseleniya k sobstvennosti i predprinimatelskoy deyatelnosti" (Changes in the population's attitude toward property and entrepreneurship), *Belorusistika. No. 14: Gosudarstennaya politika i rynochnaya ekonomika* (Belarusistics. No. 14. National policies and a market economy) (Minsk: Academy of Sciences of the BSSR, 1991), p. 95.

65. S. A. Shavel', "Sotsialnyie posledstviya perekhoda k rynku, problemy sotsialnoy zashchity naseleniya respubliki" (Social consequences of a transition to a market economy: Problems of social protection of the population of the republic), *Belorusistika. No. 14 Gosudarstennaya politika i rynochnaya ekonomika* (Belarusistics. No. 14. National policies and a market economy) (Minsk: Academy of Sciences of the BSSR, 1991), p. 118.

66. *Narodnaja hazieta,* January 17, 1992.

EIGHT

Neighbors and the World (1985–1992)

DEMILITARIZATION IN PRINCIPLE

The Greatest Concentration of Servicemen

Since the time Belarus postulated its state sovereignty on July 27, 1990, the republic's foreign policy has been guided by pronouncements of the parliament and government on matters of principle, by geopolitical realities, and by economic exigencies. In a brief statement by its parliament on October 2, 1991, "About Principles of the Foreign Policy of the Republic of Belarus," the country acceded to basic international acts such as the Universal Declaration of Human Rights and the Helsinki Final Act.[1]

In the Declaration of State Sovereignty, the Belarusan Supreme Council reaffirmed "respect for the dignity and the rights of the people of all nationalities residing in the Byelorussian SSR" (Preamble) and stated that "all questions concerning borders shall be decided only on the basis of mutual consent of the Byelorussian SSR and the adjacent sovereign states" (Article Six).[2] The latter comprise Russia to the east, Latvia and Lithuania to the north, Poland to the west, and Ukraine to the south.

An important component of Belarus's foreign policy is the republic's intention to become militarily neutral and free of nuclear arms. Article Ten of the Declaration of State Sovereignty proclaims: "No military units of other countries, their military bases and installations shall be deployed on the territory of the Byelorussian SSR without the consent of its Supreme Council. The Byelorussian SSR sets the aim of making its territory a nuclear-free zone and of becoming a neutral state."

Piotr Kraŭčanka, the foreign minister of Belarus, reported to the UN General Assembly in September 1991 that his government "has initiated the idea of creating a nuclear-free belt—from the Baltic Sea to the Black Sea—including Belarus, the three Baltic States and Ukraine."[3] In January 1992, Kraŭčanka, addressing foreign ministers of the Conference on Security and Cooperation in Europe (CSCE) countries in Prague, repeated his government's "ideal" within a somewhat enlarged scope: "a nuclear-free belt in the center of Europe, which will include the Scandinavian countries in Northern Europe, embrace the Baltic area as well as the states of Central and Eastern Europe."[4] Kraŭčanka expected the issue to be part of the agenda of a CSCE conference scheduled for July 1992.[5] However, there has been no visible diplomatic activity directed at the realization of this grand design, perhaps because of the basic contradiction between the idea of "a nuclear-free belt in the center of Europe" and the geostrategic role assigned to Belarus in the military defense mechanism of the Commonwealth of Independent States (CIS).

Although Belarus's intentions are to become a neutral and nuclear-free state, the reality is that at least half of the armed forces stationed on its territory are under the CIS command, which for all practical purposes remains in the hands of Moscow. On February 14, 1992, nine CIS states, including Belarus, Russia, and Ukraine, agreed in Miensk to appoint Marshal Yevgeniy Shaposhnikov commander-in-chief of the CIS's armed forces. However, Belarus, along with Azerbaijan, Kyrgyzstan, and Ukraine refused to sign an agreement regarding establishment of a Council of Defense Ministers of the CIS. The document was signed only by Armenia, Kazakhstan, Russia, Tajikistan, and Uzbekistan.[6] The abstaining republics were clearly guided by the desire to avoid providing any legal basis to a fact that would contradict their wish to become militarily neutral.

The Belarusans, like many Ukrainians, are well grounded in their suspicion, that "the CIS armed forces were in fact Russian armed forces in disguise."[7] And those forces have been behaving accordingly. For example, the Belarusan parliament has been kept in the dark on the actions of the military. Deputy Colonel Valery Paŭlaŭ (Pavlov) complained in February 1992 that "removal of tactical nuclear arms from its [the republic's] territory was carried out without its knowledge and without any agreement with the Republic of Belarus. ... We don't even know what, where and in what quantities was carried away," said Paŭlaŭ. "Moreover, under the guise of removal of nuclear arms from the territory of Belarus, building materials and other property is being taken away to Russia."[8]

There is no agreement among various sources as to the number of soldiers in the republic. The most oft-cited figure is 160,000. But according to the chairman of the Supreme Council of Belarus, Stanislaŭ Šuškievič, the figure is on the order of 240,000. Belarus, according to Šuškievič, has "the greatest concentration of servicemen anywhere in the world. For every forty-three citizens there is one serviceman on the territory of Belarus. No other country in the world, no other country of the Commonwealth [of Independent States], has such a large concentration."[9]

Speaking on the same subject with a correspondent from *Le Monde*, Šuškievič added that "in real figures that amounts to 180,000, to which must be added 60,000 auxiliaries."[10] A short time later, Belarusan Premier Viačaslaŭ Kiebič, while addressing a military audience on the subject of the complexity of demilitarizing Belarus, dramatized his point by a comparison. "Today," he said, "in Belarus for every forty-three inhabitants there is one military person. By comparison: in Ukraine—there is one for every ninety-eight, in Kazakhstan—one for 118, in Tajikistan—one for 528, and in Russia—one for 634."[11]

When the republic's leaders discuss the real needs of Belarus's military defense, they speak of an army numbering from 60,000 to 90,000 soldiers. And consistent with the declared sovereignty and independence, the Belarusan government is slowly moving toward estasblishment of its own army. As chairman of the parliament, Stanislaŭ Šuškievič, explained at the CIS summit in Miensk in February 1992:

Our constitutional law, the Declaration of the State Sovereignty of the Republic of Belarus, obliges us to establish our own armed forces. There is no reason to delay this question. This work must be started. We need to proceed from the realities of the present day, when we have single forces, and further develop the negotiating process in such a way that Belarus has its own armed forces.[12]

Šuškievič further noted that his republic "should not belong to any military alliances" and that he believed Belarus would be able to move to the status of a nuclear-free and neutral state in "two to three years."[13]

In April 1992 General Paval Kazloŭski replaced General Piotr Čaus as Belarus's defense minister. Upon his appointment, Kazloŭski explained the intended structure of the republic's military forces. These, according to him, would consist of a land army (about 40,000 soldiers), an air force (about 30,000), and strategic units (between 35,000 and 40,000). In short, the number of the existing military personnel would be reduced by more than 40 percent.

Speaking of the geostrategic situation of Belarus, General Kazloŭski then noted:

Most important communication lines pass across and above the Republic, and the European Community should be interested in preserving stability in our region. Avoiding the slightest displays of nuclear blackmail, *diktat*, and ultimatums in a dialogue with the West, Belarus is entitled to count on compensation for a voluntary renunciation of the status of a nuclear power. In exchange for guarantees of military-strategic security the West could offer many things. We should not be afraid of an intelligent and civilized political bargain. We should engage more boldly in a dialogue on military questions with our immediate neighbors.[14]

In March 1992 the Belarusan parliament announced its decision to create its own armed forces. "Within the next two years their numerical strength is expected to reach 90–100,000 people."[15]

Getting Rid of Tactical Nuclear Arms

From the very beginning of the formal dissolution of the Soviet Union in December 1991, the main attention of Western governments was concentrated on the nuclear arsenal of the former empire. Belarus was among the four republics possessing nuclear arms (the other three were Kazakhstan, Russia, and Ukraine). The removal of these arms was mandated by the declaration of the sovereignty and nuclear-free status of the republic.

Following long internal debates and expressions of nationalist opposition against their removal, and under pressure from the West, the parliament of Belarus decided to remove from its territory all nuclear armaments, both tactical and strategic. On January 30, 1992, Belarusan Foreign Minister Piotr Kraŭčanka informed his CSCE counterparts in Prague, "with a sense of deep satisfaction," that "by February 1 of this year the last units of tactical nuclear arms will disappear from our national territory."[16]

The deadline apparently was not met, inasmuch as Western sources reported two months later that "Belarus had transferred about seventy percent of its tactical nuclear weapons to Russia" under the terms of an agreement that all the weapons would be shipped out by July 1, 1992.[17] The latter goal was achieved ahead of time by Belarus, Kazakhstan, and Ukraine, as was reported in May: "All short-range, or tactical, nuclear weapons have already been returned to Russia by other republics where they were deployed. Russia is pledged to destroy them."[18]

Strategic Arms

Regarding strategic arms, an agreement between the United States and the four ex-Soviet nuclear republics was reached in Lisbon, Portugal, on May 23, 1992. According to its terms, Belarus, Kazakhstan, and Ukraine must destroy or transfer to Russia all strategic nuclear warheads and accede "in the shortest possible time" to the 1968 Nuclear Non-Proliferation Treaty. This agreement was an important step toward fulfillment of the Strategic Arms Reduction Treaty (START) signed by Presidents Bush and Gorbachev in July 1991, five months before the collapse of the Soviet Union. START will have to be ratified by the United States and the four ex-Soviet states before being implemented. After its ratification, the nuclear warheads on missiles and bombers in Belarus, Kazakhstan, and Ukraine must be reduced and eliminated over a seven-year period.

Meanwhile, a system of international verification and inspection will have to be put in place. Belarus and Ukraine specifically called for such a system in a letter to President Bush, sent to him because of the sensitivity of the issue. Since nuclear arms are being transferred by these republics to Russia, whose imperial ambitions and instincts are not altogether dead, the republics insist on maximum international guarantees for their security. In any case, financial and technical assistance is also sorely needed. Belarusan Foreign Minister Piotr Kraučanka warned that "evacuation of strategic nuclear weapons from Belarus could be slowed down if the West withholds certain help on which the Republic counts." The help is needed, said the minister, "for control of the export of nuclear material, decontamination of places where the weapons have been stored, and for solving social problems connected with its liquidation."[19]

"The developments today," observed the *New York Times* on May 24, 1992, "leave the United States with the prospect of having to deal by the end of the century with not four nuclear powers but just one in what was formerly the Soviet Union." An important step in that direction was made by the Supreme Council of Belarus when, on February 4, 1993, it ratified the Strategic Arms Reduction Treaty (START-I) as well as approving adherence to the Nuclear Non- Proliferation Treaty. The *New York Times* on February 8, 1993, observed editorially that Belarus was the first state in history that "committed itself to giving up ... all 81 of its nuclear-tipped SS-25 missiles." The newspaper called on Washington to "provide additional incentive for Belarus to expedite the disarming" and to "join with allies in sending a high-level aid mission to Minsk to begin working with the government on monetary and other assistance to help transform the economy."

The ratification of the START-I Treaty brought immediate results in the sphere of Belarusan-American relations. On February 9, 1993, U.S. President Bill Clinton made a telephone call to Chairman of the Belarusan parliament Stanislaŭ Šuškievič to congratulate the republic's Supreme Council on the ratification of START-I and "assured the Belarusian leader that the U.S. will provide Belarus with security guarantees." A week later, Belarus was rewarded the grant from Washington of most favored nation status in trade relations with the United States.[20]

Reality: Nuclear Hostage-Holding

Although Belarus, Kazakhstan, and Ukraine are freeing themselves of nuclear arms, they cannot be called nuclear-free states in the full sense of that term as long as they remain members of the Commonwealth of Independent States, with CIS's strategic forces on their territories. What is the status of these forces? In 1991 there were twenty-three missile bases and forty-two military airfields in Belarus.[21] How many of them will remain in the jurisdiction of Marshal Yevgeniy Shaposhnikov? (The marshal was made commander-in-chief of the CIS Unified Armed Forces by nine republics, including Belarus and Ukraine, on February 14, 1992.) Will Belarus cease being the "Western Gate" to Russia? Will Moscow forget past military marches against it from the West across Belarus?

These are geostrategic questions that the Belarusan parliament and government cannot afford to disregard. At the same time, there has been a certain duality in Miensk's political course—a vacillation between do-it-yourself independence and let's-do-it-together sovereignty—that has been influenced not only by geopolitics but by the results of the Russificatory policies of the former Soviet regime as well.[22] This observation stems partially from the realization by politicians that sovereignty in the modern world has eroded under the impact of democratic trends overflowing national borders, as exemplified by recent developments in Western Europe. Because they are aware of their European heritage, Belarusan leaders—both in the government and in the opposition—tend to model their thinking on European patterns.

The duality of Belarus's position between East and West, marked by a European proclivity, can be seen in Foreign Minister Kraŭčanka's speech at the Prague CSCE conference in January 1992. "We do not want an aggressor's military boot trampling on our lands," said the minister; "we do not want to be hostage to alien powers' nuclear ambitions or nuclear cataclysms, similar to the one in Chernobyl." At the same time, Kraŭčanka cannot see his republic as existing in the near future outside a union of former Soviet states:

> I am convinced that even if the CIS does not pass the test of endurance, the economic forces of mutual attraction and forces of reason will lead to a renewal of a similar economic and political union of eleven or some other number of states. For the next ten to fifteen years we are condemned to exist and to live together (whether someone likes it or not).[23]

ECONOMIC, POLITICAL, AND CULTURAL TIES

Within six months of Belarus's independence, the republic had been recognized by more than seventy states. Some of them were arguably prompted by the fact that Miensk was chosen as the capital of the Commonwealth of Independent States or, as Belarusan Foreign Minister Kraŭčanka hurriedly dubbed it, the "Brussels of the East." By the end of March 1992 Belarus had established diplomatic relations with thirty of

For the first time since 1921, Belarus (in 1992) has issued a postal stamp, one important attribute of the republic's sovereignty.

these states, including Australia, Brazil, China, Germany, Japan, the United States, and many other European countries.[24]

In view of the dire economic situation, the essential consideration in Miensk's flurry of diplomatic activities has been trade relations, to which Premier Viačaslaŭ Kiebič has devoted much of his traveling. Some critics have scolded him for going far afield, for traveling to such distant places as South Korea, China, Mongolia, and Thailand, where there is nothing to gain. In unison with this criticism the opposition in the Supreme Council clamors for a "return to Europe." In the parliament, Premier Kiebič responded to these voices: "As far as our paths to Europe or Asia are concerned, I think, both directions deserve our attention equally. The more so that, considering the level of economic development we now have in the area of foreign trade, a narrow path leads us to Europe while a wide road goes to Asia."[25]

Indeed, the assortment of goods that Belarus can competitively offer the saturated West European market next door is very limited. The republic would be more realistic to consider trade and other exchanges, including cultural ones, with Central and South European countries, such as Austria, Greece, and Poland, where it could find markets for both its exports and its imports. Meanwhile, certain specific trade exchanges have already been established with some distant Asian countries. Premier Kiebič's visit to China, for example, produced an accord on the barter sale of grain for which China will receive heavy trucks and potash fertilizer. China also agreed to open stores in Miensk, where Chinese goods will be sold for rubles and foreign currency.[26] What remains unclear, though, is how practical it will be to haul Belarusan goods along that "wide" and distant road to China, South Korea, or Thailand to make the exchange profitable.

Through diplomatic contacts with the European states Miensk is trying to enter the European Community, with whose world contacts and culture Belarus feels more at home. On January 30, 1992, the Republic of Belarus was accepted as a member of the Conference on Security and Cooperation in Europe. Then, on February 24, in Helsinki, Chairman of the Belarusan Parliament Stanisłaŭ Šuškievič signed the CSCE Final Act and Foreign Minister Piotr Kraŭčanka signed an agreement on cooperation between the two countries.[27] "Our goal," said Šuškievič, "is economic and political integration into the European Community while preserving and strengthening the Commonwealth of Independent States for a transitional period." He also noted that Miensk, "which today has already become the coordinating center of the Commonwealth, is prepared to take upon itself the function of an 'Eastern Brussels,' to be … the transmission link between East and West."[28]

In April 1992 a high-ranking Belarusan delegation visited Paris, where the Paris Charter for a New Europe was signed and numerous agreements were reached regarding technical and cultural cooperation.[29] Within the first seven months after Belarus proclaimed its independence, Miensk was visited by foreign ministers of France, Germany, Portugal, the United States, and other countries. Foreign Minister Kraŭčanka announced that seven Belarusan embassies would open in 1992—specifically in Belgium, Germany, Israel, Poland, South Korea, Sweden, and the United States. Nearly twenty more are planned for 1993. By mid-1992, moreover, Australia, China, Finland, Germany, Italy, Turkey, and the United States had ambassadors in Miensk.[30] On November 12, 1992, Prime Minister Kiebič was reported to have signed a document under which Belarus will open embassies and consulates in Russia, Germany, Austria, France, Belgium, Italy, Switzerland, Sweden, China, India, Kazakhstan, Latvia, Lithuania, and Ukraine before the end of the year.[31]

BELARUSAN-RUSSIAN RELATIONS

According to the Soviet census of 1989, there are 1.2 million Belarusans in the Russian Federation[32] and 1.3 million Russians in Belarus.[33] Relations between the two nationalities have been peaceful, with intermarriage a common occurrence. However, the demographic figures do not tell the entire story. There are powerful economic, military, and cultural factors, too, that keep Belarus deep in the Russian sphere of interests and influence. Historically, Moscow has viewed Belarus ("the North-Western Region," in pre-1917 terminology) as an inalienable part of Russia to be rescued and protected from a more powerful expansionist Poland. As if proof were needed, Polish expansionism has manifested itself recently in the guise of Catholicism. On the other hand, the Belarusan citizenry, steeped in Soviet dogmas about the eternal strivings of Belarusans to live together with their "Older Brother," and now frightened by the burden of Chernobyl, has been hesitant to support the drive for full separation from Russia and, for that matter, from the CIS.

Since August 1991 Belarusan-Russian relations have been shaped essentially by Belarus's economic needs and Moscow's military and strategic considerations aimed at prevention of a final disintegration of the empire. The latter constituted the basic rationale for President Yeltsin's support of Belarus's independence within the Commonwealth of Independent States. This support, however, has its limits. Soon after the emergence of the CIS, Russian Foreign Minister Andrey V. Kozyrev attended a news conference in Moscow (along with U.S. Secretary of State James A. Baker), where he stated: "Basically we do ask now for full diplomatic recognition of the independent states, those which created this commonwealth. This will help crystallize the authority which stems from the people's vote in Ukraine, Russia, and Byelorussia, and stop further disintegration."[34] To "stop further disintegration" between Russia and Belarus, Moscow imposed on Miensk an agreement concerning mutual defense. (The defense clause is notably absent from similar agreements of the Russian Federation with Ukraine and Kazakhstan, according to Piotra Sadoŭski, chairman of the Foreign Relations Committee of the Belarusan parliament.)[35]

Further Russian attempts to enwrap Belarus in a military defense network were displayed at the CIS meeting in Tashkent, Uzbekistan, in May 1992; but these efforts met with resistance. The Belarusan delegation refused to initial the three agreements dealing with collective security, chemical weapons, and border guards. Šuškievič, head of the delegation and chairman of the Belarusan parliament, explained the refusal by noting the following reasons: (1) The question of "collective defense," which in reality amounts to a military alliance, is a matter to be decided by the parliament; (2) chemical weapons are not and will not be produced in Belarus, so the issue is irrelevant; and (3) Belarus has created its own border troops.[36]

On the eve of the Tashkent conference Belarusan Foreign Minister Piotr Kraŭčanka, speaking of his republic's "unique position" as a "coordinator" of the CIS, nevertheless cautioned: "On the other hand, there are dangers of falling under the *diktat* of Russia."[37]

To some Russian leaders *diktat* comes almost instinctively. A classic example of it was an encoded telegram by Marshal Yevgeni Shaposhnikov, commander of the CIS forces, to the non-Russian republics on January 6,

1992, ordering servicemen to take the new military oath of allegiance to Russia. The noisy debates this order caused in the Belarusan parliament produced an unintended effect: "The coded telegram did something the parliamentary opposition of the BPF had not been able to achieve in many months. Even the most obstinate politicians began to incline towards the idea of Belarus's own army."[38]

Vasil Bykaŭ, the noted Belarusan writer, expressed a widely accepted view about resistance not only against the Communist mentality in Belarus but also against the Russian "imperial, nationalist thinking which accompanies it" and which, moreover, has affected even Russian democrats. "We see," says Bykaŭ, "how Russian democracy which liberated itself from Communism perhaps the most, has now found itself under the spell of an imperial mentality."[39] This state of mind creates tension, especially when territorial problems are brought up. For example, when in September 1991 President Yeltsin's press secretary said that Russia "preserves the right to raise the issue of revising the borders," observers in Miensk thought first not of Crimea, disputed between Russia and Ukraine, but of Belarus whose area was twice enlarged (in 1924 and 1926) by the inclusion of sizable segments of Belarusan ethnic territory, which had been left in the Russian Federation in 1921 in the wake of the Russo-Polish War. In November 1991 Deputy Jaŭhien Cumaraŭ alerted his colleagues in the Belarusan Supreme Council to the fact that "certain political groups in the Homiel [Gomel] Region conduct a relentless agitation among the inhabitants for holding a referendum on ... annexation to Russia."[40]

Moscow exerts an influence on Belarusan affairs not only through the "Russified" political thinking that often accompanies use of the Russian language but also through the Orthodox Church. Until 1989 Belarus constituted but one eparchy of the Russian Orthodox Church. However, due to the religious revival resulting from perestroika, the number of eparchies was increased in August 1989. Later, in February 1990, the growth of national self-awareness was reflected in the creation of the Belarusan Exarchate of the Moscow Partriarchate and the introduction of the name "Belarusan Orthodox Church" (BOC). The BOC is headed by Metropolitan Filaret (Vakhromeyev), an experienced diplomat and realistic politician of ethnic Russian background. Filaret made a number of concessions to Belarusan Orthodoxy, including institution of the Feast of All Saints of Belarus and translation of the Holy Scriptures into modern Belarusan. He even extended an official welcome to Metropolitan Mikalaj of Toronto, Canada, head of the Belarusan Autocephalous Orthodox Church (in Exile), when the latter visited Miensk in February 1992.[41]

Nevertheless, the Russian Orthodox Church in Belarus, along with a large segment of the military, remains a staunch exponent and defender of the imperial mentality. It is thus entirely conceivable that if Moscow wanted to create a disruptive situation in Belarus, it could exploit the Russophile elements in the republic to raise a host of issues, including the territorial ones.

When in March 1992 the Anticrisis Committee was established in Miensk for the defense of Belarus's sovereignty from an unnamed threat (but which was generally understood to come from Russia), it is rather telling that leaders of several dozen political organizations, including the heads of the government and the republican KGB, joined the committee. The only hold-outs were those at the helm of the Belarusan Military District (abolished shortly afterward) and the Belarusan Othodox Church.[42] Consider too, the fact that although 1.3 million Belarusans are living in the Russian Federation, many of them on Belarusan ethnic territories in the Smolensk and Bryansk areas, there are no signs of their ethnic cultural activity in terms of publications, festivals, and radio and television broadcasts. Moreover, only two self-supporting Belarusan cultural societies exist (one in Moscow and the other in St. Petersburg), whereas Belarus is teeming with Russian associations, theaters, publications, societies, and other organized bodies.

Thus Belarus, a part of "Eurasia's ethnic archipelago," is beset with a potential for conflict and violence that begs for international protection, as the *New York Times* sensibly suggested:

> Such constitutional protections need to be backed up by international guarantees, enforced by, say, NATO, the U.N. Security Council, or even some ad hoc coalition of military powers. ... The international community has a stake in the integrity of borders and in the economic and political viability of new states.[43]

BELARUSAN-POLISH RELATIONS

Unlike the numbers of Russians in Belarus and of Belarusans in Russia, the statistics concerning Poles in Belarus and Belarusans in Poland are debatable and have become a source of contention. Estimates of Belarusans in Poland vary between 150,000 and 300,000; whereas those of Poles in Belarus vary between 417,000 and 600,000.[44]

During the latter years of perestroika, Belarusan-Polish relations on the state-to-state level moved toward mutual understanding and cooperation. But this process was halted for a while when, in October 1990, Miensk raised the issue of alleged mistreatment of Belarusans in Poland's eastern province of Bielastok, thereby causing postponement of the signing of an agreement similar to those Warsaw had concluded with Kiev and Moscow. But Belarusan and Polish foreign ministers, Piotr Kraŭčanka and

Krzysztof Skubiszewski, found each other agreeable to further discussions. As a result, a Declaration on Good-Neighborly Relations and Cooperation was signed on October 10, 1991, during the visit of Belarusan Premier Viačaslaŭ Kiebič to Warsaw. The document included acceptance of the inviolability of the Polish-Belarusan border, (which had been established on August 16, 1945), as well as decisions to preserve historical and cultural monuments, widen information exchange, and enhance trade.[45]

On December 27, 1991, Poland recognized the independence of the Republic of Belarus.[46] This event led to a state visit by Premier Kiebič to Warsaw in April 1992 and the concluding of a series of agreements on political, economic, and cultural matters.

Poland is Belarus's main trading partner to the west, having replaced some of the delinquent or too-distant traders from among the CIS states. In 1991 Poland absorbed 19 percent of Belarus's exports and sold Belarus much-needed grain and sugar. Miensk has also expressed interest in using the Polish port of Gdynia, which is closer and less expensive than Ukraine's Odessa, for shipping goods. During Kiebič's visit in April 1992, an agreement concerning establishment of a Polish-Belarusan commercial bank was signed.[47]

Much more complex and tense are the nongovernmental relations between Belarus and Poland. The Belarusans living in the adjacent areas of eastern Poland, the vast majority of whom belong to the Eastern Orthodox faith, allege discrimination and at times feel threatened—especially when their churches are burned down under mysterious circumstances, as was the case in 1990.[48] On the other hand, Polish politicians and journalists have become incensed at official Miensk when it has raised the question of the Belarusan ethnic character of the Bielastok region.[49]

The problem gets more complicated on the Belarusan side of the state border, where activities of the Catholic Church and of the recently founded cultural societies have a pronounced Polish political coloration. Old clichés inherited from history are being reanimated now in the atmosphere of free expression: Whereas Eastern Orthodoxy is identified by many, either subconsciously or overtly, as the "Russian faith," Catholicism is presented as the "Polish creed." Official Moscow and Warsaw are both content with this twist of mind and have been using it for their own expansionist purposes. Occasionally, their interests seem to coincide in the face of Belarusan nationalism—a case of *divide et impera* (divide and rule). In December 1989, for example, Pope John Paul II and President Mikhail Gorbachev reached an understanding to the effect that the Vatican would send priests from Poland to work in Belarus.[50] Currently, 82 Catholic priests from Poland are engaged in pastoral activity in the Republic of Belarus. Virtually all of them are of Polish origin and possess an ideological outlook that more or less coincides with the following view expressed by the author of a "testimony" on the "Need for Ecumenism in Eastern Europe": "Catholicism and Poland have been molded from the same matter and remain in relationship to each other as God and Christ. Patriotism and Catholicism constitute a unity in the history of Poland."[51]

Polish Pope John Paul II was no less eloquent when in October 1989, after a hiatus of more than sixty years, he consecrated the first bishop for Belarus—Tadeusz Kondrusiewicz, a Belarusan-born Pole (now an archbishop with his seat in Moscow). At the consecration ceremony in St. Peter's Basilica in Rome, the pope ended his blessing of the new bishop, spoken in Italian, with a Polish-language address to the entire Polish delegation headed by then–Prime Minister Tadeusz Mazowiecki. "Gaude Mater Polonia!" exclaimed the pope. "Rejoice, Mother Poland, rejoice you sons of this land, who now have joined the fellowship of bishops of the Church of Christ in order to fulfill the apostolic mission. May God be with you, may you be accompanied on your pastoral roads by Our Lady of Jasna Gora, Queen of Poland, St. John Kenty, and all the patrons and patronesses of our Fatherland so that you may go and bring fruit."[52]

It must be pointed out that the Vatican per se is not averse to the Belarusan national revival. Radio Vatican has been broadcasting in Belarusan since the 1950s. Pope John Paul II has used the Belarusan language and demonstrated his support of Belarusanness on several occasions. And Belarusan cultural activities in Poland (a weekly newspaper, schools, radio broadcasts, etc.) receive financial support from the Polish government. But the "fruit" that Polish priests are bringing to Belarus is another matter altogether. For most of those priests, the Catholic creed and the Polish language are as indissoluble as God and Christ. And language in this case means nationality. Claims by many Poles in Poland and Belarus that Catholicism means Polishness have caused a flood of denunciatory articles in the Belarusan press. "Missionaries or Agitators?" asked the newspapers of BPF, alleging that "contemporary Catholic priests distinguish themselves by an open pro-Polish orientation."[53] And "Polish Flags Have Become an Inseparable Part of Catholic Churches," reads the heading of a speech at an all-republican conference of the Belarusan Language Association in Miensk.[54]

Priests, as a rule, hold sway over the sentiments of their parishioners. In most cases spiritual shepherds are obeyed and emulated. For this reason, public support for the Belarusan language in church life, in both Orthodox and Catholic parishes, has been sparse and Belarusization superficial. Identification of Orthodoxy with Russianness and Catholicism with

Polishness is deep-seated in the popular mind. In fact, Belarusan renewal is an uphill struggle precisely because it has to deal with the heavy burden of past centuries—a burden not easily discarded.

However, there were some signs in the latter half of 1992 indicating that the heads of both the Orthodox and Catholic churches in Belarus were coming to terms with the idea of a Belarusan political state. Thus Metropolitan Filaret, the exarch of the Moscow Patriarch in Belarus and a native Russian, in a letter (dated October 30, 1992) to this author, expressed his wish for "fruitful work so that our Belarusan language may always resound and our independent Belarus may flourish." On the other side, Archbishop Kazimir Sviontak, who, in January 1992, replaced Bishop Tadeusz Kondrusiewicz as the leader of Belarusan Catholics, was reported "to favor the national renewal of Belarus." The archbishop uses the Belarusan language in public prayers and in August 1992 prohibited his priests and parishioners "from 'decorating' Catholic churches with attributes (flags, coats-of-arms, portraits of presidents) of a neighboring state." The "principledness" of the archbishop evoked "displeasure in those who would like to transform the Catholic church into a Polish shop."[55]

One may assume that continuing clashes between Belarusan national interests and Polish Catholicism in Belarus will be resolved with more efficiency and permanency now that the Vatican and the Republic of Belarus have established diplomatic relations "desiring to develop their mutual and friendly relations."[56]

BELARUSAN-UKRAINIAN RELATIONS

According to the Soviet census of 1979, there were 231,000 Ukrainians in Belarus and more than 406,000 Belarusans in Ukraine.[57] Friendly relations between the two nationalities, who over the centuries have faced similar adversities in their struggle for self-assertion, have been marked by political solidarity during the perestroika years as well. However, because of the more advanced national development of Ukraine (a result of geography, history, and its considerably larger demographic base) the political course undertaken by Kiev has been "too radical" for official Miensk. Belarusan Foreign Minister Piotr Kraŭčanka explained to a Belarusan-American audience in New York in February 1992 that his government cannot conduct a policy vis-à-vis Russia similar to that of Ukraine because Belarus is eight times more economically dependent on Russia than is Ukraine. And because Russia and Ukraine are Belarus's two principal trading partners, this dependency explains the distance that Miensk officially maintains in the face of the contentious relations between Russia and Ukraine over the Black Sea fleet, Crimea, the economy, nuclear arms, and other important matters. Also, herein lies the reason for which the Belarusan press is reticent not only on Ukrainian-Russian issues but also on the subject of Belarusan-Ukrainian relations in general, including the day-to-day lives of the two minorities in each of the republics.

During the perestroika years of the pre-independence period, Belarusan-Ukrainian cooperation developed along unofficial lines. For instance, the leaders of the national fronts of both republics, together with their conterparts from the three Baltic states (Estonia, Latvia, and Lithuania), held several conferences on a grand project of the so-called Baltic to Black Sea Union. At one such meeting, held in Miensk on November 23–24, 1990, the five sides, having pronounced "the lack of a perspective for the continued existence of the USSR," expressed their demand for a withdrawal of Soviet troops from the Baltic–to–Black Sea region and agreed on establishing a commonwealth of the five states.[58]

The traditional Belarusan-Ukrainian closeness has survived the bumps and strains of the transformation. The imperial danger emanating from the Kremlin and the large Russian minorities in both republics has dictated a delicate solidarity.

Indeed, Ukraine was the first among the states to establish diplomatic relations with the Republic of Belarus.[59] Having proclaimed their independence one after another (on August 24, 1991, in Kiev, and the next day in Miensk), the two republics exchanged ratified copies of a treaty of friendship and cooperation within ten days.[60]

To allay the economic shock caused by the transition to a free market, Belarus and Ukraine signed an agreement in October 1991 on "principles of economic cooperation between the enterprises and organizations of the two sovereign republics for 1992." They also published an "Appeal" to their industrial leaders and working collectives, asking them "to create a Most Favored Nation climate while negotiating contracts about supplying technical and consumer goods."[61]

In March 1992, as the economic fabric of the former Soviet republics was further unraveling, the Ukrainian parliament responded to Russia's "liberalization" of prices by deciding on a complete withdrawal from the ruble and the introduction of its own currency. "Ukraine: A Course for Separation," alerted *Zviazda*, as a warning to its readers against an influx into the republic of worthless "Ukrainian" rubles. Of course, good-neighborly relations should dictate a civilized way of handling such matters as a change in national currency. But after all, the newspaper concluded, "One must take into consideration human psychology which had been shaped in the former Union and oriented toward the fact that the State will cheat you in any event. Be it Ukrainian or Belarusan. ..."[62]

A high-ranking Belarusan delegation visited Kiev in April 1992 to prevent, to the extent possible, any manifestations of this "human psychology." On the agenda were balance of payments, property rights, supply contracts, and the mutual exchange of trade representations.[63]

BELARUSAN-LITHUANIAN RELATIONS

The Soviet census of 1979 indicated that there were 58,000 Belarusans in Lithuania and nearly 7,000 Lithuanians in Belarus.[64] The latter figure has been disputed by unofficial Lithuanian sources that claim "at least 30,000" Lithuanians in Belarus[65] and others "up to 50,000."[66]

As described in Chapter 1, the history of the Belarusan and Lithuanian peoples has been inextricably intertwined along the lines of ethnogenesis, terminology, institutions, and territory. Between the last two world wars, the Belarusan-Lithuanian border was changed or obliterated by the Russians and the Poles without any consultation with the local inhabitants. The consequences of these violent territorial settlements and of the forcible "acculturation" of the local population brought normalization of Belarusan-Lithuanian relations in the post-Soviet period to a bumpy start. Subservient to Moscow, the Presidium of the Belarusan Supreme Council reacted to Lithuania's proclamation of independence on March 11, 1990, by claiming the Vilnia region as part of Belarusan ethnic territory. The Belarusan Popular Front, including its group of Supreme Council deputies, in solidarity with the Lithuanian independent movement, Sajudis, denounced its government's territorial claim as "political blackmail" and dispatched a delegation to Vilnia where, together with a group of Lithuanian parliamentarians, a common "Statement" was issued. In it the authors wrote that "the city of Vilnia has, since the times of the Grand Duchy of Lithuania, been the cultural center of both peoples" and that "the Vilnia region from ancient times has been an area of settlement and ethnic contacts of Belarusans and Lithuanians" who, however, because of Polonization and Russification, "had and have experienced difficulty in defining and preserving their national identity."

The "Statement" recommended a solution to the problem: Maintain the territorial status quo, but mutually guarantee "creation and support [each side for the other] of schools, publications, radio and TV programs, national cultural centers and societies" as well as bilateral cultural organizations and publications.[67]

When in January 1992 Lithuanian President Vytautas Landsbergis and his Belarusan counterpart, Stanislaŭ Šuškievič, met in Miensk for a working session, they agreed on the need for the "free development of the culture of national minorities" and struck a common position vis-à-vis Polish expansion in their territories. First, the two leaders rejected the idea of local autonomy for national minorities in their republics (such autonomy being an outcome the Poles would like to see in Lithuania and, potentially, in Belarus). Second, they recognized that "interethnic tensions could be caused by attempts to interpret confessional particularities as national-ethnic" (e.g., "the Polish faith").[68] Third, both leaders claimed that the Polish minority in Lithuania consists fundamentally of indigenous inhabitants, who consider themselves Poles exclusively because of their Catholic religion (the everyday language of these "Poles" is a dialect of Belarusan).

But the squabble does not end there. Now, Belarusans and Lithuanians have to settle an argument among themselves as to the ethnic authenticity of these people: Are they Belarusans or Slavicized Lithuanians? Obviously, Lithuanian authorities and Belarusan organizations in Vilnia do not see eye to eye here. Slowly, however, the two sides, facing a more aggressive Polish expansionism, have been moving toward an understanding that includes mutual concessions. The Belarusans in Lithuania have their cultural societies in Vilnia as well as radio and television broadcasts that are partially funded by the state. At the same time, in some primary schools in Belarus along the Lithuanian border, the Lithuanian language is being taught to children and Lithuanian Catholic priests serve in Belarusan parishes.

The road to cooperation is not entirely smooth, however. In February 1992, for example, to the surprise of many, Western agencies reported Belarusan Foreign Minister Kraŭčanka's "claim to Lithuania's border territory" along with a complaint that the Lithuanians "had refused to negotiate."[69] However, Kraŭčanka's statement, whatever its purpose, was immediately countered by Belarusan Supreme Council Chairman Šuškievič, who "denied reports that Belarus is claiming part of Lithuanian territory."[70]

While the issue of overlapping territorial claims and counterclaims (with dissemination of appropriate maps as a backup) continues to be hotly debated in Belarusan, Lithuanian, and Polish publications, the governments in Miensk and Vilnia are prudently laying the foundation for a civilized solution to their knotty bilateral relations. The latest chapter in this process was the signing in April 1992 of an Agreement on Principles of Trade and Economic Cooperation between the two republics. Belarusan Premier Kiebič and Lithuanian President Landsbergis also discussed the issue of the common border, which has never been demarcated precisely and is now being worked on by a bilateral commission.[71]

The relations between the two republics have improved since the November 1992 victory in Lithuania's parliamentary elections by the Democratic Labor Party (former Communists), led by Algirdas Brazauskas. The visit to Belarus by Brazauskas in December 1992 was followed by the establishment of diplomatic relations between the two countries.

BELARUSAN-LATVIAN RELATIONS

According to the Soviet census of 1979, there were 112,000 Belarusans in Latvia and 2,617 Latvians in Belarus.[72] As is true of Lithuania and the Bielastok region in Poland, most of the Belarusans in Latvia living on the other side of the state border are of local origin. Those in Riga came later, during the Soviet period. Many Belarusans came to Latvia immediately after the end of World War II from West Belarus, either to escape persecution or in remembrance of the fact that people from the former Polish state, of which they were a neglected part, used to travel to Latvia to work there.

The Latvians, who in their republic constitute a majority of only 52.5 percent (34 percent are Russians), have been restrictive in their requirements for citizenship and strict in their enforcement of cultural legislation. As a result, some non-Latvians, including Belarusans, have complained of discrimination. To avoid any territorial claims (in view of the fact that the Belarusan-Latvian border has not been demarcated precisely), a mixed commission started work on the issue of the border at the beginning of 1992.

Miensk is interested in maintaining good relations with Latvia as a matter both of principle and economics. In December 1991, Latvian Prime Minister Ivars Godmanis, inspired by similar motives, came to Miensk to sign an accord regarding fulfillment of the supply agreements for 1992. The daily *Zviazda* responded by observing: "The northern neighbor is for our land a window onto the Baltic Sea and Northern Europe, and a fitting partner with a developed economy."[73] Soon after, a trip to Riga was made by a Belarusan delegation headed by Supreme Council Chairman Stanislaŭ Šuškievič and the signing of a Declaration of Principles of Good-Neighborly Relations that recognized not only the sovereignty of both countries but also their pledge of noninterference. The Belarusan delegation was especially gratified by the prospect of leasing sea docks in Latvia for a Belarusan fishing fleet, as well as by the designation of transit routes for its overseas imports and exports.[74] These steps were followed by a protocol signing in Riga in April 1992 pertaining to the establishment of diplomatic relations. A similar agreement was also concluded with Estonia.[75]

BELARUSAN-JEWISH RELATIONS

The first Jewish communities appeared in the Belarusan cities of Hrodna (Grodno) and Biareście (Brest) at the end of the fourteenth century. Later, the number of Jews settled throughout Belarus increased to 350,000 in 1863, 890,000 in 1897, and to 1,250,000 in 1914 (This last figure represented about 14 percent of the entire population.)[76]

At the end of the nineteenth century and during the postrevolutionary years before World War II, Jews were the second largest ethnic group in Belarus, making up between 50 and 60 percent of the population of Belarusan cities and towns. However, as a result of the genocide during World War II and their emigration in the latter years, their numbers have sharply declined. According to the Soviet census of 1989, Jews were the fifth largest group in the republic, numbering 112,000 (1.1 percent of the population).[77]

Belarusan-Jewish relations have traditionally been favorable, primarily because of the socioeconomic function served by Jewish middlemen and artisans in relation to the largely rural Belarusan segment of the population. This long symbiotic cohabitation had not been without impact on the character of Belarusan Jews. As noted by Samuil Agurski, a professor at Hebrew University and son of a Belarusan-born revolutionary and historian: "Belarusan Jews in their shtetl-deep mass were able to make close contact with Belarusans and appropriate some of their spiritual qualities, such as benevolence, trust, patience, and tolerance."[78] Another factor contributing to the peaceful and businesslike relations between Belarusans and Jews is their shared historical background: Both groups were discriminated against by uncongenial political regimes serving either Polish or Russian imperial interests. Over the last century, moreover, Belarusan culture and the cause of national renewal have been enhanced by such Jewish talents as painters Marc Chagall, Yuri Pen, and Barys Žaboraŭ, sculptor Zair Azhur, writer Žmitrok Biadula, and literary critic Ryhor Biarozkin.

Perestroika itself has further enhanced Belarusan-Jewish relations. Strains caused by the anti-Semitism of the old totalitarian regime are now being allayed. Direct contacts between Belarus and Israel have been established for the first time in history. And a new cultural society, "Belarus-Israel," became active in 1992, with Leanid Levin, Distinguished Architect of the republic, at its head.[79]

In November 1991 Prime Minister Kiebič and a group of Supreme Council deputies took part in a Jewish religious ceremony in the city of Valožyn, famous for its yeshiva. Following the ceremony, which commemorated the dead at a Jewish cemetery that had fallen into disrepair, the premier promised to restore the cemetery.[80] Meanwhile, one can observe not only more public openness in discussions of anti-Semitism but also greater displays of friendliness toward the Jewish population. For example, the newspaper *Zviazda*, writing on behalf of the Supreme Council and the Council of Ministers, greeted its readership on January 1, 1992, in Belarusan, Russian, Polish, Ukrainian, and Yiddish. (All except Ukrainian were official languages in Soviet Belarus during the 1920s.) In addition, Jews have been freely emigrating from Belarus, for the most part to Israel.

In May 1992, a high-ranking Belarusan delegation visited Israel. On the eve of his departure for Israel, Prime Minister Viačaslaŭ Kiebič expressed hope that his republic would be able to develop cooperation with Israel in a number of fields, including conversion of military plants, trade, agriculture, health care, and tourism. The visit resulted in the establishment of diplomatic relations between the two states. Belarus has the distinction of being the country where many outstanding Israelis were born, among them David Ben-Gurion, Golda Meir, Menachem Begin, and former premier of Israel, Itzhak Shamir. The latter visited his native city of Pružany at the invitation of the Belarusan government in September 1992. A month earlier, his successor in the premiership, Shimon Peres, visited Belarus as Israel's foreign minister.

Jewish cultural and social life in independent Belarus has entered a new and more dynamic phase. The daily *Zviazda* of October 16, 1992, quoted Alexandr Halperin, a representative of the Jewish communities in the republic, as saying that "in Belarus a process of rebirth of Jewish life is actively developing." There were at that time "nearly seventy" Jewish organizations of which half were "republicwide."

BELARUS WITHIN THE CONTEXT OF THE WORLD

In the modern world—particularly in the context of the complex passage of Eastern Europe from communism to democracy, threatened by the disruptive forces of chauvinism—Belarus can be viewed as a laboratory of changes, to which a careful evolutionary approach must be taken. Located in the geographic middle of the European continent and straddling the East and West, Belarus has been the arena for hundreds of military battles and encounters of sundry tongues and creeds. By necessity, the Belarusan people have become deeply imbued with a tolerance of other people's views and needs. Their historical experience demonstrates that force and violence do not solve problems but, rather, only postpone and aggravate them. This experience has translated into political cautiousness, gradualism, and an evolutionary methodology in solving problems. One of the best examples of this deliberate approach is the 1990 "Law About Languages," which allows up to ten years to learn Belarusan. Taught throughout their history by suffering and sacrifice, the Belarusans have indeed developed a deep sense of humanity. A common appeal among them, when asking an unresponsive fellow for a favor, is "Please be human"(*Nu, budź ty čalaviekam*). It is no accident that Vasil Bykaŭ (Bykov), foremost contemporary Belarusan author, depicts in his World War II novellas a central is-

Concert at the site of the ruins of the old castle in Navahradak in the summer of 1992. Photo by Siarhiej Hryc. Courtesy of *Narodnaja hazieta* (People's newspaper).

sue of our times: the preservation of one's humanity in the face of savage war.

Of modest size and economic potential on the world scale, Belarus epitomizes both the woes of history and the predicaments of the modern age. It lost more than 2 million people to Stalinist genocide and as many more in the whirlwind of World War II. Twenty-five percent of its present-day population of more than 10 million, including 800,000 children, live in an area affected by 70 percent of the nuclear fallout from Chernobyl. Yet amidst all its shortages and dire needs, and beset by a burdensome legacy of yesteryear that has significantly slowed progress, the republic continues to display an overall calmness (sometimes mistakenly interpreted as meekness and docility) that could well serve as an example for others.

The Belarusan capital of Miensk has been selected as the coordinating center for the Commonwealth of Independent States and as the site of a UNICEF regional office. As a beneficial result of these events, and of perestroika more generally, the outside world is finally beginning to become acquainted with this East European nation that had been all but hidden in the shadow of a military superpower. Emerging from behind the information curtain as an independent state, Belarus will gradually present itself to the world in all of its colors and shades, offering humanity both its historic experience and its peaceful nature.

NOTES

1. *Viedamasci Viarchoŭnaha Savieta Respubliki Bielaruś* (Proceedings of the Supreme Soviet of the Republic of Belarus), No. 30 (Minsk: Supreme Council of the Republic of Belarus, 1991), pp. 31–32

2. *Declaration of State Sovereignty of the Byelorussian Socialist Republic adopted by the Supreme Soviet of the BSSR on July 27, 1990,* Press Release of the UN Mission of the Byelorussian Soviet Socialist Republic (n.d.).

3. *Statement by Pyotr K. Kravchanka, Minister for Foreign Affairs of the Republic of Belarus in the General Debate at the 46th Session of the United Nations General Assembly* (Minsk: Bielaruś, 1991), p. 24.

4. *Litaratura i Mastactva* (Literature and art), Minsk, March 20, 1992.

5. *Zviazda* (Star), Minsk, March 28, 1992.

6. *Narodnaja hazieta* (People's newspaper), Minsk, February 18, 1992.

7. Roman Solchanyk, "Ukraine and Russia: The Politics of Independence,"*RFE/RL Research Report*, Vol. 1, No. 19 (Munich, May 8, 1991), p. 15.

8. FBIS-SOV-92-030, February 13, 1992, p. 81.

9. FBIS-SOV-92-032, February 18, 1992, p. 60.

10. *Le Monde,* quoted by FBIS-SOV-92-037, February 25, 1992, p. 62. Deputy Uladzimir Hrybanaŭ (Gribanov), who has the military rank of a major, specifies a much higher figure. In an interview, he said: "According to my calculations, there are 400,000 military personnel on the territory of Belarus. The statistics of the Commander of the [Military] District, General Kostenko, reduces the number to 180,000." See *Narodnaja hazieta,* January 17, 1992.

11. *Zviazda,* February 13, 1992.

12. FBIS-SOV-92-032, February 18, 1992, p. 60.

13. *Narodnaja hazieta,* February 18, 1992.

14. *Belta,* Minsk, April 21, 1992.

15. Moscow Teleradiokompaniya Ostankino, Television First Program, in Russian March 19, 1992; text quoted in FBIS-SOV-92-055, March 20, 1992, p. 72.

16. *Litaratura i Mastactva,* March 20, 1992.

17. *New York Times,* April 1, 1992.

18. *New York Times,* May 24, 1992.

19. *Zviazda,* March 28, 1992.

20. FBIS-SOV-93-027, February 11, 1993, p. 39; and FBIS-SOV-93-032, February 19, 1993, p. 50.

21. *Naviny BNF* (News of the BPF), Miensk, September 6, 1991.

22. A poll conducted in February 1992 in twenty-five localities of Belarus asked the question: "Do you agree that in order to solve the crisis the Republic must quit the CIS?" The results indicated that 61.0 percent of the respondents were against quitting, 15.7 percent were in favor of quitting, 18. 9 percent had difficulty answering, and 4.7 percent were partially for and against quitting. See *Respublika,* Minsk, February 19, 1992.

23. *Litaratura i Mastactva,* March 20, 1992.

24. *Čyrvonaja zmiena* (Red generation), Minsk, March 23–29, 1992.

25. *Siomaja siesija Viarchoŭnaha Savieta Respubliki Bielarus Dvanaccataha sklikannia* (Seventh Session of the Twelfth Supreme Council of the Republic of Belarus), Bulletin No. 5 (Minsk: Supreme Council, 1991), p. 20.

26. *Izvestiya,* February 8, 1992; text quoted in FBIS-SOV-92-030, February 13, 1992, p. 82.

27. *Interfax News Bulletin,* February 26, 1992.

28. *TASS,* Minsk, February 24, 1992

29. *Narodnaja hazieta,* April 10, 1992.

30. FBIS-SOV-92-052, March 17, 1992.

31. FBIS-SOV-92-219, November 12, 1992.

32. *Argumenty i fakty* (Arguments and facts), No. 33 (Moscow, August 18–24, 1990).

33. H. I. Kaspiarovič, "Etnademahrafičnyja pracesy i mižnacyjanalnyja adnosiny ŭ BSSR" (Ethnodemographic processes and interethnic relations in the BSSR), *Viesci AN BSSR. Sieryja hramadskich navuk* (Proceedings of the Academy of Sciences of the BSSR: Social sciences series), No. 5 (Minsk: Academy of Sciences of the BSSR, 1990), p. 83.

34. *New York Times,* December 16, 1991.

35. *Naviny BNF,* No. 6 (September 1991).

36. *Belta,* Minsk, n.d. (reported by correspondent Vladimir Glod).

37. *Zviazda,* Minsk, May 16, 1992.

38. *Narodnaja hazieta,* January 10, 1992.

39. *Litaratura i Mastactva,* February 7, 1992.

40. *Zviazda,* November 13, 1991.

41. Thomas E. Bird, "Religion and Nation-Building in Today's Belarus," paper presented at the Belarusan Session of the conference of the Canadian Association of Slavists, Charlottetown, Prince Edward Island, June 3, 1992, pp. 3–4.

42. *Čyrvonaja zmiena,* March 23–29, 1992.

43. *New York Times* (Editorial), June 8, 1992.

44. For information regarding the number of Poles in Belarus, see Kaspiarovič, *op. cit.,* p. 83; and *Bielarus* (The Belarusan), No. 384 (New York, November 1991.)

45. *Narodnaja hazieta,* October 17, 1991.

46. *Narodnaja hazieta,* February 12, 1992.

47. *Zviazda,* April 25, 1992.

48. *Bielarus,* No. 377 (New York, January 1991).

49. *Bielarus,* No. 376 (New York, December 1990).

50. Bird, *op. cit.,* p. 2.

51. Eugene Mannoni, "O Potrzebie ekumenizmu w Europie Wschodniej" (About the need for ecumenism in Eastern Europe), *Libertas,* No. 1 (Paris, 1984), p. 91.

52. *L'Osservatore Romano,* Rome, October 22, 1989.

53. *Naviny BNF,* No. 7 (November 1991).

54. *Litaratura i Mastactva,* May 29, 1992.

55. *Litaratura i Mastactva,* August 28, 1992.

56. *Osservatore Romano,* Weekly Edition, No. 46 (November 18, 1992).

57. *Etnahrafija Bielarusi. Encyklapiedyja* (Minsk: Belarusan Soviet Encyclopedia, 1989), pp. 59, 504.

58. *Sovetskaya Belorussiya,* Minsk, October 15, 1991. Publication of the resolutions adopted at the Miensk conference was delayed in the Belarusan press by almost a year because of Communist censorship.

59. *Čyrvonaja zmiena,* March 23–29, 1992.

60. *Zviazda,* September 3, 1991.

61. *Zviazda,* October 31, 1991.

62. *Zviazda,* March 28, 1992.

63. *Zviazda,* April 8, 1992.

64. *Etnahrafija Bielarusi. Encyklapiedyja,* pp. 59, 292.

65. Jonas Papartis, "*Samizdat* Report on Lithuanian Minority in Belorussia," Radio Liberty Research (RL 102/79), Munich, Germany, March 26, 1979, p. 4.

66. Julian Birch, "Border Disputes and Disputed Borders in the Soviet Federal System," *Nationalities Papers,* Vol. 15, No. 1 (New York, Spring 1987), p. 60.

67. *Naviny BNF,* No. 2 (Miensk, April 23, 1990).

68. *Sovetskaya Belorussiya,* January 9, 1992.

69. *Reuters,* Minsk, February 24, 1992.

70. *RFE/RL Daily Report,* No. 39 (Munich, February 26, 1992), p. 3.

71. *Zviazda,* April 4, 1992.

72. *Etnahrafija Bielarusi. Encyklapiedyja,* pp. 59, 286.

73. *Zviazda,* December 12, 1991.

74. *Zviazda,* December 17, 1991.

75. *Narodnaja hazieta,* April 9, 1992.

76. *Etnahrafija Bielarusi. Encyklapiedyja,* p. 556.

77. Kaspiarovič, *op. cit.,* p. 83.

78. *Litaratura i Mastactva,* October 18, 1991.

79. *Holas Radzimy* (Voice of the homeland), February 20, 1992.

80. *Zviazda,* November 12, 1991.

APPENDIX

Major Dates in Belarusan History

With Some References to Western History

6th–7th centuries: Penetration of Slavs into the territory of future Belarus, already settled by Baltic tribes.

8th–9th centuries: Massive settlements of East Slavic tribes (Kryvičans, Drehovičans, and Radzimičans) on the territory of Belarus and their assimilation of the Balts.

800: Charlemagne crowned emperor in Rome.

862: First mention of Polacak (Polotsk) in the chronicle *Tale of the Bygone Years.*

10th century: The city of Polacak (Polotsk) in Northern Belarus becomes the predominant center of power on Belarusan territory, competing with Novgorod and Kiev.

962: Otto the Great of Germany (936–973) crowned in Rome as ruler of the "Holy Roman Empire."

976–1025: Byzantium at the peak of its power under Emperor Basil II.

980(?): Death of Prince Rahvalod at the hands of Vladimir of Novgorod, the future Kievan overlord. (Rahvalod was the first known ruler of Polacak and the father of Rahnieda, whom Prince Vladimir forced to become his wife.)

980: First mention of the city of Turaŭ in a chronicle.

987: Accession of Hugh Capet to the throne in Paris marks the founding of France.

988: Christianization of Kiev by Prince Vladimir (Volodymyr).

992: Polacak becomes the seat of a diocese.

ca. 1000: Death of Princess Rahnieda, divorced by Vladimir and exiled from Kiev to the town of Iziaslaŭ (in Belarus), named after their first-born son.

1003–1004: Rule in Polacak of Iziaslaŭ's son, Prince Bračyslaŭ, who extends his principality's territory eastward in a struggle with Novgorod and Kiev.

1019: First mention of the city of Bieraście (Brest) in the chronicle *Tale of the Bygone Years.*

1044–1101: Rule in Polacak of Bračyslaŭ's son, Usiaslaŭ, an outstanding figure in Belarusan history.

1044–1066: Erection in Polacak of St. Sophia Cathedral to match similar buildings in Novgorod and Kiev, as a symbol of independent power.

1054: Formal schism between Greek and Roman churches.

1067: The bloody Battle of Niamiha near Miensk (Minsk) between the army of Prince Usiaslaŭ and the coalition of Kievan princes (described in the classic poem *The Lay of Igor's Host*).

First mention of the city of Orša (Orsha) in the chronicle *Tale of the Bygone Years*.

1095: First Crusade preached by Pope Urban II.

1097: First mention of the city of Pinsk in the chronicle *Tale of the Bygone Years*.

Meeting of princes in Liubech reconfirms independence of all Ruśian principalities from the Kievan center.

12th century: Break-up of the Polacak principality into several appanages, which war among themselves and against Kiev.

1120–1173: Life of St. Euphrosyne, granddaughter of Prince Usiaslaŭ.

ca. 1130–ca. 1182: Life of St. Kiryla (Cyril), bishop of Turaŭ.

1161: Craftsman Lazar Bohša makes a gem-studded cross for Princess Euphrosyne (later canonized) that will become the most cherished national relic in Belarus. (The cross disappeared during World War II.)

1180s: First expeditions of German missionaries up the Dvina River. (The missionaries obtained permission from "King Waldemar" [Uladzimier] of Polacak to proselytize among the Livs.)

1201: German missionaries found the city of Riga, Latvia's capital today.

1202: The religious order of the Knights of the Sword established by the Germans in Riga to spearhead Christianization; armed clashes between Polacak and the German knights.

1204: Sack of Byzantium by the Crusaders and establishment of the Latin Empire in the East.

1210: Peace treaty between Bishop Albert of Riga and Prince Uladzimier of Polacak.

1214: Polacak loses to the Knights of the Sword its western vassal cities (Kukenois and Hercyke) on the banks of the Dvina.

1215: Magna Carta signed in England.

1228: Polish Prince Konrad of Mazovia invites to his realm the German Christian warriors known as the Knights of the Cross, who make constant military incursions into Lithuanian, Belarusan, and Muscovite lands.

1236: Military debacle of the Knights of the Cross in Lithuania at the Battle of Siauliai.

1237: Merger of the Knights of the Sword and the Knights of the Cross into one Teutonic Order.

1240: Destruction of Kiev by the Mongols.

1240–1263: Rule of Mindoŭh (Mindaugas), who consolidates east Lithuanian and west Belarusan territories into the Grand Duchy of Lithuania and Ruś, with a capital in Navahradak.

1300: Dante and Giotto mark dawn of the Renaissance.

1315–1341: Rule of Grand Duke Hedymin (Gediminas), who transfers the capital of the Grand Duchy of Lithuania and Ruś from Navahradak to Vilnia (Vilnius) in 1323.

1341–1377: Rule of Grand Duke Alhierd (Algirdas), who expands eastward the territory of his duchy, thereby clashing with neighboring Muscovy.

1374 (or 1375): Elevation of Kipryjan by Constantinople to the rank of metropolitan of the Grand Duchy of Lithuania and Ruś in counteraction to the Metropolitan of Moscow.

1385: Alhierd's son, Grand Duke Jahaila (also known as Jogailo or Jagiello; baptized Wladyslaw, 1385–1434), concludes a personal union with Poland by marrying the Polish queen and promising to Catholicize Lithuania.

1387: King Jahaila's first charter favoring Catholic lords.

The city of Vilnia is granted self-rule privilege.

1388–1392: King Jahaila's nephew, Vitaŭt (Vytautas or Witold), fights the king's brother, Skirhaila, over the rule of the Grand Duchy.

1390: Self-government bestowed on the city of Bieraście (Brest).

1391: Self-government bestowed on the city of Hrodna (Grodno).

1392: Grand Duke Vitaŭt (d. in 1430) recognized by King Jahaila as the independent ruler of the Grand Duchy.

1410: The great Battle of Grunwald, during which the united armies of Poland and the GDL crush the Germans of the Teutonic Order.

1415: Act of Horodlo furthers the union of the GDL with Poland and confirms privileges of the Catholic lords vis-à-vis those belonging to the Orthodox Church.

A council of Orthodox bishops in Navahradak consecrates Ryhor Tsamblak as the metropolitan of the Grand Duchy of Lithuania and Ruś.

Burning of John Hus, Czech forerunner of Protestantism.

1432, 1434, 1447: Royal charters establish equality of feudal lords of both Catholic and Orthodox confessions.

1453: In France, end of the One Hundred Years' War.

In Byzantium (Constantinople), conquest by the Ottoman Turks.

1458: The Kievan Metropolitanate with its seat in Navahradak becomes separate from Muscovy, where an independent Metropolitanate has been in existence since 1448.

1468: King Kazimir's Code of Laws (*Statut Kazimira*), the first code of criminal and procedural laws of the Grand Duchy of Lithuania (written in Belarusan) in which punishment is individualized.

1472: Grand Duke Ivan III of Muscovy takes a Byzantine wife, and Moscow is soon proclaimed the "Third Rome."

1480: Muscovy free of the Tatar dependency.

1492: Columbus reaches America, initiating the Spanish overseas empire.

1494: To prevent border clashes with the Muscovites, the GDL's Grand Duke Alexander marries Helene, daughter of the ruler of Muscovy.

1498: Self-government privilege granted to Polacak.

1499: Self-government privilege granted to Miensk.

1500: Beginning of defensive wars of the Grand Duchy of Lithuania, Ruś, and Samogitia against Muscovy.

early 16th century: First Belarusan printing shop founded in Vilnia.

1514: Battle near Orša, where an 80,000-strong Muscovite army is crushed by the much smaller force of the GDL and Poland—a date celebrated in today's Belarus.

1517: Luther's *Ninety-Five Theses* precipitate the Protestant Reformation.

1517–1519: Francišak Skaryna (ca. 1490–1552?) of Polacak translates and publishes the Bible in the Belarusan vernacular in Prague.

1523: Publication in Cracow of Nicolai Husoŭski's *Carmen de Bisontis* (in Latin), a classic poetic description of the times.

1529: Adoption by the Diet of the GDL of the first code of laws, the "Statute of the Grand Duchy of Lithuania," written in Belarusan.

ca. 1538–1593: Life of Symon Budny, an ardent propagator of the Reformation in Belarus.

ca. 1538–1603(?): Life of Vasil Ciapinski, translator into Belarusan of certain books of the New Testament.

1540: Society of Jesus (Jesuits) founded by Ignatius Loyola.

1543: *The Revolutions of Heavenly Bodies,* by Poland's Nicolas Kopernik, marks the advent of modern science.

1558–1583: The Livonia War of Muscovy's Ivan the Terrible is waged, with the aim of gaining access to the Baltic Sea.

1560s: Wave of conversion of Belarusan gentry to Calvinism.

1563: Polacak occupied by the Russian army; civil population and Jews massacred.

Issuance of a royal charter making the rights of Orthodox subjects equal to those belonging to the Catholic Church, thus reinforcing the striving of the Orthodox gentry for a fuller union with Poland.

1566: Second edition of the "Statute of the Grand Duchy of Lithuania."

1569: Political union of the Grand Duchy of Lithuania, Ruś, and Samogitia with Poland; establishment of the Commonwealth of Poland.

Arrival of the first Jesuits in Vilnia; start of the Counter-Reformation in the GDL.

1577: Mahileŭ (Mogilev) receives a charter of self-government.

1579: Polacak taken back from Muscovites by the army of King Stefan Batory.

Founding of the Vilnia Academy (later, Vilnia University) by the Jesuits.

1581: Establishment of the Tribunal of the GDL, an appellate court that fortified the rights of the gentry by virtually annulling the legal immunity of the great magnates.

Pinsk receives a charter of self-government.

Jesuit college opened in Polacak.

1584: Jesuit college opened in Niaśviž.

First Orthodox Brotherhood established in Vilnia (an example followed by other cities) to promote education among the Orthodox and to counteract the missionary activities of the Catholic Church.

1588: Promulgation of the third, revised and enlarged edition of the "Statute of the Grand Duchy of Lithuania," which remains in force in the Russian Empire until 1840.

Defeat of the Spanish Armada.

Elizabethan England flourishes.

1589: Establishment of the Moscow Patriarchate, which proceeds to claim allegiance of the Orthodox population of the GDL.

Introduction of *Liberum Veto* rule into the Commonwealth of Poland, where the Diet can pass laws only by unanimity; as a result, the legislative process is effectively paralyzed and the state is weakened.

1596: Establishment of the Uniate Church in the GDL by the Council of Brest, whereby the Orthodox hierarchy recognizes the authority of Rome while preserving the Eastern Rite in the Liturgy.

1597: Viciebsk (Vitebsk) receives a charter of self-government.

1607: Founding of Jamestown in Virginia, first of the thirteen English colonies in America.

1603–1613: Muscovy's "Time of Troubles," when a Polish king of Swedish lineage, Sigismund III, tries to be accepted as Russia's tsar.

1613: Election of the first Romanov tsar in Russia.

1620: Reestablishment of the Orthodox hierarchy in Kiev for Ukraine and Belarus, to replace the hierarchs who joined the Uniate Church.

1622: King Sigismund III prohibits any public polemics against the Catholics.

1623: Reacting to religious persecutions of Orthodox Christians, inhabitants of Viciebsk revolt and kill the Uniate archbishop, Jazafat Kuncevič. Religious strife intensifies between the Orthodox and the Uniates; the government sides with the latter.

1632–1634: War of the Commonwealth with Muscovy.

1648: In Western Europe, Peace of Westphalia marks the end of the Thirty Years' War.

1654: Bohdan Khmelnitsky unites Ukraine with Russia.

1654–1667: War of the Commonwealth with Russia; loss of Smolensk to Muscovy.

1661: Beginning of the personal rule of King Louis XIV in France.

1666: *Liberum Veto* rule extended to local diets of the gentry, resulting in increased anarchy within the state.

1686: Russo-Polish "Eternal Peace": Russia retains Smolensk, Chernigov, and Kiev, and obtains from the patriarch of Constantinople the right to consecrate a metropolitan for "Kiev and All of Ruś" in Moscow.

1688–1689: "Glorious Revolution" in England establishes the supremacy of the Parliament.

1696: By a decision of the Warsaw General Confederation, the Ruś'ian (Old Belarusan) language is replaced by Polish in official documents of the Grand Duchy of Lithuania. The Latin alphabet replaces the Cyrillic in popular usage.

1699: Peace of Karlovitz ends the threat to Europe of Ottoman Turkey.

1700–1721: Northern War of Russian Tsar Peter I (1682–1725) and the rise of Russia.

1708: Occupation of Mahiloŭ (Mogilev) by the Swedes.

1709: Defeat of the Swedes by Peter I in the Battle of Poltava in Ukraine.

1710: Inclusion of Riga in the Russian state.

1713: Peace of Utrecht closes the War of the Spanish Succession and removes the French threat to a balance of power.

1751: Publication of the *Encyclopédie* commences, marking the dawn of the Enlightenment.

1762–1796: Reign of Empress Catherine II of Russia.

1763: Russian trade consulates established in the East Belarusan cities of Viciebsk and Škloŭ, marking the westward advance of Moscow's expansion.

The Seven Years' War ends with victory for Britain and Prussia, and with French losses in North America and India.

1767: Confederation of Orthodox gentry in Sluck plays into the hands of Catherine II in her design to partition the Commonwealth of Poland and the Grand Duchy of Lithuania.

1772, 1793, 1795: Three partitions of the Polish Commonwealth among Russia, Prussia, and Austria. All of Belarus is incorporated into the Russian Empire, with the exception of a small northwestern corner, taken by Prussia.

1776: Most Belarusan cities and towns are deprived of their Magdeburg Statutes of self-government.

Proclamation of the independence of the United States of America.

1789: Onset of French Revolution.

American Constitution adopted.

1791: The Constitution of May 3 merges the Polish Crown and the Grand Duchy of Lithuania, Ruś, and Samogitia into a unitary state.

1792: Constitution of May 3 is abrogated.

1794: Anti-Russian uprising led by Tadeusz Kosciuszko, scion of Polonized Belarusan gentry family.

Decree of Empress Catherine II barring Jews, who were numerous in Belarus, from settling in Russian provinces; Pale of Settlement established.

1803: The Vilnia Imperial University is founded and becomes a hotbed of Polish, Belarusan, and Lithuanian youth movements.

1807–1884: Life of Vincuk Dunin-Marcinkievič, first major Belarusan writer of the "Renewal" period.

1812: Napoleon's march into Russia.

1815: Napoleon defeated at the Battle of Waterloo; Europe reshaped by the Congress of Vienna.

1820: Jesuit schools in Belarus closed down.

early 1820s: *Aeneid Turned Inside Out* (a travesty of Virgil's *Aeneid*) written in the Belarusan vernacular, marking the beginning of the modern period in Belarusan literature.

1823: Russian government clamps down on clandestine student societies; tsarist ukase prohibits youth from Belarus to be sent for study abroad.

Monroe Doctrine opposes European intervention in affairs of the Americas.

1830–1831: Anti-tsarist insurrection in Poland, Belarus, and Lithuania.

1831: Abrogation of the "Statute of the Grand Duchy of Luthuania" in Viciebsk and Mahiloŭ gubernias.

1832: Vilnia Imperial University closed down as part of the measures taken to thwart the insurrection of 1830–1831.

1836: Tsarist ukase prohibits use of Polish language in schools of Belarus and orders use of Russian as the exclusive language of instruction.

1839: Religious union with Rome of 1596 renounced by a council of bishops in Polacak; burning of Uniate books; forcible return of Uniates to Russian Orthodoxy.

1840: Abrogation of the "Statute of the Grand Duchy of Lithuania" in the western part of Belarus, and prohibition of the use of the terms *Belarusan* and *Lithuanian* in reference to the northwestern gubernias.

1840–1900: Life of Francišak Bahuševič, the "father" of modern Belarusan literature.

1840: Another anonymous poem, *Taras on Parnassus,* confirms the growth of Belarusan vernacular as a vehicle for literary expression.

1848: Wave of liberal and nationalistic revolutions in Europe.

1853–1856: Crimean War, pitting Russia against France and England, exposes Russia's backwardness.

1859: Use of the Latin alphabet in Belarusan literary works prohibited by Russian censors.

1861: Abolition of serfdom in Russia.

Civil War in the United States.

1862: Construction of first railroad through Belarus, connecting St. Petersburg and Warsaw.

1862–1863: Publication by Kastuś Kalinoŭski of *Peasants' Truth,* the first clandestine Belarusan newspaper.

1863–1864: Massive anti-tsarist uprising in Poland, Belarus, and Lithuania, led in Belarus by Kastuś Kalinoŭski.

1864–1876: Opening of teachers' seminaries in Maladečna, Niaśviž, Śvislač, and Polacak.

1864–1915: The Vilnia Archeological Commission publishes forty-nine volumes of documents pertaining to Belarusan history.

1867: Canada becomes a British Dominion.

Russia sells Alaska to the United States.

1870: Publication of *The Dictionary of the Belarusan Language* by Ivan Nasovič.

Franco-Prussian war leads to completion of the unification of both Germany and Italy.

1876–1916: Life of Aloiza Paškievič (pseudonym: Ciotka), Belarusan writer, publisher, and revolutionary activist.

1881: Assassination of Tsar Alexander II by Social-Revolutionaries, one of whom was Belarusan Ihnat Hryniavicki.

1881–1919: Life of archeologist Ivan Luckievič, one of the founders of the Belarusan Socialist Hramada and organizer of the *Our Soil* publication.

1881–1931: Life of Usievalad Ihnatoŭski, a leading Belarusan historian and statesman.

1882–1942: Life of Janka Kupala, the foremost writer and national leader of the Belarusans.

1882–1956: Life of Jakub Kolas, one of Belarus's greatest poets and civil leaders.

1883–1938: Life of Vaclaŭ Lastoŭski, historian, lexicographer, and ideologue of the Belarusan "Renewal."

1884: Clandestine magazine *Clamor* published by Belarusan students in St. Petersburg, putting "the first stone in the foundation of the federated independence of Belarus."

1886–1941: Life of Źmitrok Biadula (Samuil Plaŭnik), writer and civic activist.

1887–1920: Life of Aleś Harun, poet and political activist.

1891: Clandestine publication of Francišak Bahuševič's collection of poems *The Belarusan Fife,* which was seminal for the Belarusan "Renewal" movement.

1891–1917: Life of Maksim Bahdanovič, Belarusan poet.

1893–1939: Life of Maksim Harecki, writer and historian of Belarusan literature.

1902: Founding of the Belarusan Revolutionary Hramada, renamed in the following year as the Belarusan Socialist Hramada, which spearheaded the establishment of a Belarusan political state.

1903–1922: Academician Jaŭchim Karski publishes his monumental three-volume study, *The Belarusans.*

1904–1905: Russo-Japanese War.

Revolution in Russia leads to the establishment of the Russian Parliament (the State Duma), and lifts the prohibition against printing in the Belarusan language.

1906–1915: Appearance in Vilnia of the weekly *Our Soil,* which becomes the rallying point of the Belarusan national cause.

1907–1911: Conservative regime of Premier Stolypin in Russia.

1910: Publication of *Short History of Belarus* by Vaclaŭ Lastoŭski, first historian to view Belarus's past as a self-contained unit.

1913–1915: Appearance in Vilnia of *The Belarusan,* a Catholic weekly.

1914: Onset of World War I.

1915–1918: West Belarus occupied by the Germans.

1916: Belarusan delegation at the international conference in Lausanne, Switzerland, lobbies for an independent Belarus.

1917: In March, the Russian Revolution causes Tsar Nicholas II to abdicate.

In November, Lenin's Bolsheviks seize power.

In December, the First All-Belarusan Congress in Miensk (on the Russian side of the Russo-German front) proclaims a republican government in Belarus and is disbanded by Bolsheviks.

1918: In January, President Wilson's Fourteen Points include defense of people's right to self-determination.

On February 21, the Executive Committee of the Council of the First All-Belarusan Congress declares itself the Provisional Authority in Belarus.

On March 3, the Russo-German armistice signed at Bieraščie (Brest-Litovsk), disregards both Belarus's right to representation and its territorial integrity.

On March 9, the Executive Committee of the Council of the First All-Belarusan Congress declares Belarus a Democratic Republic.

On March 25, in Miensk, the Executive Council of the First All-Belarusan Congress declares the independence of the Belarusan Democratic Republic under German occupation.

Onset of Civil War in Russia.

1919: In January, the Belarusan Soviet Socialist Republic is proclaimed by a Bolshevik conference in Smolensk. The conference declares itself to be the first congress of the Communist Party of Belarus.

In February, the short-lived Lithuano-Belarusan Soviet Socialist Republic is founded.

The Peace Treaty of Versailles ends World War I.

1919–1921: The Russo-Polish War results in the partitioning of Belarus between the Belarusan Soviet Socialist Republic and Poland.

1920: Patriarch Tikhon of Moscow gives his blessings for the use of the Belarusan language in sermons and some liturgical services and for the publication of the Bible in Belarusan.

1921: October 30 marks the opening of the Belarusan State University in Miensk.

1921–1928: New Economic Policy (NEP) in the Soviet Union is marked by relative tolerance of private initiative and cultural liberalism.

1922: January 30 marks the opening in Miensk of the Belarusan Institute of Culture, which becomes the center of scholarly activity of the Belarusan intelligentsia.

Restoration of the Belarusan Metropolia in Miensk with Archbishop Melchisadek elected Metropolitan of Miensk and All Belarus.

In elections to the Polish Parliament, Belarusans win 11 seats in the lower house and 3 in the upper house.

On December 30, the Union of Soviet Socialist Republics is founded.

1924: In West Belarus, Polish authorities close 400 Belarusan schools and suspend more than 15 Belarusan newspapers.

On January 21, Lenin dies.

On March 3, the parts of regions (gubernias) of Viciebsk, Homiel, and Smolensk inhabited by Belarusans are transferred from the Russian Federation to the Belarusan SSR.

On July 15, by a decree of the government of the Belarusan SSR, the equal rights of the four principal languages of the Republic (Belarusan, Polish, Russian, and Yiddish) are confirmed.

1925: In October, after a conference in Berlin, several members of the Belarusan government-in-exile return to Soviet Belarus.

1926: In May, the Excelsior literary club is founded in the BSSR to stimulate high standards and national values in literature and art.

June marks the beginning of legal activities by the Belarusan Peasant-and-Workers' Hramada, a massive leftist political movement in West Belarus.

On December 6, Rečyca and Homiel (Gomel) counties are transferred from the Russian Federation to the Belarusan SSR.

1927: In January, massive arrests of the leaders of the Belarusan Peasant-and-Workers' Hramada are made by Polish authorities.

Reaffirmation in Miensk of autocephaly of the Belarusan Orthodox Church.

1928: In December, the Institute of Belarusan Culture is renamed the Belarusan Academy of Sciences, with Usievalad Ihnatoŭski as president.

1929: The peak of the newspaper campaign against "Belarusan National Democracy" in the BSSR, and the beginning of repressions of the Belarusan intelligentsia.

1930: In Poland, the parliament is disbanded and opposition leaders of the center-left coalition are arrested and imprisoned.

1931: On February 2, Usievalad Ihnatoŭski, president of the Belarusan Academy of Sciences in Miensk, commits suicide in protest against persecution; intelligentsia in the BSSR are subject to massive arrests and imprisonment.

1933: August 26 marks Soviet decree concerning the Belarusan language, which is artificially brought closer to Russian.

1934: Creation by administrative decision of a concentration camp in Bereza Kartuska in Poland, for detainment of opposition activists.

1935: In the general elections in Poland, Belarusans lose the last seat they held in the Polish Parliament.

1936: Closure by the Polish authorities of the Belarusan Institute of Economy and Culture and the Belarusan School Society in Vilnia.

1937–1941: Operation of Soviet death camp in Kurapaty near Miensk, where up to 250,000 civil victims may have been executed. More than 2 million people are estimated to have perished in Belarus as a result of Stalinist genocide.

1938: Presidential decree in Poland enabling the state to interfere in matters of the Polish Autocephalous Orthodox Church, to which a majority of Belarusans in Poland belonged.

1939: On August 23, Soviet-German nonaggression pact is signed.

On September 1, Germany attacks Poland and World War II begins.

On September 17, Red Army moves into West Belarus and West Ukraine as Polish resistance to Germany collapses.

On October 10, Moscow transfers Vilnia from the Belarusan SSR to the Lithuanian SSR.

1941–1944: The German occupation of Belarus results in the deaths of 2.2 million people, the destruction of 209 cities and townships and 9,200 villages, and uncounted material losses.

1942: From August 30 to September 2, the All-Belarusan Orthodox Council (Sabor) in Miensk proclaims the autocephaly of the Belarusan Orthodox Church.

1943: At the Teheran Conference (November 27 to December 2), Stalin insists on retaining within the USSR those territories of West Belarus and Ukraine taken from Poland.

1944: At the Moscow Conference (October 9–22), the Polish delegation agrees to accept the Curzon Line as Poland's eastern frontier.

1945: At the Yalta Conference (February 2–11), Soviet domination over Eastern Europe is established.

On April 25, delegates from Belarus and Ukraine are invited to the San Francisco Conference. Recognized for their role in the war effort, both countries become members of the United Nations.

On May 7, World War II ends in Europe.

On May 24, Stalin makes his famous toast to the Russian people "as the guiding force of the Soviet Union" and opens up the government's Russification drive.

1946–1948: A thorough purge of the Communist Party of Belarus results in the replacement of most leading Communists in Belarus by Russians.

1947: In February, the Central Committee of the Communist Party of Belarus discusses the question of the struggle against "bourgeois nationalism."

1948: April 1 marks the start of the six-month Soviet blockade of Berlin, a major cold war crisis.

1951: On April 20, a decree of the Ministry of Education of the BSSR cancels the requirement to pass a Belarusan language test in the republic's schools, in the majority of which Russian is the language of instruction.

1953: On March 5, Stalin dies.

1956: On February 14–25, the Twentieth Congress of the Communist Party of the Soviet Union is held. It is here that Soviet leader Nikita Khrushchev denounces some of Stalin's crimes.

Anti-Communist uprisings in Poland (in June) and Hungary (in October).

1959: In January, Nikita Khruschchev's pronouncement in Miensk—"The sooner we all start speaking Russian, the faster we shall build Communism"—accelerates the Russification of Belarus.

1964: In October, Nikita Khrushchev is ousted from power in the Kremlin.

Authoritarianism and conservatism return under the rule of Leonid Brezhnev (1964–1982).

1965: On March 30, Piotr Mašeraŭ (Masherov) becomes first secretary of the CPB, a post he occupies until his death in October 1980.

1968: In August, the Soviet Union invades Czechoslovakia.

mid-1960s to mid-1970s: Nationalist ferment among Belarusan scholars, students, and writers leads to a series of administrative reprisals.

Belarus is well on its way to becoming a major industrial region of the Soviet Union, specializing in machine and precision instrument building.

1971: Twenty years after the German invasion, Belarus reaches its prewar level of population: 9.1 million people.

1975: The Helsinki Agreement is signed, highlighting the human rights issues in Eastern Europe and opening up communication channels between West and East.

1979: Establishment at the Belarusan State University of "The Belarusan Shop," a student movement championing renewal of Belarusan culture.

1985: In January, the *Talaka* (Together) movement, launched by young patriots in Miensk, struggles for preservation of national monuments and historical traditions.

In February, the Heritage Club in Miensk begins its "informal" activities, stressing recovery of the national heritage.

In March, Mikhail S. Gorbachev is elected secretary general of the Communist Party, marking the beginning of perestroika (restructuring) of the Soviet system.

In July, Gorbachev visits Belarus, where a regional Party leader, Jafrem Sakałoŭ, catches his eye and in January 1987 becomes first secretary of the Communist Party of Belarus.

1986: On April 20, young participants in the folkloric Spring Festival in Miensk are beaten up by *afgantsy* (veterans of the Afghan War) for their alleged Belarusan nationalism, at the instigation of the city's Communist Party organization.

On April 26, Chernobyl suffers a nuclear accident; 70 percent of the radioactive fallout falls on Belarusan territory.

On December 15, a collective letter is sent by the Belarusan intelligentsia to Gorbachev, pleading for the prevention of the "spiritual extinction" of the Belarusan nation and spelling out a program for the renewal of Belarus.

1987: In January, the Communist Party Central Committee approves a plan to give voters a choice of candidates in local elections.

On November 1, at an unauthorized rally in Miensk in observance of the traditional day of *Dziady* (All Souls' Day), the Soviet regime is accused of genocidal policies in Belarus.

On December 26–27, more than thirty independent Belarusan youth groups hold their first "General Diet" to bring about fundamental changes and accelerate national renewal.

1988: On June 3, the Miensk literary weekly *Literature and Art* publishes evidence (submitted by Zianon Paźniak and Jaŭhien Šmyhaloŭ) of the unearthing of 500 mass graves of victims of Stalinist repression, in Kurapaty near Miensk.

On June 19, approximately 10,000 people participate in a demonstration commemorating the killings at Kurapaty and demanding the creation of an investigatory commission.

On October 19, at a rally of intelligentsia in Miensk, the "Martyrology of Belarus" is established to commemorate the victims of Communism, and an organizational committee is set up for creation of the Belarusan Popular Front.

On October 30, military troops in Miensk violently disperse a mass demonstration commemorating the victims of Stalinism.

1989: January 14–15 marks the second convention of representatives of sixty-six Belarusan youth groups in Vilnia (Vilnius), Lithuania, in support of Belarusan "Renewal"; authorities in Miensk deny permission for the convention to be held in the capital.

On February 2, the Society of Belarusan Culture is established in Vilnia, Lithuania.

On February 19, about 45,000 demonstrators at the Dynama Stadium in Miensk support the call of the BPF Organizing Committee to speed up democratic reforms.

On March 26, in an election to the Congress of People's Deputies of the USSR (the first multichoice contest permitted since 1917), conservative candidates win a vast majority of seats.

On June 24–25, the Belarusan Popular Front "Renewal" is formally established, with Zianon Paźniak as president.

On June 27, the Belarusan Language Society is founded, with formal support for the language's renewal from the Central Committee of the Communist Party of Belarus.

On July 26, a mass rally in Miensk demands creation of a commission to investigate the Chernobyl coverup.

On July 28, Mikalaj Dziemianciej (Dementei) is elected speaker of the Supreme Council of the BSSR; but he resigns on August 25, 1991, when his siding with the putsch leaders is revealed.

Communist governments in Eastern Europe collapse throughout the second half of the year, after Gorbachev announces that he will not use force to save them.

In December, the Communist Party of Lithuania breaks with Moscow; Gorbachev denounces the move.

1990: In January, a confrontation occurs between Gorbachev and the Lithaunians over the issue of Lithuania's independence.

Ethnic violence erupts in Azerbaijan.

On January 26, the Supreme Council of the Belarusan SSR passes the "Law About Languages of the BSSR," making Belarusan the official language of the republic.

On March 3, elections to the Supreme Council of the BSSR takes place under conditions favoring the Communists, who win a majority of seats.

On March 11, Lithuania declares independence.

March 15 marks the abrogation of the Sixth Article of the Soviet Constitution guaranteeing the Communists monopoly of power.

On March 29, the Presidium of the Supreme Council of the BSSR issues a statement indicating that if Lithuania secedes from the Soviet Union, the Vilnia region should be returned to the Belarusan SSR. A diplomatic stir results.

In June, the Warsaw Pact pronounces the end of ideological conflict with the West.

On June 23, Viačaslaŭ Kiebič (Kebich) is appointed prime minister of Belarus.

In July, the Democratic Opposition group—consisting of twenty-seven Belarusan Popular Front members and seven other democrats—formalizes itself within the Supreme Council of the BSSR.

Boris Yeltsin, leader of the Russian Republic, quits the Communist Party to become Gorbachev's chief rival.

On July 27, the Supreme Council of the BSSR adopts the Declaration of State Sovereignty of the Belarusan Soviet Socialist Republic.

In September, the government approves "The National Program on the Development of the Belarusan Language and the Languages of Other Nationalities of the BSSR."

On November 28, at the Belarusan Communists' Party Congress, First Secretary of the CPB Jafrem Sakałoŭ warns that "chauvinism, nationalism, and separatism are on the rise." Sakałoŭ's successor, Anatol Malafiejeŭ (Malofeyev), calls for rapprochement with the intelligentsia.

In December, the Congress of People's Deputies convenes in Moscow to discuss revamping of the system and the concept of a new union treaty between Moscow and the republics.

On December 18, Belarus and Russia sign a treaty on political noninterference and economic cooperation.

On December 29, Belarus and Ukraine sign a treaty on trade.

1991: On January 14, the City Council of Miensk adopts a resolution condemning the central government's use of force in Lithuania.

In February, Gorbachev visits Belarus, including the territories affected by the Chernobyl radiation, and calls for a new Union Treaty.

On March 17, the preservation of the Soviet Union is approved in an All-Union referendum.

In April, massive demonstrations (caused by steep price rises on many consumer goods) take place in Miensk and Orša.

On June 12, Russia proclaims independence.

On July 26, Communist leaders overwhelmingly approve Gorbachev's new Party platform, which abandons Marxist dogma.

On August 19, a group of conservative leaders in Moscow initiate a putsch, while leaders of the Belarusan Popular Front call for mass protests. Some journalists denounce the putsch. The government in Miensk, siding with the putschists, calls for calm.

On August 20, Estonia declares independence.

On August 21, the putsch fails and Gorbachev returns to Moscow.

Latvia declares independence.

On August 22, President Yeltsin disbands Communist Party cells in the Soviet armed forces on Russian territory.

Lithuania outlaws the Communist Party.

On August 24, Gorbachev resigns as leader of the Soviet Communist Party and recommends the disbandment of its Central Committee.

Ukraine declares independence.

On August 25, Belarus declares independence. Speaker of the Supreme Council, Mikalaj Dziemianciej (Dementei), is forced to resign. The Communist Party of Belarus secedes from the CPSU.

On August 28, Belarusan Prime Minister Viačaslaŭ Kiebič (Kebich) publishes a statement indicating that he and his entire cabinet have "suspended" their Communist Party membership.

On August 29, the Supreme Council of the USSR suspends Communist Party activities and freezes its bank accounts.

On September 3, Poland recognizes the independence of Belarus.

The government of Miensk changes the city's official appellation of Minsk to the historic name of Miensk (also spelled Mensk).

On September 6, the Soviet Union recognizes the independence of Lithuania, Latvia, and Estonia.

On September 17–19, the Supreme Council of Belarus elects Stanislaŭ Šuškievič (Shushkevich) as speaker, replaces the Soviet flag and coat-of-arms with national symbols, and changes the name of the state from the Belarusan Soviet Socialist Republic to the Republic of Belarus.

On October 18, some republics (including Belarus) sign a treaty with Gorbachev, creating an economic union.

On November 16, Russia's President Yeltsin challenges Gorbachev's Union and assumes control by decree over the Soviet money supply and foreign trade.

On December 1, Ukrainian voters approve Ukraine's independence in a referendum.

On December 4, the Supreme Council of Belarus endorses the Union Treaty.

On December 8, Russia, Belarus, and Ukraine form the Commonwealth of Independent States. The Soviet Union comes to a virtual end.

On December 23, Switzerland recognizes the independence of Belarus.

On December 25, the United States recognizes the independence of Belarus, along with that of Russia, Ukraine, Armenia, and Kazakhstan. Gorbachev resigns as president of the Soviet Union.

1992: On January 1, the Belarusan Parliament votes to subordinate to the republic's government all former Soviet troops, with the exception of the nuclear forces. It also adopts the text of a military oath on allegiance to the Republic Belarus.

On January 30, Belarus becomes a member of the Conference on Security and Cooperation in Europe (CSCE).

From February to April, at the initiative of the Belarusan Popular Front, more than 440,000 signatures are collected for a referendum on new elections to the Supreme Council.

On March 18, the Supreme Council of Belarus directs the government to begin immediately forming its national armed forces.

On May 23, Belarus, Kazakhstan, and Ukraine agree to destroy or turn over to Russia all strategic nuclear warheads.

On May 26, Belarus establishes diplomatic relations with Israel.

On July 7, Belarus becomes a full member of the International Monetary Fund and the International Bank for Reconstruction and Development.

On July 20, Belarus concludes an agreement with Russia as the basis for a military and political alliance.

On September 25–29, widespread festivities are held in Miensk and Polacak marking the millennium of Christianity in Belarus.

On October 29, the Supreme Council (in which ex-Communists make up 86 percent of its deputies) overwhelmingly rejects the Opposition's demand to hold a referendum on new elections and decides to concentrate on adopting a new constitution.

On November 11, Belarus and the Vatican establish diplomatic relations.

On December 19–20, for the first time in the post–World War II period Belarusans from all the former Soviet republics and Poland hold their convention in Miensk.

On December 31, officers and soldiers of Belarus's armed forces (those with Belarusan citizenship) swear allegiance to the Republic of Belarus.

Belarus and Lithuania establish diplomatic relations.

1993: On January 3, the United States and Russia sign the START-I agreement providing for a sharp reduction of nuclear weapons.

On February 4, the Belarusan parliament ratifies the first Strategic Arms Reduction Treaty (START-I) and approves adherence to the Nuclear Nonproliferation Treaty. By the year 2000 Belarus should be free of all nuclear arms.

On February 4, the Supreme Council of Belarus repeals the decree "On Temporary Ban of the activities of the Communist Party of Belarus–Communist Party of the Soviet Union on the Territory of the Republic of Belarus," which had been imposed on August 25, 1991.

On March 21–25, for the first time in the history of Soviet Belarus the anniversary of the proclamation of the independence of the Belarusan Democratic Republic (March 25, 1918) is openly celebrated in Miensk and other cities of the republic.

· GLOSSARY ·
OF BELARUSAN NAMES

Spelling in This Book	Alternative Spellings
Baranavi;acky	Baranovichi, Baranowicze
Belarus	Byelorussia, Belorussia, Byelarus, White Russia, Whiteruthenia
Biarezina	Berezina
Brest	Biareście, Bieraście
Homiel	Gomel
Hrodna	Grodno, Harodnia, Horadnia, Horadzien
Kalinoŭski Kastuś	Kalinovski Konstantin, Kalinowski Konstanty
Kiebič ViačaslaŭK	ebich Viacheslav
Kraŭčanka	Kravchanka, Kravchenko
Mahiloŭ	Mogilev, Mahileŭ
Miensk	Minsk, Mensk
Navahradak	Navahrudak, Novogrudok, Nowogródek
Orša	Orsha, Vorša
Paźniak Zianon	Pazniak Zenon, Pozniak, Pozdniak
Polacak	Polotsk, Polack
Skaryna Francišak	Skorina Francysk
Sluck	Slutsk, Slucak
Šuškievič Stanislaŭ	Shushkevich Stanislav
Turaŭ	Turov
Viciebsk	Vitebsk
Vilnia	Vilnius, Wilno, Vilna

· Bibliography ·

Abdiralovich, Ignat. "Izvechnyi put'. Opyty belorusskogo mirovozzreniya," (The eternal path: An essay on the Belarusan worldview." *Nioman* 11 (1990):162–179.

Abecedarski, Laŭren. *U sviatle nieabvieržnych faktaŭ* (In the light of undeniable facts). Minsk: Vydaviectva "Holas Radzimy," 1969.

Academy of Sciences of the Belarusan SSR. *Bielaruskaja Savieckaja Encyklapiedyja*, Vols. 1–12. Minsk: Vydaviectva "Bielaruskaja Savieckaja Encyklapiedyja," 1969–1975.

_____. *Historyja Bielaruskaj SSR u piaci tamach* (History of the Belarusan SSR in five volumes). Minsk: Vydaviectva "Navuka i technika," 1972–1975.

_____. *Istoriya Belorusskoy SSR*. Minsk: Izdatel'stvo "Nauka i tekhnika," 1977.

_____. Department of Scientific Information on the Social Sciences. *Referatyŭny zbornik. Bielarusistyka. No. 10. Historyja* (Reference series. Belarusan studies. No. 10. History). Minsk, 1991

_____. Department of Scientific Information on the Social Sciences. *Referatyŭny zbornik. Bielarusistyka. No. 9. Sieryja 7. Sacyjalohija* (Reference series. Belarusan studies. No. 9. Series 7. Sociology). Minsk, 1991.

Adamovič, Anton. *"Jak duch zmahańnia Bielarusi" Da 100-ch uhodkaŭ naradžeńnia Ivana Luckieviča* ("Like the spirit of Belarus's struggle" [On the centenary of Ivan Luckievič's birth]). New York: Vydaviectva "Bielarus," 1983.

_____. *Opposition to Sovietization in Belorussian Literature (1917–1957)*. New York: Scarecrow Press, 1958.

Afanasy, Archbishop. *Belaruś v istoricheskoy gosudarstvennoy i tserkovnoy zhizni* (Belarus in historical, state, and church life). Buenos Aires, 1966.

Aleksandrovič, Sciapan Ch., Aleh A. Lojka, and Viačaslaŭ P. Rahojša, compilers. *Bielaruskaja litaratura XIX stahoddzia. Chrestamatyja* (Belarusan literature of the nineteenth century: A reader). Minsk: Vydaviectva "Vyšejšaja škola," 1971.

Alekseyev, Leonid V. *Polotskaya zemlya (Ocherki istorii severnoy Belorussii) v IX–XIII vv.* (The Polacak land: An outline of the history of northern Belarus in the ninth to thirteenth centuries). Moscow: Izdatel'stvo "Nauka," 1966.

Aleksiutovič, Mikola. "A dzie ž iscina abjektyŭnaja?" (And where is the objective truth?). *Polymia* (Flame) 5 (1966):179–185.

Aničenka, U. V., and K. S. Usovič. *Kalasy rodnaj movy* (Ears of corn of the native language). Minsk: Vydaviectva "Univiersiteckaje," 1990.

Antonovich, T., et al., "V poiskakh utrachennogo vremeni" (In search of the lost time). *Kommunist Belorussii* 1 (January 1990):64–71.

Argumenty i fakty (Arguments and facts) 1 (1991).

Astroŭski, Radaslaŭ, ed. *Druhi Usiebielaruski Kanhres. Matarjaly* (Second All-Belarusan Congress: Materials). Publication of the Belarusan Central Council, 1954.

Babosov, Yevgeny. "Pochemu my okazalis' na obochine NTR?" (Why have we found ourselves on the sidelines of the scientific revolution?) *Kommunist Belorussii* 8 (August 1991): 35–41.

Bahrovich, Andrej. *Žycharstva Bielaruskaje SSR u śviatle pierapisu 1959 hodu* (The population of the Belarusan SSR in the light of the 1959 census). New York: Kreceuski Foundation, 1962.

Bahuševič, Francišak. *Tvory* (Works). Minsk: Vydaviectva "Mastackaja litaratura," 1967.

Bardach, Juliusz. *Studia z ustroju i prawa Wielkiego Ksiestwa Litewskiego XIV–XVII w.* (Studies on the administration and laws of the Grand Duchy of Lithuania from the fourteenth to seventeenth centuries). Warsaw: "Państwowe Wydawnictwo Naukowe," 1970.

Bazarevič, M. "Slova Kolasa natchniala Klimuka" (The poems of Kolas inspired Klimuk). *Litaratura i Mastactva* (Literature and art), October 24, 1975.

Belarusan Soviet Encyclopedia. *Francysk Skaryna i jaho čas. Encyklapiedyčny daviednik* (Francis Skaryna and his time: Encyclopedic reference book). Minsk: Vydaviectva "Bielaruskaja Savieckaja Encyklapiedyja," 1988.

Belorusskiy delovoy vestnik (Belarusan business herald) 2 (1991).

Bergman, Aleksandra. *Sprawy bialoruskie w II Rzeczypospolitej* (Belarusan affairs in the second republic). Warsaw: Państwowe Wydawnictwo Naukowe, 1984.

Bez-Karnilovich, Mikhail. *Istoricheskiye svedeniya o primechatelneyshikh mestakh v Belorussii* (Historical information on the most remarkable locations in Belarus). St. Petersburg: "In the Printing Shop of the Third Department of His Imperial Majesty's Own Chancellery," 1855.

Bič, P. "Kab zakon zapracavaŭ" (So that the law may work). *Naša Slova. Biuleteń Tavarystva Bielaruskaj Movy* (Our language: The Bulletin of the Belarusan Language Society) 7 (September 1990): 9–10.

Bielarus (The Belarusan), a monthly of the Belarusan American Association. New York.

Bielaruski čas (Belarusan times), a newspaper of the labor unions of Belarus. Minsk.

Birch, Julian. "Border Disputes and Disputed Borders in the Soviet Federal System." *Nationalities Papers* 1 (Spring 1987):43–70.

Bird, Thomas E. "Orthodoxy in Byelorussia: 1917–1980." *Zapisy Bielaruskaha Instytutu Navuki i Mastactva* (Annals of the Byelorussian Institute of Arts and Sciences) 17 (1983):144–208.

_____. "Religion and Nation-Building in Today's Belarus." Paper presented at the Belarusan session of the Conference of the Canadian Association of Slavists, Charlottetown, Prince Edward Island, June 3, 1992.

Birnbaum, Henrik. "Some Aspects of the Slavonic Renaissance," *Slavonic and East European Review* 108 (January 1969):37–56.

Birzhi i banki (Money markets and banks), a business newspaper. Minsk.

Borushko, V. F. *Belorussiya: lyudi, sobytiya, fakty* (Belarus: People, events, and facts), 3rd ed. Minsk: Izdatel'stvo "Bielaruś," 1988.

Brinton, Crane, John B. Christopher, and Robert Lee Wolf. *A History of Civilization*, Vol. 2, 3rd ed. Englewood Cliffs, N.J.: Prentice-Hall, 1967.

Brzezinski, Zbigniew K. *The Permanent Purge: Politics in Soviet Totalitarianism*. Cambridge, Mass.: Harvard University Press, 1956.

Budovnits, I. U. *Obshchestvenno-politicheskaya mysl' drevney Rusi* (The sociopolitical thought of ancient Ruś). Moscow: Academy of Sciences of the USSR, 1960.

Byelorussian Business Herald (a newsletter on business, economic, and political development in Byelorussia and the Commonwealth) 2 (December 1991).

Byelorussian Soviet Socialist Republic, Mission to the United Nations. *Statement by H. E. Mr. Vyacheslav Kebich, Chairman of the Council of Ministers of the Byelorussian SSR in the General Debate at the 45th Session of the UN General Assembly*. Press Release No. 45. New York, September 26, 1991.

Bykov, Vasil'. "Myortvym–nye bolno, bolno zhivym" (The dead feel no pain, but those living do). *Nioman* 1 (1992): 141–147.

Carr, Edward Hallett. *What Is History?* New York: Vintage, 1961.

Central Board of Statistics of the Belarusan SSR. *Narodnoye khozyaystvo Belorusskoy SSR v 1985 g. Statisticheskiy ezhegodnik* (The National Economy of the Belarusan SSR. Statistical yearbook). Minsk: Izdatel'stvo "Bielaruś," 1986.

Central Statistical Board at the Council of Ministers of the USSR. *Narodnoye obrazovaniye, nauka i kultura v SSSR. Statisticheskiy sbornik* (National education, science, and culture in the USSR: Book of statistics). Moscow: Izdatel'stvo "Statistika," 1971.

Čakvin, I. U. "Litviny, lićviny." *Etnahrafija Bielarusi. Encyklapiedyja*. Minsk: Bielaruskaja Savieckaja Encyklapiedyja (1989):291–292.

Čakvin, I. U., and I. A. Jucho. "Bielaja Ruś." *Etnahrafija Bielarusi. Encyklapiedyja*. Minsk: Bielaruskaja Savieckaja Encyklapiedyja (1989):77.

Cieraškovič, Paval U. "Asnoŭnyja tendencyi razviccia bielaruskaha etnasu ŭ epochu kapitalizmu" (The main trends of development of the Belarusan ethnos in the epoch of capitalism). *Viesci AN BSSR. Sieryja hramadskich navuk* (Proceedings of the Academy of Sciences of the BSSR: Social sciences series). 5 (1986):89–96.

Conquest, Robert. "Coming to Terms with the Past." *National Review* (March 10, 1989):14–16.

Čyrvonaja zmiena (Red generation), a Belarusan youth newspaper. Minsk.

Dallin, Alexander. *German Rule in Russia, 1941–1945: A Study of Occupation Policies*. London: Macmillan, 1957.

Declaration of State Sovereignty of the Byelorussian Socialist Republic Adopted by the Supreme Soviet of the BSSR on July 27, 1990. Press Release of the UN Mission of the Byelorussian Soviet Socialist Republic. New York, n. d.

Dobry viečar (Good evening), a Minsk city newspaper, 1991.

Dovnar-Zapolsky, Mitrofan. "Osnovy gosudarstvennosti Belorussii" (The grounds for Belarus's statehood). *Nioman* 2 (1990):132–139.

Dundulis, Bronius. *Napoléon et la Lituanie en 1812*. Paris: Alcan, 1940.

Entsiklopedicheski Slovar' (Encyclopedic dictionary), Vol. 5. St. Petersburg: Brockhaus-Yefron, 1891.

Fedorovich, V. "Vremya li delat' stavki?" (Is it time to make bets?). *Chelovek i ekonomika* (Man and economy). 12 (1991):20–21.

Foreign Broadcast Information Service. *Daily Report. Soviet Union.* Washington: U.S. Government Publication, 1991, 1992.

Glenny, Michael. "Writing in Belorussia," *Partisan Review* 2 (Spring 1972):255–263.

Grekov, I. B. *Vostochnaya Yevropa i upadok Zolotoy Ordy [na rubezhe XIV–XV vv.]* (Eastern Europe and the fall of the Golden Horde [at the turn of the fourteenth and fifteenth centuries]). Moscow: Izdatel'stvo "Nauka," 1975.

Gritskevich, Anatol' P. *Chastnovladel'cheskiye goroda Belorussii v XVI–XVIII vv.* (Privately owned cities of Belarus in the sixteenth to eighteenth centuries). Minsk: Izdatel'stvo "Nauka i tekhnika," 1975.

Gritskevich, Valentin P. *Razmeri i prichiny massovogo begstva russkikh zhiteley v Litvu i Belorussiyu vo vtoroy polovine XVIII veka [po opublikovannym russkim istochnikam]* (Dimensions and reasons for the mass flight of Russian inhabitants to Lithuania and Belarus in the second half of the eighteenth century [according to Russian published sources]). (Photostat copy of an unpublished article in possession of this author.)

Halak, Leanid. *Uspaminy* (Memoirs), Part 1. New York: Letapis, 1982.

Halecki, Oscar. *Borderlands of Western Civilization: A History of East Central Europe.* New York: Ronald Press, 1952.

Holas Radzimy (Voice of homeland), "A Weekly for Countrymen Outside the Fatherland." Minsk.

Homan (Clamor), a Belarusan semi-weekly published in Vilnia in 1916–1918.

Hryckievič, Anatol' P. "Relihijnaje pytannie i znieśniaja palityka caryzmu pierad padzielam Rečy Paspalitaj" (The religious question and the foreign policy of tsarism before the partition of the Commonwealth). *Viesci Akademii navuk BSSR. Sieryja hramadskich navuk* (Proceedings of the Academy of Sciences of the BSSR: Social sciences series) 6 (1973):62–71.

Husoŭski, Mikola. *Piesnia pra zubra* (The song of the bison). Minsk: Vydaviectva "Mastackaja litaratura," 1973.

Ihnatoŭski, Usievalad. *Karotki narys historyi Bielarusi* (A short outline of the history of Belarus), 5th ed. Minsk: Vydaviectva "Bielaruś," 1991.

_____. "Bielaruskaje nacyjanalnaje pytańnie i Kamunistyčnaja partyja. Tezisy" (The Belarusan national question and the Communist Party). *Volny Ściah* (The free banner). 6/8 (December 25, 1921):38–40.

Inorodetz. *La Russie et les peuples allogènes* (Russia and the peoples of the outlying areas). Berne, 1917.

Institute of Party History at the Central Committee of the Communist Party of Belarus. *Kommunisticheskaya Partiya Belorussii v rezolutsiakh i resheniyakh syezdov i plenumov TsK* (The Communist Party of Belarus: Resolutions and decisions of congresses and plenums of the Central Committee), 6 vols. Minsk: Izdatel'stvo "Bielaruś," 1973–1987.

Jermalovič, Mikola. *Staražytnaja Bielaruś. Polacki i novaharodski pieryjady* (Ancient Belarus: The Polacak and Novaharodak periods). Minsk: Vydaviectva "Mastackaja litaratura," 1990.

Jucho, Iosif. *Krynicy bielaruska-litoŭskaha prava* (Sources of the Belarusan-Lithuanian laws). Minsk: Vydaviectva "Bielaruś," 1991.

Kabysh, Simon. "The Belorussians." In Nikolai K. Deker and Andrei Lebed, eds., *Genocide in the USSR*. New York: Scarecrow Press, 1958. Pp. 77–78.

Kamienskaja, N. V., et al., eds. *Historyja Minska*. Minsk: Vydaviectva "Navuka i technika," 1967.

Karsky, Yevfimiy F. *Belorusy. Khudozhestvennaya literatura na narodnom yazyke* (Belarusans: Literature in the vernacular), Vol. 3, Part 3. Petrograd: Rossiyskaya Akademiya Nauk, 1922.

_____. *Etnograficheskaya karta belorusskago plemeni* (Ethnographic map of the Belarusan people). Petrograd: Belarusan Regional Committee of the All-Russian Soviet of Peasant Deputies, 1917.

Kaspiarovič, H. I. "Etnademahrafičnyja pracesy i mižnacyjanalnyja adnosiny ŭ BSSR" (Ethnodemographic processes and national relations in the BSSR). *Viesci AN BSSR. Sieryja hramadskich navuk* (Proceedings of the Academy of Sciences of the BSSR: Social sciences series) 5 (1990):78–85.

Kiebič, Viačaslaŭ. "Pa pryrodzie svajoj ja aptymist …" ("By nature I am an optimist. …" Interview in *Bielaruś* 1 (January 1992):4–5, 22–3.

Kipel, Vitaŭt, and Zora Kipel, eds. *Byelorussian Statehood: Reader and Bibliography*. New York: Byelorussian Institute of Arts and Sciences, 1988.

Kiselev, K. V., ed. *Belorusskaya SSR na mezhdunarodnoy arene* (The Belarusan SSR in the international arena). Moscow: Izdatel'stvo "Mezhdunarodnyie otnosheniya," 1964.

Kisialoŭ, Hienadź, compiler. *Pačynalniki. Z historyka-litaraturnych mataryjalaŭ XIX st.* (Initiators: From the nineteenth-century literary material pertaining to history). Minsk: Vydaviectva "Navuka i technika," 1977.

Kohn, Hans. *Nationalism: Its Meaning and History*. New York: Van Nostrand, 1955.

Kommunist Belorussii, a monthly of the Central Committee of the Communist Party of Belarus. (Appearing since October 1991 as *Bielaruskaja dumka*.)

"Kontseptsiya pod skal'pelem nauki. Diskussiya" (A conception under the scalpel of science: A discussion). *Kommunist Belorussii* 4 (April 1990):34–41.

Kopyssky, Z. Yu. *Ekonomicheskoye razvitiye gorodov Belorussii (XVI–XVII vv.)* (Economic development of Belarusan cities [sixteenth to seventeenth centuries]). Minsk: Izdatel'stvo "Nauka i tekhnika," 1966.

Kosman, Marceli. *Historia Bialorusi*. Wroclaw–Warsaw: Wydawnictwo Ossolińskich, 1979.

"KPB v zerkale statistiki" (Communist Party of Belarus in the mirror of statistics). *Kommunist Belorussii* 5 (1990):27–29.

Kravchanka, Pyotr K. *Statement by Pyotr K. Kravchanka, Minister for Foreign Affairs of the Republic of Belarus in the General Debate at the 46th Session of the United Nations General Assembly*. Minsk: Bielaruś, 1991.

Krukovsky, A. S. "Spetsifika sotsialnykh otnosheniy na sele v usloviyakh perekhoda k rynku" (The specificity of social relations in the countryside during the transition to a market economy). *Belorusistika* 14 (1991):123–135.

Krushinsky, S. *Byelorussian Communism and Nationalism: Personal Recollections*, Mimeographed Series No. 34. New York: Research Program on the USSR, 1953.

Kryžanoŭski, Mikalaj. "Čamu nie palapšajecca stan našaj ekanomiki?" (Why is the state of our economy not improving?") *Mienski viesnik* (The Miensk herald). March 1992.

Kryzhanovsky, A. "Polyusa glasnosti" (The extremities of glasnost). *Kommunist Belorussii* 1 (January 1990):49–53.

Labyncaŭ, Juryj. *Pačataje Skarynam. Bielaruskaja drukavanaja litaratura epochi Reniesansu* (What was begun by Skaryna: Printed works of Belarusan literature in the period of the Renaissance). Minsk: Vydaviectva "Mastackaja litaratura," 1990.

Latyšonak, Aleh. "Bielastoččyna i narodziny bielaruskaj dumki" (The Bielastok region and the birth of Belarusan thought). *Bielaruskija naviny. Biuleteń Bielaruskaha Demakratyčnaha Abjadniańnia* (Belarusan news. Bulletin of the Belarusan Democratic Union) 2 (July 1991):20–24.

Lenin, Vladimir I. "K istorii natsional'noy programmy v Avstrii i Rossii" (Toward a history of the national program in Austria and Russia). *Polnoye sobraniye sochineniy* (Complete works), Vol. 24, 5th ed. Moscow: Gosudarstvennoye izdatel'stvo politicheskoy literatury, 1961. Pp. 313–315.

_____. "Kriticheskiye zametki po natsional'nomu voprosu" (Critical notes on the nationality question). *Polnoye sobraniye sochineniy* (Complete works), Vol. 24, 5th ed. Moscow: Gosudarstvennoye izdatel'stvo politicheskoy literatury, 1961. Pp. 113–150.

Letter to a Russian Friend. A 'Samizdat' Publication from Soviet Byelorussia. London: Association of Byelorussians in Great Britain, 1979.

Lewandowski, Józef. *Federalizm. Litwa i Białoruś w polityce obozu belwederskiego* (Federalism: Lithuania and Belarus in the policy of the Józef Pilsudski camp). Warsaw: Państwowe Wydawnictwo Naukowe, 1962.

Listy da Harbačova. Vydańnie druhoje, z pierakladam na anhielskuju movu (Letters to Gorbachev: Second edition with original text and English translation). London: Association of Byelorussians in Great Britain, 1987.

Listy da Harbačova (Letters to Gorbachev), Issue 2. London: Association of Byelorussians in Great Britain, 1987.

Litaratura i Mastactva (Literature and art), "A Newspaper of the Creative Intelligentsia of Belarus." Minsk.

Lojka, Aleh A., Viačaslaŭ P. Rahojša, compilers. *Bielaruskaja litaratura XIX stahoddzia. Chrestamatyja* (Belarusan literature in the nineteenth century: A reader), 2nd ed. Minsk: Vydaviectva "Vyšejšaja škola," 1988.

Lubachko, Ivan S. *Belorussia Under Soviet Rule, 1917–1957.* Lexington: University of Kentucky Press, 1972.

Lukashuk, Aleksandr. "Zharkoye leto 53-go. Zametki na polyakh stenogramy iyun'skogo (1953) plenuma TsK KP Belorussii" (The hot summer of 1953: Notes in the margin of the verbatim report on the June 1953 Plenum of the CC of the CP of Belarus). *Kommunist Belorussii* 7 (1990):69–75; 8 (1990):73–82.

Lyakh, I. "Speshit' nel'zya i medlit' nevozmozhno" (Haste is not allowed and lingering is impossible). *Chelovek i ekonomika* (Man and economy) 10 (1991):1–2.

Lysenko, O. F. *Goroda Turovskoy zemli* (Cities of the Turov land). Minsk: Izdatel'stvo "Nauka," 1974.

Mannoni, Eugene. "O potrzebie ekumenizmu w Europie Wschodniej" (About the need for ecumenism in Eastern Europe." *Libertas* 1 (1984):90–97.

Marcinkievič, F. S. "Ekanamičnaje razviccio Bielarusi ŭ sastavie SSSR" (Economic development of Belarus within the USSR). *Viesci Akademii navuk BSSR. Sieryja hramadskich navuk* (Proceedings of the Academy of Sciences of the BSSR: Social sciences series) 6 (1972):16–29.

Marples, David R. "Post-Soviet Belarus' and the Impact of Chernobyl'." *Post-Soviet Geography* (formerly *Soviet Geography*), vol. 33, No. 7 (Silver Spring, MD, September 1992), pp. 419–431.

Martyraloh (Martyrology), a samizdat magazine of the Belarusan Civic Historico-Educational Society of Remembrance of Victims of Stalinism. Miensk.

McMillin, Arnold B. *The Vocabulary of the Byelorussian Literary Language in the Nineteenth Century.* London: Anglo-Byelorussian Society, 1973.

———. *A History of Byelorussian Literature: From Its Origins to the Present Day.* Giesen, Germany: Wilhelm Schmitz, 1977.

Mienski, Jazep. "The Establishment of the Belorussian SSR." *Belorussian Review* 1 (1955):5–33.

Mihalisko, Kathleen. "Belorussia as a Soviet Sovereign State: An Interview with Henadz' Hrushavy," *Report on the USSR* 35 (August 31, 1990):11–16.

Mikalajčanka, Aliaksandar. "Epicentr, što pryvioŭ Bielaruś da svabody" (The epicenter that led Belarus to liberty). *Polacak* 9 (1991):4–8.

Narodnaja hazieta (People's newspaper), daily newspaper of the Supreme Council of Belarus.

Nastaŭnickaja hazieta (Teachers' newspaper), a semi-weekly of the Ministry of Education of the Republic of Belarus. Minsk.

Naviny Bielaruskaha Narodnaha Frontu "Adradžeńnie" (News of the Belarusan Popular Front "Renewal"), an irregular newspaper. Miensk.

"Nekotoriye aktualnyie voprosy ideologicheskoy raboty v sovremennykh usloviyakh [v poryadke orientirovaniya dla sekretarey partiynykh komitetov]" (Some current questions of ideological work under contemporary conditions [A guide for the secretaries of party committees]) *Belorusskaya Tribuna* 3 (December 18, 1988):5.

New York Times. Editorial. June 8, 1992.

Niamiha, H. "Education in Belorussia Before the Rout of 'National Democracy': 1917–1930." *Belorussian Review* 1 (1955):34–66.

Nioman (Nieman), a literary monthly of the Belarusan Writers' Union. Minsk.

Niva (Soil), weekly newspaper of the Belarusan Socio-Cultural Society in Bielastok, Poland.

Ochmański, Jerzy. *Historia Litwy.* Wroclaw–Warsaw: Wydawnictwo Ossolińskich, 1982.

Olshansky, P. N. *Rizhski mir* (The Treaty of Riga). Moscow: Izdatel'stvo "Nauka," 1969.

Osservatore Romano, Weekly Edition (semi- official Vatican newspaper), No. 46 (November 18, 1992).

Papartis, Jonas. "Samizdat Report on the Lithuanian Minority in Belorussia." *Radio Liberty Research* 102/79 (March 26, 1979).

Paźniak, Zianon. "Paviedamlennie ab tavarystvie ('Martyraloh Bielarusi')" (Announcement on the society ["Martyrology of Belarus"] *Martyraloh* 1 (1989):1–4.

_____. "Jakaja pazicyja u apazicyi?" (What is the position of the opposition?). Interview with People's Deputy Zianon Paźniak in *Litaratura i Mastactva* (Literature and art), August 10, 1990.

Pertsev, V. N., et al., eds. *Dokumenty i materialy po istorii Belorussii, 1900–1917* (Documents and material for the history of Belarus: 1900–1917), Vol. 3. Minsk: Izdatel'stvo Akademii nauk BSSR, 1953.

Picheta, Vladimir I. *Belorussiya i Litva XV–XVI vv. (issledovaniya po istorii sotsialno-ekonomicheskogo, politicheskogo i kulturnogo razvitiya)* (Belarus and Lithuania of the fifteenth to sixteenth centuries [Studies in the history of socioeconomic, political and cultural development]). Moscow: Izdatel'stvo Akademii nauk SSSR, 1961.

Platonov, Rostislav. "K novomu urovnyu issledovaniy" (Toward a new level of research). *Kommunist Belorussii* 6 (1991):73–77

Pogonowski, Iwo. *Poland: A Historical Atlas*. New York: Hippocrene Books, 1987.

Polymia (Flame), a literary monthly of the Belarusan Writers' Union. Minsk.

Prahramnyja dakumienty Bielaruskaha Narodnaha Frontu "Adradžeńnie" (The Programmatic Documents of the Belarusan Popular Front "Renewal"). Minsk, 1989.

Praškovič, Mikola. "Slova pra Afanasija Filipoviča" (A word about Afansij Filipovič). *Polymia* (Flame) 12 (1965):174–177.

Rabochaya tribuna, a daily newspaper. Moscow, December 28, 1990.

Radio Liberty. "Kratkiye soobshcheniya ITAR-TASS" (Brief news of ITAR-TASS). *Russia and CIS Today.* May 11, 1992.

_____. *Materyjaly Bielaruskaha Manitorynhu* (Materials of Belarusan monitoring), No. 229/66 (March 2, 1992).

Rasolka, Michail. "Deputackija hulni 'Viasna-90'" (Deputy Games, "Spring-90"). *Krynica* 7 (July 1990): 3–4.

Respublika, "A Newspaper for Those Who Make Independent Decisions." Minsk.

Rich, Vera, transl. *Like Water, Like Fire: An Anthology of Byelorussian Poetry from 1828 to the Present Day.* London: George Allen & Unwin, 1971.

Sambuk, Susanna M. *Revolutsionnyie narodniki Belorussii 70-ye–nachalo 80-kh godov XIX v.* (Revolutionary populists of Belarus: The 1870s–Beginnings of the 1880s). Minsk: Izdatel'stvo Akademii nauk BSSR, 1972.

Sedov, Valentin V. *Slavyane Verkhnego Podneprov'ya i Podvin'ya* (The Slavs of the Upper Regions of the Dnieper and Dvina rivers). Moscow: "Nauka" Publishers, 1970.

Selskaya gazeta, an agricultural newspaper. Minsk.

Šerech, Yuri. *Problems in the Formation of Belorussian.* Supplement to *Word,* Journal of the Linguistic Circle of New York 9 (December 1953):1–109.

Shavel, A., and O. T. Manayev, eds. *Molodezh i demokratizatsiya sovetskogo obshchestva. Sotsiologicheskiy analiz* (Youth and the democratization of Soviet society: A sociological analysis). Minsk: Izdatel'stvo "Nauka i tekhnika," 1990.

_____. "Sotsialnyie posledstviya perekhoda k rynku, problemy sotsial'noy zashchity naseleniya respubliki" (The social consequences of a transition to a market economy and problems of social protection of the population of the republic). *Belorusistika* 14 (1991): 111–122.

Slay, Ben, and John Tedstrom. "Privatization in the Postcommunist Economies: An Overview." *RFE/RL Research Report* 17 (April 24, 1992):1–8.

Smirnov, A. F. *Vosstaniye 1863 goda v Litve i Belorussii* (The Uprising of 1863 in Lithuania and Belarus). Moscow: Izdatel'stvo Akademii nauk SSSR, 1963.

Smirnova, R. A. "Izmeneniye otnosheniy naseleniya k sobstvennosti i predprinimatel'skoy deyatel'nosti" (Changes in the population's attitude toward property and entrepreneurship). *Belorusistika* 14 (1991):68–75.

Smith, Hedrick. *The New Russians*. New York: Random House, 1990.

Solchanyk, Roman. "Ukraine and Russia: The Politics of Independence." *RFE/RL Research Report* 19 (May 8, 1991): 13–16.

Sovetskaya Belorussiya, daily newspaper of the Council of Ministers of Belarus and the editorial staff of *Sovetskaya Belorussiya*. Minsk.

Stankievič, Adam. "'Mužyckaja Praŭda' i 'Homon'" ("Peasants' truth" and "Clamor"). *Kalośsie* (Ears of grain) 1 (1935):34–39.

Starčanka, Uladzimir. "Ci josč šanc pieramahčy?" (Is there a chance to prevail?) *Litaratura i Mastactva* (Literature and art), May 5, 1991.

State Committee of the Republic of Belarus for Statistics and Analyses. *Statisticheskiye dannyie ob ekonomike Respubliki Belaruś v 1991 godu* (Statistical data on the economy of the Republic of Belarus in 1991). Minsk, 1991.

———. *O rabote narodnogo khozyaystva Respubliki Belaruś v yanvare-oktyabre 1991 g.* (On activity in the national economy of the Republic of Belarus from January to October 1991). Minsk, 1991.

Statut Vialikaha Kniastva Litoŭskaha 1588. Teksty. Deviednik. Kamientaryi (The Statute of the Grand Duchy of Lithuania. Texts. References. Commentaries). Minsk: Bielaruskaja Savieckaja Encyklapiedyja, 1989.

Suhl, Yuri, ed. *They Fought Back: The Story of the Jewish Resistance in Nazi Europe.* New York: Crown Publishers, 1967.

Sulzberger, C. L. "Two Chinas with One Voice." *New York Times*, October 8, 1971.

Supol'naść (Togetherness), an irregular *samizdat* bulletin of the Coordinating Council of the Confederation of Belarusan Societies. Minsk, 1989.

Supreme Council of the Republic of Belarus. *Otchetnyi doklad Vremennoy komissii Verkhovnogo Soveta Respubliki Belarus po otsenke deystviy chlenov GKChP i podderzhavshikh ikh obshchestvenno-politicheskikh obrazovaniy, organov gosudarstvennoy vlasti i upravleniya, dolzhnostnykh lits i grazhdan* (Report of the Ad Hoc Committee of the Supreme Council of the Republic of Belarus on estimating actions related to the State Emergency Committee and the support of it by civic-political structures, organs of government and administration, officials, and citizens). Minsk, dated before December 17, 1991.

———. *Dzieviataja siesija Viarchoŭnaha Savieta Respubliki Bielaruś Dvanaccataha sklikannia* (Ninth Session of the Twelfth Supreme Council of the Republic of Belarus) 24 (April 7, 1992).

———. *Niečarhovaja šostaja siesija Viarchoŭnaha Savieta BSSR Dvanaccataha sklikannia* (Sixth Extraordinary Session of the Twelfth Supreme Council of the BSSR). *Biuleteń* 2 (September 17, 1991).

————. *Siomaja siesija Viarchoŭnaha Savieta Respubliki Bielaruś Dvanaccataha sklikannia* (Seventh Session of the Twelfth Supreme Council of the Republic of Belarus). 5 (November 17,1991).

Svaboda (Liberty), "A Belarusan Newspaper." Miensk.

Taraškievič, Branislaŭ. *Vybranaje* (Selected). Minsk: Vydaviectva "Mastackaja litaratura," 1991.

Tarasaŭ, Kastuś. *Pamiać pra lehiendy. Postaci bielaruskaj minuŭščyny* (Remembrance of legends: Personalities of the Belarusan past). Minsk: Vydaviectva "Polymia," 1980.

Tolochko, P. P. *Drevnyaya Ruś. Ocherki sotsialno-politicheskoy istorii* (Ancient Ruś: An outline of sociopolitical history). Kiev: Vydavnytstvo "Naukova dumka," 1987.

Tomaszewski, Jerzy. *Mniejszości narodowe w Polsce XX wieku* (National minorities in twentieth-century Poland). Warsaw: Editions Spotkania, 1991.

Turevich, Art. "Elections in Byelorussia." *Byelorussian Review* 1 (Spring 1990):5–8.

Turonek, Jerzy. *Białoruś pod okupacja niemiecka* (Belarus under the German Occupation). Warsaw–Wroclaw: "Wers," 1989.

Ulashchik, Nikolai N. *Vvedeniye v izucheniye belorussko-litovskogo letopisaniya* (Introduction to the study of the Belarusan-Lithuanian chronicles). Moscow: Izdatel'stvo "Nauka," 1985.

————. *Ocherki po arkheografii i istochnikovedeniyu istorii Belorussii feodal'nogo perioda* (An outline of the archaeography and sources of the History of Belarus of the feudal period). Moscow: Izdatel'stvo "Nauka," 1973.

————. *Predposylki krestyanskoy reformy 1861 g. v Litve i Zapadnoy Belorussii* (Bases of the land reform of 1861 in Lithuania and West Belarus). Moscow: Izdatel'stvo "Nauka," 1965.

Ulicionak, Aliaksandr. *Inšadumcy. Hutarki z tymi, kaho jašče ŭčora klejmavali 'demahohami'* (Dissidents: Interviews with those who only yesterday were branded "demagogues"). Minsk: "Bielaruś," 1991.

Urban, Michael. *An Algebra of Soviet Power: Elite Circulation in the Belorussian Republic, 1966–1986.* Cambridge, England: Cambridge University Press, 1989.

Urban, Paval. "The Twentieth Party Congress and the National Question." *Belorussian Review* 4 (1957): 83–95.

————. "Belorussian Opposition to the Soviet Regime." *Belorussian Review* 6 (1958):30–44.

Vakar, Nicholas. "The Name 'White Russia,'" *American Slavic and East European Review,* 8 (October 1949):201–213.

————. *Belorussia: The Making of a Nation.* Cambridge, Mass.: Harvard University Press, 1956.

Viedamasci Viarchoŭnaha Savieta Bielaruskaj SSR (Proceedings of the Supreme Council of the Belarusan SSR). Nos. 1–28 (December 5, 1990–October 5, 1991).

Viedamasci Viarchoŭnaha Savieta Respubliki Bielaruś (Proceedings of the Supreme Council of the Republic of Belarus). Nos. 29–36 (October 15, 1991–December 25, 1991).

Volacič, Mikola. "The Curzon Line and Territorial Changes in Eastern Europe." *Belorussian Review* 2 (1956):37–72.

_____. "The Population of Western Belarus and Its Resettlement in Poland and in the USSR." *Belorussian Review* 3 (1956):5–30.

Wilinbachow, W. "Struktura kultury staroruskiej w wiekach X–XII" (The structure of Old-Ruśian culture in the tenth to twelfth centuries). *Kwartalnik Historyczny.* 79 (1972):832–842.

Yakovenko, Vasil. "Nye day solgat', sovest'. Interv'yu pisatela Vasilya Yakovenko" (Don't let me lie, conscience: An interview with writer Vasil' Yakovenko). *Kommunist Belorussii* 12 (1989):70–74.

Yaroś, Anatoly, "Kakiye my—takoye vremya" (As we are, so are the times). *Kommunist Belorussii* 9 (September 1990):4–14.

Yukho, I. A. *Pravovoye polozheniye naseleniya Belorussii v XVI v.* (The legal status of the population of Belarus in the sixteenth century). Minsk: Izdatel'stvo BDU, 1978.

Zaprudnik, Jan. "Development in Belorussia Since 1964." In George W. Simmons, ed., *Nationalism in the USSR and Eastern Europe in the Era of Brezhnev and Kosygin.* Detroit: University of Detroit Press, 1977. Pp. 105–114.

_____. "Dziaržaŭnaść Bielarusi u dasavieckuju paru" (The statehood of Belarus in the pre-Soviet period). *Zapisy Bielaruskaha Instytutu Navuki i Mastactva* (Annals of the Byelorussian Institute of Arts and Sciences) 15 (1977):3–22.

_____. "Inakodumstvo v Bilorusi" (Dissent in Belarus) *Sučasnist'* (Modern times) 7–8 (1979):158–169.

_____. "Belorussian Reawakening." *Problems of Communism* 4 (July–August 1989):36–52.

Zaprudnik, Jan, and Thomas E. Bird. *The 1863 Uprising in Byelorussia: "Peasants' Truth" and "Letters from Beneath the Gallows." Texts and Commentaries.* New York: Kreceuski Foundation, 1980.

Znamya yunosti (The banner of youth), "A Socio-Political Newspaper of the Republic of Belarus." Minsk.

Zviazda (Star), a daily newspaper, published by the Supreme Council and the Council of Ministers of the Republic of Belarus, and the editorial staff of *Zviazda*. Minsk.

· About the Book ·
and Author

Belarus—sometimes called "the Western Gate of the Soviet Union"—has been placed by history between powerful states to the east and west. Soldiers of Muscovy and Poland, of Napoleon and Hitler, and of Alexander I and Stalin have all left their mark. Its territory has been laid claim to by both the Russians and the Poles, and religious and political echoes of their challenges continue to be heard. In this timely volume, Jan Zaprudnik—himself a native Belarusan—paints a vivid picture of the complex past of Belarus (formerly known as Belorussia), paving the way for his analysis of the challenges now facing the republic in the wake of a disintegrated Soviet Union.

In recent years Belarus has been less visible to the world than the Baltic republics to the north or Ukraine to the south, yet this multi-ethnic republic has undergone a significant demographic, social, cultural, and political evolution since 1956. A proclamation of state sovereignty in July 1990 combined with the accelerated fragmentation of the Soviet Union to push Belarus along the uncertain road to independence—a process that culminated with a declaration of full independence in August 1991.

Although perestroika has contributed to a dramatic rise in national consciousness among the people of Belarus, the nation-state has been notable in its quest for interethnic coexistence and for peaceful solutions to the problems brought about by democracy and independence.

Jan Zaprudnik, a historian by training, spent thirty-seven years with Radio Liberty as a commentator on Soviet and international politics. A graduate of the Catholic University of Louvain, Belgium (Licencié en sciences historiques, *cum laude*, 1954), he received his doctorate in history from New York University (1969). He taught Russian and Soviet history at Queens College of the City University of New York (1970–1975). Among the publications to which he contributed chapters or articles on Belarus are *Handbook of Major Soviet Nationalities, Nationalism in the USSR and Eastern Europe, Encyclopedia of World Literature in the 20th Century, Belorussian Review, Annals of the Byelorussian Institute of Arts and Sciences, Problems of Communism,* and *Nations and Politics in the Soviet Successor States.*

· Index ·